The Future of Food Tourism

ASPECTS OF TOURISM

Series Editors: Chris Cooper, *Oxford Brookes University, UK*, C. Michael Hall, *University of Canterbury, New Zealand* and Dallen J. Timothy, *Arizona State University, USA*

Aspects of Tourism is an innovative, multifaceted series, which comprises authoritative reference handbooks on global tourism regions, research volumes, texts and monographs. It is designed to provide readers with the latest thinking on tourism worldwide and push back the frontiers of tourism knowledge. The volumes are authoritative, readable and user-friendly, providing accessible sources for further research. Books in the series are commissioned to probe the relationship between tourism and cognate subject areas such as strategy, development, retailing, sport and environmental studies.

Full details of all the books in this series and of all our other publications can be found on http://www.channelviewpublications.com, or by writing to Channel View Publications, St Nicholas House, 31–34 High Street, Bristol BS1 2AW, UK.

ASPECTS OF TOURISM: 71

The Future of Food Tourism

Foodies, Experiences, Exclusivity, Visions and Political Capital

Edited by

Ian Yeoman, Una McMahon-Beattie, Kevin Fields, Julia N. Albrecht and Kevin Meethan

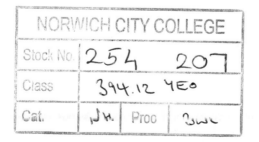
CHANNEL VIEW PUBLICATIONS
Bristol • Buffalo • Toronto

Library of Congress Cataloging in Publication Data
The Future of Food Tourism: Foodies, Experiences, Exclusivity, Visions and Political
Capital/Edited by Ian Yeoman, Una McMahon-Beattie, Kevin Fields, Julia N. Albrecht
and Kevin Meethan.
Aspects of Tourism: 71
Includes bibliographical references and index.
1. Food tourism. 2. Food tourism—Forecasting. I. Yeoman, Ian.
TX631.F87 2015
394.1'2–dc23 2015008252

British Library Cataloguing in Publication Data
A catalogue entry for this book is available from the British Library.

ISBN-13: 978-1-84541-538-9 (hbk)
ISBN-13: 978-1-84541-537-2 (pbk)

Channel View Publications
UK: St Nicholas House, 31–34 High Street, Bristol BS1 2AW, UK.
USA: UTP, 2250 Military Road, Tonawanda, NY 14150, USA.
Canada: UTP, 5201 Dufferin Street, North York, Ontario M3H 5T8, Canada.

Website: www.channelviewpublications.com
Twitter: Channel_View
Facebook: https://www.facebook.com/channelviewpublications
Blog: www.channelviewpublications.wordpress.com

The policy of Multilingual Matters/Channel View Publications is to use papers that are
natural, renewable and recyclable products, made from wood grown in sustainable for-
ests. In the manufacturing process of our books, and to further support our policy, preference is given to printers that have FSC and PEFC Chain of Custody certification. The FSC
and/or PEFC logos will appear on those books where full certification has been granted
to the printer concerned.

Typeset by Techset Composition India (P) Ltd., Bangalore and Chennai, India.

Printed and bound by CPI Group (UK) Ltd, Croydon, CR0 4YY

To the best redhead in New Zealand who is often the lucky (and sometimes unlucky) recipient of my experimental cooking and food adventures whilst exploring and writing this book. Ian Yeoman

*To the best chef in my world, my husband, Graham.
Una McMahon-Beattie*

To all the friends I've broken bread with at gastronomy-related conferences and events. Kevin Fields

To the hosts at great wineries now and in the future. Julia Albrecht

To Sally and Joe for putting up with me. Kevin Meethan

Contents

Figures, Tables, Images

Figures

Tables

Images

Contributors

Editors

Ian Yeoman is a specialist travel and tourism futurologist who believes in Star Trek, is an eternal optimist, crazy about Sunderland AFC and enjoys cooking. Ian is a trainee professor at Victoria University of Wellington who commutes and holidays around the world.

Una McMahon-Beattie (PhD) is Professor and Head of the Department for Hospitality and Tourism Management at Ulster University (UK). Her research interests include tourism and event marketing, revenue management and tourism futures. She is an editor/author of a number of books, book chapters and journals articles in these areas.

Kevin Fields worked in the hospitality industry before entering academia 23 years ago. He taught at three universities across hospitality, events and tourism courses – with specific interests in business tourism and food-related tourism. Now semi-retired, he retains an interest in the industry through occasional consultancy.

Julia N. Albrecht is a senior lecturer at the University of Otago, New Zealand. Her academic interests include tourism strategy and planning, visitor management and tourism in wine destinations. Julia has published in leading journals such as *Annals of Tourism Research* and *Journal of Sustainable Tourism*.

Kevin Meethan is an associate professor at Plymouth University. He has broad and interdisciplinary research interests including cultural change and global–local relations in tourism. He is an active member of the International Sociological Association and is founding editor of the *Journal of Tourism Consumption and Practice* (www.tourismconsumption.org/).

Chapter Authors

Stephen Boyd is Professor of Tourism in the Department of Hospitality and Tourism Management, University of Ulster. Prior to joining Ulster, he taught in England and New Zealand. He has written widely on many areas, including national parks and tourism, dark heritage and community-driven tourism. He is currently writing on tourism and trails.

Tobias Danielmeier is a principal lecturer at Otago Polytechic and senior lecturer in architecture at Victoria University of Wellington, New Zealand. Tobias' architecture projects have been awarded many design and innovation awards. His research investigates the design of contemporary winery architecture and spatial strategies of place performance and performativity.

Tara Duncan is a lecturer in the Department of Tourism at the University of Otago in Dunedin, New Zealand. A human geographer by background, Tara's research focuses on the intersections between mobilities, transnationalism and tourism as well as the everyday spaces and practices within tourism, hospitality and leisure.

Harvey Ells, in addition to teaching at the University of Brighton, UK on a range of retail and food modules, has worked extensively with a number of SMEs in diversifying and marketing their food offers. His current research interests include charity retailing, food SME branding and the role of food street markets within the new food economy.

Warwick Frost is an associate professor in the Department of Managing and Marketing at La Trobe University, Australia. His research interests include heritage, events, nature-based attractions and the interaction between media, popular culture and tourism. Warwick is a co-editor of the Routledge Advances in Events Research series.

Christine Hansen is past Director of Academics and an assistant professor for Embry-Riddle Aeronautical University, and currently teaches at Hawai'i Pacific University. She holds a PhD in political science and three other Master's level degrees. She recently appeared on 'The Future of Education' segment of Thinktech Hawai'i.

Brian Hay is an honorary professor in the School of Management and Languages at Heriot-Watt University. Before moving into academia, he worked for some 20 years as Head of Research at VisitScotland.

Karen Hurley is a research associate in the School of Environmental Studies at the University of Victoria, British Columbia, Canada. She is an ecofeminist futures specialist whose research and writing focuses on envisioning food, agriculture and nature within positive and diverse futures. Karen also works with First Nations in protecting their territories (www.ecoandjustfutures.ca).

Jennifer Laing is a senior lecturer in the Department of Management and Marketing at La Trobe University, Australia. Her research interests include travel narratives, the role of events in society, heritage tourism and gastronomy. Jennifer is a co-editor of the Routledge Advances in Events Research series.

Christina M. Minihan has a PhD from Colorado State University and is an instructor at the University of Northern Colorado. Her current research is focused on culinary tourism applied to both breweries and restaurants. She is also a small business entrepreneur.

Gianna Moscardo is a professor in the College of Business, Law and Governance at James Cook University, Australia. Her research interests include understanding tourist behaviour and experiences and evaluating tourism as a sustainable development strategy.

John D. Mulcahy has an MA (Gastronomy) and an MSc (Mgt), informed by his experience as a pub, restaurant and food service operator on three continents, as an educator, and with the Irish National Tourism Development Authority. His interest is in Irish food and its significance for society. For more, see ie.linkedin.com/in/gastronomy/

Joseph T. O'Leary is Professor in International Tourism at Colorado State University. His research interests are in recreation and tourism behaviour and the use of large data resources. He teaches undergraduate and graduate courses, most recently in the Master of Tourism Management distance education programme.

David Scott is a lecturer at Southern Cross University in Australia. David's research critically explores the social and cultural aspects of tourism and hospitality. His research utilises mobile methodologies to develop a critical understanding of the experiences and performativity of hospitality and the role of food in the tourism experience.

Carol Wheatley has a BSc (Hons) in Pharmaceutical Chemistry (UK) and an MBA (NZ). Her background includes self-employment within the pharmaceutical and veterinary industries. She is currently freelancing in editing, proofreading, publishing, research and writing; contributing to a number of publications, such as *Tourism2050: Scenarios for New Zealand*.

Eunice Eunjung Yoo is a lecturer in the School of Hospitality and Tourism Management at the University of Surrey. Her research interests centre on socio-cultural aspects of food in tourism and hospitality, in that food has acquired cultural and symbolic significance as it carries on its multiple functions in socio-cultural settings and has made its way into the cultures of people.

Foreword: To Boldly Go...

If anyone had told me 10 years ago that I would be lucky enough to head the world's largest association of food tourism industry professionals, I would have politely disagreed, saying that would never happen. Yet at just over 10 years old, our industry is still the fastest growing sector of the tourism industry and there seems to be no end in sight to its growth. I'm often asked to what we can attribute this tremendous growth, and the reasons are many. Certainly the pervasiveness of online food imagery and the popularity of celebrity chef television programming has helped. Yet the most obvious reason is also the most elusive: 100% of visitors must eat. Not every visitor will play golf or go shopping, but everyone has to eat. Therefore eating and drinking are an experience that all visitors share. While that seems obvious, often we forget it because of the ubiquity of eating. Most of us eat three times per day, if not more. Eating is both the most mundane and the most popular experience in which visitors can partake.

None of us has a crystal ball and peering into the future has yet to become a perfected science. Still, with 10 solid years as a formal industry, we as academics, researchers and practitioners can begin to predict what the food tourism industry's second decade will hold. Just like a child growing into his or her teenage years, food tourism is still finding its position in the tourism and hospitality industries. This sounds odd to current food tourism professionals because we saw the potential for the industry years ago. And because of this experience and vision, it is these leaders who are exactly the ones we want showing us how the future will unfold.

The Future of Food Tourism will serve as a solid, strategic guide of topics for future food tourism research. The very topics presented in this book are poised to inform opinion at the very least, and in the best of worlds, drive change in governmental policy and consumer behaviour. *The Future of Food Tourism* presents a smorgasbord of topics from which additional academics and researchers can choose for further embellishment. Just like a chef who takes a recipe and makes it his or her own by adding and subtracting ingredients, techniques and standards, so will those reading this book be inspired to take the understanding of our industry to the next level.

The eclectic range of topics which make up the chapters of this text should ensure that everyone with an interest in food tourism will find something relevant to them, whether their interests are niche or mainstream.

Erik Wolf
Executive Director,
World Food Travel Association,
Portland, Oregon, USA

Part 1

The Past, Present and Future

1 An Introduction to the Future

Ian Yeoman, Una McMahon-Beattie,
Kevin Fields, Julia N. Albrecht and
Kevin Meethan

Highlights

- Food tourism as political capital; food tourism as a visionary state; what it means to be a foodie; the drive for affluence and exclusivity; and fluid experiences in a post-modernist world are identified as the five core *drivers of change* that will shape the future of food tourism.
- Seventeen chapters portray the future of food tourism through recording how the past shapes the present, providing projections of the future, analysing key issues and concepts and highlighting future research avenues.
- With a systematic and pattern-based approach, this book presents an explanation of how and why change could occur and what the implications might be for the future of food tourism.

The Evolutionary Future of Food Tourism

The future

Pictures of the future can be large abstractions without explanation or truth. But in reality the future is an abstraction that has not happened. Pondering the future does not require truth nor explanation but to others it is all about truth and explanation. Confused, we are! Fundamentally is it a combination of truthfulness and plausible explanation. Our bias is towards explanation, as explanation is the rigour of science.

A future based upon prediction is founded upon certainty and a short time horizon whereas a science fiction future suspends all belief systems and looks for an explanation for how something could occur (Bergman *et al.*, 2010).

Looking towards the future means understanding how change could occur, why it will occur and when it will occur. It is a combination of understanding dynamics, drivers, trends and pure speculation. Whether it is the price of wheat, changes in demography or pattern of affluence, sustainable agricultural production or tourist values, this book delves into the 'big picture' and explains what the future of food tourism could be.

The Past to the Present of Food Tourism

Food and tourism are the central features of this book. These topics have been around since the beginning of time:

> It was the German bishop Johannes Fugger, in the 12th century who was journeying to Rome, his servant travelled a few days ahead to select suitable places to stay at, eat and drink. The servant would chalk 'Est' (Latin for 'This is it') on the doors of places deemed suited to the bishop's taste. The inn in Montefiascone impressed the servant so much that he wrote 'Est! Est!! Est!!!' Legend has it that the bishop returned to Montefiascone on his way back from Rome to stay there for the rest of his life. (Domenico, 2001: 123)

Given that destinations generally provide visitors with food and drink, it is surprising that academic interest in food tourism is relatively recent. After all, food tourism refers to anything from street vendors and produce markets to high-end restaurants and large-scale food festivals. It comprises locally grown ingredients and regional cuisine as well as foodstuffs provided by global chains. Tikkanen (2007) even relates different types of food tourism to Maslow's hierarchy of needs, thereby validating the view that food and culinary tourism are not necessarily associated with high-priced visitor experiences only. Furthermore, food is undoubtedly an important part of the visitor experience (Cohen & Avieli, 2004); it is partaken on a daily basis and many take a great deal of pleasure in its consumption.

Indeed, one does not even need to travel exclusively in search of culinary experiences in order to become a food tourist: Yun et al. (2011) declare that only 'deliberate' food tourists travel specifically to seek out certain foods or ingredients. 'Opportunistic' food tourists may look for food and drink at a destination that they have selected for other reasons, and 'accidental' food tourists participate in food and drink just because it is there and they need to (Yun et al., 2011).

Other recent developments intensify the current surge in interest in food tourism both within destinations and academia. The emergence of celebrity chefs from the late 1990s onwards has increased awareness of food as a potential lifestyle factor. Chefs like Gordon Ramsay and Jamie Oliver in the United Kingdom and Rachael Ray and Mario Batali in the United States have

contributed significantly to consumers' knowledge of food and their appreciation of the provenance of ingredients. Not least due to the desire for authentic
travel experiences, travel to places where ingredients or 'branded' food and
drink such as Champagne or Parma originate is more popular than ever.
Indeed, food tourism is one of the prime examples of a (supposed) niche product that allows visitors to take in all relevant aspects of a destination: product,
process, place and people (Mason & Mahoney, 2007). Another important
factor is the status that can be associated with travelling specifically in search
of food or produce; while eating a Big Mac in as many countries as possible
(Osman et al., 2014) may not improve one's standing among one's peers, an
annual trip to sample the latest release of Beaujolais nouveau might.

The possible benefits for destinations are evident and can include
increased visitor arrivals and lengths of stay; a new competitive advantage or
unique selling proposition; more sales across the complete range of travel
products including hospitality (both accommodation and meals/drinks),
transport and retail; increased community pride, positive media coverage as
well as tax revenue. While urban destinations such as for example New York
or Sydney can add food tourism to their portfolio of tourism products, food
tourism can open up previously non-existent streams of revenue for emerging destinations in agricultural regions.

It is surprising, then, that research on food tourism took off relatively
late. Though there were some isolated case studies exploring food in the
context of, mostly rural, tourism between the 1970s and the year 2000, food
tourism as a subject of academic study gained in importance over the last 15
years. Topic areas covered include considerations of the definition of food
tourism as well as related typologies (e.g. Hall & Sharples, 2003; Long, 2004),
food tourism in the context of the wider destination (e.g. Hall et al., 2003;
Mak et al., 2012), food and wine clusters, regional development (e.g. Boyne
& Hall, 2004; Hashimoto & Telfer, 2006), destination identity (e.g. Hall et al.,
2008; Sims, 2009, 2010), as well as critical perspectives on the role of food in
tourism (e.g. Cohen & Avieli, 2004). Fundamentally, we have argued that
food tourism has a history, is part of societies' culture and – because of the
relationship between food, communities and tourism – a topic of economic
development to political leaders. Isn't this exciting, read on!

The Future of Tourism: An Overview

The past, present and future

The first section sets the scene, focusing on how history shapes the present and, based on this, what the future could be. In Chapter 2, 'The "Past"
and "Present" of Food Tourism', Boyd argues that current food tourism trends
have a historical context and explores why food tourism has developed into

its present form as production, consumption and experience. Boyd highlights the importance of the concepts of 'local' and 'authenticity' for the future of food tourism. Yeoman and McMahon-Beattie in Chapter 3, 'The Future of Food Tourism: The Star Trek Replicator and Exclusivity', portray two futures. First, they explore how science could change the food production process from a traditional land-based system to a laboratory-based one. Second, recognising the impact of food scarcity, they explore how food becomes an exclusive experience for rich tourists.

Food tourism

The second section explores the concepts and issues raised in section one and follows a scenario analysis from a supply perspective. Hansen in Chapter 4, 'The Future Fault Lines of Food', delves into the food supply chain arguing the today's food is bland because of production systems and processes, thus speculating that the opportunity for food tourism is in developing flavours and senses that enhance the experience. Ells in Chapter 5, 'The Impact of Future Food Supply on Food and Drink Tourism', continues to focus on the supply chain and argues that the future of food tourism will involve an increasing number of food policy networks and actors within government, supply chains and consumer-centred groups working together to create a visionary future. Chapter 6, 'Future Consumption: Gastronomy and Public Policy' by Mulcahy argues that gastronomy has significance to all people at some level, and it can transform a state – each citizen and organisation doing their part, so that, collectively, the nation benefits, thus identifying the political, social, economic and cultural importance of food tourism. Danielmeier and Albrecht in Chapter 7, 'Architecture and Future Food and Wine Experiences', note how the role of place is and will be used to create uniqueness and points of difference in the architectural design of experiences in wineries. Hurley in Chapter 8, 'Envisioning AgriTourism 2115: Organic Food, Convivial Meals, Hands in the Soil and No Flying Cars', creates a utopian future that is based on an ecologically sound and socially just industry. Meethan in Chapter 9, 'Making the Difference: The Experience Economy and the Future of Regional Food Tourism', argues that future tourism developments need to be expressed in the context of globalisation thus shaping national and regional identity. Whereas, Fields in Chapter 10, 'Food and Intellectual Property Rights', argues the use of these tools is better positioned for the protection of history, culture, tradition and society than using them for the promotion of tourism.

Food tourism and the future tourist

In this section, a scenario analysis perspective delves into demand side issues, starting with Chapter 11, 'Back to the Future: The Affective Power of Food in Reconstructing a Tourist Imaginary', by Scott and Duncan, whose contribution revolves around how we see food as a significant motivation to travel, and so the chapter focuses on future food experiences through the tourist imaginary. Thus, Scott and Duncan suggest that food tourists make sense of the world around them an inherently imaginative process. In Chapter 12, 'The Changing Demographics of Male Foodies: Why Men Cook But Don't Wash Up', Yeoman and McMahon-Beattie argue that men see cooking as a leisure activity whereas washing up is a chore. From a food tourism perspective they highlight three dimensions: namely, authentic food experiences, the masculinity of celebrity and media, and men as foodies in the sense that cultural capital defines their identity and status. In Chapter 13, 'The New Food Explorer: Beyond the Experience Economy', Laing and Frost's contribution to the future of food tourism is to highlight the emergence of the food explorer as a niche market. The chapter identifies nine trends from slow food, artisan or organic food and produce, a desire for hands-on experience, sustainability, niche spaces, the exclusivity of the extreme, a preference for independent or experimental ordering or tasting, the view that local is best, and a rise in interest of foraging. Hay in Chapter 14, 'The Future of Dining Alone: 700 Friends and I Dine Alone!', notes that the known long-term changes in the structure of the population, the changing construct of the meaning of 'family' and the expected growth and dominance of single-person households in the Western world will all have a profound impact on the future evolution of the single diner states. Moscardo and colleagues in Chapter 15, 'Dimensions of the Food Tourism Experience: Building Future Scenarios', use both existing food tourism research and a study of tourist reviews to develop a conceptual model of food tourism organised around key consumption experience dimensions, including: learning destination place, personality, fun and stage.

Research directions

In the final section, two chapters conceptualise the future. Yoo in Chapter 16, 'Food in Scholarship: Thoughts on Trajectories for Future Research', contributes to tourism scholarship through the adoption of an interdisciplinary lens that links tourism and food studies, focusing on the elements of food as cultural heritage, food in scholarship, food as tourism attractions and a marketing tool, and tourist food consumption behaviour and dining experience. Finally Yeoman and colleagues in Chapter 17, 'The Future of Food Tourism: A Cognitive Map(s) Perspective', bring the book to a close by concluding the future of food tourism is clustered into five themes which are explained in further detail in the next section.

The Future of Tourism: Or Proposition

The aggregate contribution of this book to the future of food tourism is represented by Figure 1.1. These are the *drivers of change* that will affect future discourses, actions and behaviours in food tourism. *Food Tourism as Political*

Figure 1.1 Drivers of change

Capital notes that tourism incorporates discourses of economic, social and cultural benefit, which in itself results in political capital (Bourdieu, 1984). Food and agriculture are traditionally strong economic sectors with a strong political capital presence, thus when combined with tourism, food tourism is a beneficiary. *Food Tourism as a Visionary State* comes about as political capital takes the form of visions and utopias as food tourism is often portrayed through the words – 'authenticity', 'sustainability' and 'activism'. Food tourism takes the form of a collective vision of utopia where the problems of humankind and climate change can be addressed.

Foodies are those tourists who are passionate about food and food is their main reason for travel (Yeoman, 2000). *What it Means to be a Foodie* is derived from the fact that food is the foodies' avenue to cultural capital, where cultural production is increasingly becoming the dominant form of economic activity and securing access to the many cultural resources and experiences becomes an important aspect in shaping identity. The political drive for economic growth means that destinations will concentrate on high-spending markets (Yeoman, 2012), hence *The Drive for Affluence and Exclusivity*. Yeoman (2012) points out that with the arrival of mass tourism for the middle classes the definition of luxury becomes diluted and luxury providers need to redefine luxury as exclusivity. Yeoman recognises in a future society where food is scarce that the ingestion of food will reshape social and economic capital. Thus strategies will be based upon attracting more high-value, high-spending food tourists.

Increased affluence alters the consumer balance of power as new forms of connection and association allow a liberated pursuit of personal identity which is fluid and less restricted by background or geography. Tomorrow's tourist wants dynamic escapist experiences but at the same time social responsibility and authenticity. This is about diversity of experiences through sampling a wide range of novel and familiar experiences (Yeoman, 2008). *Fluid Experiences in a Post-Modernist World* means undertaking an authentic Turkish cooking class but at the same learning to cook with liquid nitrogen.

Concluding Thoughts

The Future of Food Tourism presents a systematic and pattern-based explanation of how and why change could occur and what the implications could be. The only question that remains unanswered is when this change will occur. From a futures perspective, the editors' and contributors' approach to the future has focused on explanation; here we look for the causes, trends and theoretical concepts that explain change, thus adopting a sense-making process to justify and explore the future. Explanation is at the centre of rigorous research. We explain how the past has shaped the present and will continue into the future. Scenarios are used to explore alternative futures and we reflect on the issues that contributors think will be of importance. In conclusion, we identity the forces of change around which discourses about the future of food tourism will take place. We may not be right about the future, but at least we have attempted to explain it. So, enjoy the future of tourism as the future is the only place you can travel to!

References

Bergman, A., Karlsson, J. and Axelsson, J. (2010) Truth claims and explanatory claims: An ontology typology of future studies. *Futures* 42, 857–865.

Bourdieu, P. (1984) *Distinction: A Social Critique of the Judgement of Taste*. Cambridge, MA: Harvard University Press.

Boyne, S. and Hall, D. (2004) Place promotion through food and tourism: Rural branding and the role of websites. *Place Branding* 1 (1), 80–92.

Cohen, E. and Avieli, N. (2004) Food in tourism – Attraction and impediment. *Annals of Tourism Research* 31 (4), 755–778.

Domenico, R. (2001) *The Regions of Italy: A Reference Guide to History and Culture*. New York: Greenwood.

Hall, C.M. and Sharples, L. (2003) The consumption of experiences or the experience of consumption? An introduction to the tourism of taste. In C.M. Hall, L. Sharples, R.D. Mitchell, N. Macionis and B. Cambourne (eds) *Food Tourism Around the World: Development, Management and Markets* (pp. 1–24). Oxford: Butterworth-Heinemann.

Hall, C.M., Sharples, E., Mitchell, R., Cambourne, B. and Macionis, N. (eds) (2003) *Food Tourism Around the World: Development, Management and Markets*. Oxford: Butterworth-Heinemann.

Hall, C.M., Mitchell, R.D., Scott, D.G. and Sharples, L. (2008) The authentic experience of farmers' markets. In C.M. Hall and L. Sharples (eds) *Food and Wine Festivals and Events Around the World: Development, Management and Markets* (pp. 197–231). Oxford: Butterworth-Heinemann.

Hashimoto, A. and Telfer, D.J. (2006) Selling Canadian culinary tourism: Branding the global and the regional product. *Tourism Geographies: An International Journal of Tourism Space, Place and Environment* 8 (1), 31–55.

Long, L.M. (2004) *Culinary Tourism*. Lexington: University of Kentucky Press.

Mak, A.H.N., Lumbers, M. and Eves, A. (2012) Globalisation and food consumption in tourism. *Annals of Tourism Research* 39 (1), 171–196.

Mason, C. and O'Mahoney, B. (2007) On the trail of food and wine: The tourist search for meaningful experience. *Annals of Leisure Research* 10 (3–4), 498–518.

Osman, H., Johns, N. and Lugosi, P. (2014) Commercial hospitality in destination experiences: McDonald's and tourists' consumption of space. *Tourism Management* 42, 238–247.

Sims, R. (2009) Food, place and authenticity: Local food and the sustainable tourism experience. *Journal of Sustainable Tourism* 17 (3), 321–336.

Sims, R. (2010) Putting place on the menu: The negotiation of locality in UK food tourism, from production to consumption. *Journal of Rural Studies* 26, 105–115.

Tikkanen, I. (2007) Maslow's hierarchy and food tourism in Finland: Five cases. *British Food Journal* 109 (9), 721–734.

Yeoman, I. (2008) *Tomorrow's Tourist: Scenarios and Trends*. Oxford: Elsevier.

Yeoman, I. (2012) *2050 – Tomorrow's Tourism*. Bristol: Channel View Publications.

Yun, D., Hennessey, S.M. and MacDonald, R. (2011) Understanding culinary tourists: Segmentations based on past culinary experiences and attitudes toward food-related behaviour. Paper presented at the International CHRIE Conference-Refereed Track. Paper 15. See http://scholarworks.umass.edu/refereed/ICHRIE_2011/Friday/15

2 The 'Past' and 'Present' of Food Tourism

Stephen Boyd

Highlights

- This chapter aims to provide a narrative on the evolution of the interest towards food in relation to tourism.
- It traces the emergence of food research within tourism academe from the 1970s to the present day, outlining a range of themes and issues that emerged within the discourse.
- The chapter is arranged around the following broad issues: the position of food within society and as part of the 'experience economy' and the 'new tourist', examining the definition of food tourism, and the emergence of a number of subtypes, assessing the benefits of food tourism as image and destination branding, promotion of local foods as tourist products and experiences, local foods as an integral element of economic development strategies, and sustainability challenges.
- The timeline for research into food tourism does not allow for traditional demarcation of the historical past with the present, so for the purposes of this chapter, the author makes the argument that the past relates to the period prior to 2000 and the present extends back to the start of the millennium.
- The 'past' of food tourism is focused more on scholarly interest in food as part of rural tourism research, with limited studies specifically addressing food tourism per se.
- In contrast, the 'present' of food tourism witnessed the field developing into a distinct subset of niche tourism, where scholarly research has delved into a plethora of areas and issues including food consumption, tourism experience, marketing and branding, importance of local foods, food markets, trails and networks. Alongside the broadening base of topics and issues, in the early part of the 2000s a number of landmark texts appeared on food tourism and related terms (Boniface, 2003; Hall et al., 2003; Hjalager & Richards, 2002; Long, 2004).

The 'Past' of Food Tourism

Emergence of food tourism within tourism academe

A review of 'food tourism' across CAB Direct (a resource database) that contains over 9 million bibliographic and full-text applied life sciences articles revealed that prior to the 1970s there were no food tourism publications. The first publication to appear was by Brown (1974) in an agricultural economics conference which charted the growth and structure across both the agricultural sector and tourism industry in Jamaica, where the focus was on the impact of the tourist industry upon Jamaica's agricultural sector. The reference to food tourism was at a tangent to the wider competition for resources and production of food aimed at the tourist market. Between 1980 and 1990, only six additional publications appeared, where the focus was on case studies that examined the interface between tourism and food production, food as part of tourism consumption, and the extent to which demand could be met by local supply (for example the work by Bélisle, 1983). These were case study driven and focused on the Caribbean and Jamaica in particular. Another 11 publications appeared between 1991 and 2000, where the focus was on the linkages between tourism and food production (Telfer & Wall, 1996), food tourism and heritage and culture (Hughes & Leslie, 1995; Reynolds, 1993) and food tourism with healthy eating and health tourism (Šimundić & Stipetić, 1996). The work by Telfer and Wall (1996) was seminal as it illustrated the connection between food and sustainable tourism and was perhaps the first major publication that addressed the importance of local food.

With the emergence of research that focused on food tourism as a separate entity, many scholars continued to subsume discussion of food as part of research on rural tourism and the countryside. A number of scholarly texts emerged towards the end of the 1990s which focused on rural tourism, but the mention of food as attraction was somewhat peripheral to describing this type of tourism (Sharpley & Sharpley, 1997), and the relationship between rural areas and tourism and recreation in general (Butler *et al.*, 1998).

Beggière (1998: 21) had noted that 'rural areas [were] now increasingly seen as places for entertainment, leisure activities, second homes and as an alternative to urban residential areas', and that food tourism was part of wider cultural heritage that could be internalised and digested, which offered the potential for communities as a sizeable source of income. Socher and Tschurtschenthaler (1994) had earlier stressed that agriculture in its broadest terms could offer tourism not only simple but also intangible products such as the protection and construction of excellent landscapes. Perhaps an exception was the work of Hall and Macionis (1998) who stressed that while the rural setting served as the destination, a key tourist activity was food centred, involving a range of experiences such as enjoying gourmet experiences, attending farmers markets, visiting farms (as part of farm tourism), attending cookery courses, food festivals and food special events. For the most part research on rural tourism remained with a strong focus on the farm as offering an opportunity for diversification and as offering a distinct marketing strategy for farm tourism (Hjalager, 1996).

An argument could be made that it would not be until the end of the 1990s that research into food tourism would start to develop a stronger theoretical base around the importance that food played within society, the role of food as part of the emerging 'experience economy' (Pine & Gilmore, 1999) and as a sub-element of what Poon (1993) had earlier described as the 'new tourist', with their specific interests and characteristics.

Food within society, the 'new tourist' and food as part of the 'experience economy'

In her seminal work, Poon (1993) recognised that tourism was changing from what had been dubbed 'old tourism' to 'new tourism', the former characterised as mass, standardised and rigidly packaged holidays, whereas the latter found the emergence of tourism that was being recognised as offering flexibility, segmentation and offering more authentic tourism experiences. The interest within academe with food and its relationship with tourism clearly related to this new paradigm emerging; she called it the 'new tourism common sense', whereby the industry needed to recognise the needs of their customers and create packages and experiences for target groups. Food had emerged by the end of the 1990s as commonplace within society with the appearance of celebrity chefs (Jamie Oliver and Rick Stein, to name only two); and food-related television (FRT) had benefited from cookery demonstrations beamed into English-speaking households by pioneers such Fanny Cradock in the 1950s and Delia Smith in the 1970s. In addition, some regions were being branded around food (e.g. parma ham, Northern Italy). Food had clearly emerged as part of the intangible experience of tourists within destinations. Reynolds (1993) commented that tourists were looking for authentic food experiences as part of sustainable culture, based on eating local foods and frequenting local eating places and avoiding fast-food establishments that served only to standardise food and position tourists in an environmental bubble away from locals and their eating spaces.

Focus on the intangible experiences, though hard to quantify, was a key factor in the economic growth of regions, and the emergence of a new realm of economic output, namely experiences (Pine & Gilmore, 1999). Pine and Gilmore have argued that experiences were an existing but previously unarticulated genre of economic output that was a distinct offering from services that focused on memorable experiences, offered sensations around events and activities that were personalised around the traits of guests/tourists. Food by the end of the last millennium had become an important element of the experience economy, elevating the act of simply eating for sustenance and allowing tourists to become part of the environment they are visiting. Fields (2002) would later suggest that tourists started to eat like locals, even if the most basic of meals became a novel gastronomic experience. Richards (2002) would also later claim that the convergence of food and tourism was closely linked to the experience economy, both demonstrating similar qualities of having production–consumption chains that resulted in the creation of experiences, and where thinking on food tourism became more complex, subdividing into culinary tourism (Long, 2004) and gastronomy tourism (Hjalager & Richards, 2002). This specialisation and division helped to mark what the author here terms the 'present era' of food tourism.

The 'Present' of Food Tourism

There was considerable growth of food tourism-related publications across the first decade of the new millennium. Fifty-four specific works had emerged which was a five-fold increase on the previous decade. This trend has continued from 2011 to the present day (2013) with an additional 24 publications resulting, demonstrating that a sizeable cluster of food tourism researchers has emerged as mentioned earlier in this chapter; the maturing of the field was evidenced in the publication of tourism texts specifically focused on food and wine (Boniface, 2003; Hall *et al.*, 2003; Hjalager & Richards, 2002; Long, 2004). This maturing of the field is self-evident in the range of topics and subtopics that have received scholarly attention post millennium, as shown in the following areas: food tourism typologies; towards a definition and subtypes; food as part of destination image, attraction, marketing and sustaining regional identity; food tourism as part of wider attraction (heritage, culture, special interest); food tourism motivation, experience and consumption; food and wine clusters and network development; local food networks and products and as regional development tool; traceability, health, hygiene and impediments to local cuisine; slow food and tourism; food tourism in protected areas and as part of community development (including food festivals); and the carbon footprint of food production and consumption.

Space does not permit a detailed discussion of each of the above so the remainder of this section teases out some of the developments with respect to what the author considers are the most pertinent areas that have helped shape the research field around food tourism post 2000. What the above list however demonstrates is the broad spectrum of research that has taken place with regard to food tourism.

Defining food tourism and emergence of subtypes

By the year 2000, it could be argued the 'new' tourist had become well established in the psyche of travellers as well as the industry, and that destinations were emerging that offered tourists distinct choices and experiences. The idea that a destination could be viewed as a 'food specialised locale' played into the wider change that was happening where there was a shift away from mass tourism towards niche forms of tourism. Novelli (2005) argued that the concept of 'niche tourism' was founded on the basis of the term 'niche marketing' whose role was to modify products to specific needs and expectations of consumers and market segments. She made the distinction between 'niche tourism products' and 'niche tourism markets'. Wine and gastronomy were recognised as micro niche tourism products that fitted within the macro 'rural' niche market. Other 'macro' markets included cultural, environmental and urban, and it was somewhat surprising that food and wine were not thought to pervade the 'urban' niche market.

Awareness, interest and the enjoyment of food have coincided with the increased consumption of tourism and therefore it was perhaps inevitable that they would combine and be referred to as food, culinary, gourmet or gastronomic tourism. These terms have been used interchangeably in the scholarly literature, and while they are similar they are not the same and the fact that food was such an integral part of the tourist experience was perhaps the reason it had been neglected and was viewed as just another incidental part of the tourist experience. Hall and Sharples (2003: 10), in an early definition, positioned food tourism as part of niche or special interest tourism, stating it involves the 'visitation to primary and secondary food producers, food festivals, restaurants and specific locations to experience a particular type of food or the produce of the specific region'. The primary factor stressed in this definition is that food must be the primary motivation to visit a region in order for it to become food tourism; it is important at the same time to stress that food tourism can complement other elements of the overall tourist experience. While there is the need to make the distinction between food and non-food tourists, there can be no doubt that a certain amount of ambiguity exists as all tourists eat, and expenditure on food is high for most tourists.

Gastronomy or gourmet tourism is particularly difficult to define as difference often arises within academe linking the concept to the art, science and culture of food. Gastronomy has different traditions in space and over time, with the world separated into gastronomic regions (Hall et al., 2003). It could be argued that all food tourists are the reserve of the gourmand as this entails an appreciation and understanding of many types of cooking as well as food production; blending tradition with culture and heritage. However, according to Lacy and Douglas (2002: 8) 'every tourist is a voyeuring gourmand' as they all in one way or another seek to experience unique and authentic food while visiting specific destinations and regions. Hall and Mitchell (2005: 74) classed gourmet tourism as consisting of 'visits to expensive and or highly rated restaurants, wineries and festivals'.

A midway position is that of 'culinary tourism'. The term culinary is much easier to define as the word translated quite literally means 'for or of the kitchen'. It refers to cooked food, finished food, and is linked to the gastronomy of a region. Long (2004: 21) defined culinary tourism as 'the intentional, exploratory participation in the foodways of an other – participation including the consumption, preparation, and presentation of a food item, cuisine, meal system or eating style considered to belong to a culinary system not one's own'.

Richards (2002) used the 'experience economy' to tease out the differences between food tourism, culinary tourism and gastronomy tourism. With regard to production–consumption, food tourism is positioned at the production end of the continuum, and gastronomy tourism at the consumption end of the spectrum, with culinary located in between. Food tourism relates to ingredients, whereas culinary tourism relates to dishes and meals, with gastronomy tourism focused on offering gastronomic experience. With respect to food tourism, he argues that the focus is on quality of opportunity compared to gastronomy tourism which has its focus on quality of experience. As one moves from food tourism to gastronomy tourism, he makes the argument that added value is increased, moving from commodities through goods and services to experiences.

What is not disputed in the literature is the value of the quality of food and gastronomy as well as the experience, either as a secondary motivation or one that is designed to offer added value. Quan and Wang (2004: 300) recognised the intrinsic relationship that existed between tourism and food, stressing that 'the total quality of the tourist experience relies on the mutual support and reinforcement between both dimension [food as daily experience of tourists and the main motivation and peak experience sought]'.

More recent research has broadened early statements of defining terms to stress the experiential dimension, as opposed to motivation. For example, Everett (2008: 338) makes the argument that food tourism can be a 'conceptual vehicle with which to explore issues of multisensory experience, embodied engagement and non-representable knowledge generation thus problematizing the dominance of the visual sense in tourism studies'. This elevates the desired experience above the visual gaze of tourists to a sensory one. Henderson's (2009) typology of food tourism products takes this sensory element into consideration when she states the importance of cookery schools in destinations and cooking holidays, often linked to celebrity chefs.

Food tourism interest, destination marketing and branding

Hall and Sharples (2003) have conceptually argued that as you move from food/gastronomic through culinary tourism to rural and urban tourism the level of interest in food tourism declines, but the volume of visitors increases where the former (food/gastronomic tourism) is the primary focus of holiday activity, compared to the secondary focus for culinary tourism.

As the subject started to become more specialised, research focused on how regions could capitalise on their food resource as a marketing and branding tool. Henderson (2004) argued that in the case of Singapore, tourism promotion could centre on the idea of 'eating out' in order to gain competitive advantage, whereas Frochot (2003) stressed how food is a powerful visual image in tourism promotional material. Quan and Wang (2004) noted that food experiences in tourism could be marketed as 'peak experience', but should be viewed alongside 'consumer experience' as being integrated as a structured and integrated whole. Okumus et al. (2007) undertook comparative case study research (Turkey and Hong Kong) and suggested blending local with international cuisine for marketing purposes. Research emerged that demonstrated the association that was being made between food and tourism at various levels, namely a theoretical level (academe), strategic level (policymakers) and applied level (practitioners) (e.g. Boyne et al., 2003). Hall (2003) offered an overview of contemporary practices and trends in the marketing of food (including wine) tourism, where he stressed the role of food and wine in destination marketing and the role of government in promoting food and wine tourism and the broader development of marketing policies; issues which would be later addressed by Croce and Perri (2010).

Branding of gastronomy was given global presence when in 2005 UNESCO (United Nations Educational, Scientific and Cultural Organization) launched its Global Alliances Creative Cities Network that recognised cities worldwide with reputations as centres of excellence in a range of areas, including gastronomy. In order to qualify, cities had to demonstrate they met the following criteria: evidence of traditional food markets, a traditional food industry and a tradition of hosting gastronomic festivals. To date, only four cities have been given the label of city of gastronomy, Popayan, Colombia (2005), Chendu, China (2010), Östersund, Sweden (2012) and Jeonju, South Korea (2012).

Segmentation is important to branding and it is often assumed that certain types of tourism qualify as 'special interest' over mainstream tourism products. McKercher et al. (2008) however have challenged conventional thinking on segmentation, asking if food tourism is a form of special interest tourism, and if it is not best viewed in the context of 'other' products a destination can offer, given that tourists rarely choose destinations based on a single activity. Based on their case study of Hong Kong, they argue that direct marketing organisations should only market single activities (like food tourism) if the activity appeals to a group of visitors currently not being attracted to the destination and the destination has the ability to deliver high-quality products and services. More recent research has examined tourists' behaviour in regard to gourmet, culinary and wine tourism, outlining the

challenges and potential of marketing food tourism in destinations, acknowledging that food has clear potential as a form of destination identity (Lin
et al., 2011) and could be implemented within specific destinations (e.g. Black
Forest) (Beer et al., 2012).

Local foods as tourist products, experiences and economic development strategies

A major recent focus of food tourism research has been the unique position of local foods as a tourist product, experience and strategy towards
economic development at the regional level. The World Tourism
Organisation hosted a conference on local food and tourism in Cyprus in
2000, addressing issues such as local food within tourism policies, local
food and culture and the economy (e.g. Enright et al., 2003), and local food
and tourism promotion. Research started to uncover the potential that
local food and drink could help differentiate destinations by developing a
'sense of place', which offered a unique visitor experience but at the same
time provided economic benefits to local communities (Haven-Tang &
Jones, 2005). Later on, Everett (2008) would argue that local food tourism
initiatives (food producers) offered visitors the opportunity to move beyond
just gazing towards postmodern touristic consumptive activity and an
embodied experience, as food producers looked to negotiate a balance
between the operation of their business and the drive towards developing
new arenas of consumption.

With respect to economic development thinking and strategy, a
number of strands of research can be identified. Lothian and Siler (2003)
advanced some early thinking on applying Porter's model of industrial
clusters to the linkages between the food, drink and tourism sectors, and
that regions can gain a competitive advantage if they set up successful
industrial clusters. Hall (2004) would later apply cluster and network
theory to both small food and wine businesses and to leading food and
wine tourism regions in New Zealand. Another strategy, particularly in
frontier regions, has been to place importance on local fairs, food festivals
and markets to promote local quality agrifood products to visitors (Chang,
2011). A final strategy that is emerging is the use of local foods and food
heritage as an opportunity to create as well as revive cultural identity and
subsequently strengthen the economic development base at a regional level
(Vittersø & Amilien, 2011).

Food tourism, sustainability and its carbon footprint

It has been somewhat surprising that the contribution of food to sustainable tourism has received scant attention, given the resource implications of tourism as an activity. An exception to this has been the work of

Rand and Heath (2006) who argued that local and regional food held great potential to contribute to the sustainable competitiveness of a destination. Sustainability requires that any impediments need to be overcome, and Cohen and Avieli (2004) note that while food is an attraction for tourists, it can also be an obstacle or even a concern as tourists find themselves in unfamiliar destinations where hygiene standards may be poor, and tourists' knowledge of local cuisine is limited. Other research has examined food insecurity that has come about as a result of the transformation of regions towards tourism and certain niche forms (e.g. ecotourism and adventure tourism) as is the case of rural Costa Rica (Himmelgreen *et al.*, 2006). Food tourism has also been examined from the perspective that it can sustain regional identity, especially given the role it can play in rural regeneration and agricultural diversification, helping to forge closer relationships between production and consumption in the countryside (Everett & Aitchison, 2008). Local foods have an important role to play in the sustainability of destinations. Sims (2009) argues that local foods appeal to visitors' desires for authenticity. Based on comparative case studies of the Lake District and Exmoor in Britain, Sims argues that local food has the potential to enhance the visitor experience by connecting consumers to the region and its perceived culture and heritage, using food to establish the 'local' in the region's food commodity chain.

Food production and consumption in tourism are of critical relevance to sustainability, yet they have received relatively scant attention in the tourism literature. Equally scant has been the coverage given over to the climate change dimension of food. Gössling *et al.* (2011) however note that food production and consumption have a range of sustainability implications, including their contribution to global emissions of greenhouse gases (GHGs). They argue the need for greater climate change mitigation by restricting those foodstuffs in destinations that entail higher GHG emissions, and by moving towards climatically sustainable food management through the adoption of food management strategies they term the '3 Ps': purchasing, preparation and presentation. They raise challenging questions of tourists and their willingness to pay premiums for organic or locally produced food, as well as challenges to producers for their commitment to sustainable food management. While organic food, produced on a local-regional scale, is an effective countertrend to globalisation and the rise of homogeneity of foodstuffs for a certain section of the tourism marketplace, Mak *et al.* (2012) argue that the common perception of globalisation as a threat to local gastronomic identities should be used as an impetus to open up new opportunities for the reinvention of local gastronomic products and identities, thereby ensuring the sustainability of local regions.

As stated at the outset of this section, research into food tourism post 2000 has been extensive, and the above themes demonstrate the diversification of the field and the healthy debate and discussion that has ensued.

Concluding Remarks

This chapter has set out the narrative of the evolution, development and specialism of food tourism. Like all areas of scholarly research, there has been a maturing of the field over time as more scholars have become interested in studying the topic, moving away from defining and categorising types to examining a plethora of issues and themes considered relevant to food tourism. So what broad trends and issues may become apparent in the future as this field of inquiry matures? If we accept the old adages that 'one can learn from the past and the present' and 'the future is a representation of the past' then what is clearly developing is the recognition of the primacy of the 'local' in production, marketing, experience and consumption. It is unlikely that this will diminish, as more destinations look to capitalise on the uniqueness of local traditional food and cuisine styles in order to seek competitive advantage and provide authentic experiences. Another trend to be anticipated in the future is greater attention paid to the food carbon footprint, addressing the current dearth of research in this area at present, though what is emerging has created a base on which this issue must be further examined; ensuring the offer is grounded in the 'local' in the future will combat claims of creating large carbon footprints. A third trend will be to see research that examines the food tourist, understanding the requirements of the casual as well as the serious food tourists and how they consume a more diverse product base including food events, festivals and trails.

Food will remain embedded as part of the market triumvirate of sightseeing, shopping and eating at destinations, so greater attention must be given to how we promote food tourism in the future, recognising that the futures we create will have been shaped by traditions and practices of our past and present.

References

Beer, C.L., Ottenbacher, M.C. and Harrington, R.J. (2012) Food tourism implementation in the Black Forest destination. *Journal of Culinary Science and Technology* 10 (2), 106–128.

Bélisle, F.J. (1983) Tourism and food production in the Caribbean. *Annals of Tourism Research* 10 (4), 497–513.

Bessiére, J. (1998) Local development and heritage: Traditional food and cuisine as tourist attractions in rural areas. *Sociologia Ruralis* 38 (1), 21–34.

Boniface, P. (2003) *Tasting Tourism: Travelling for Food and Drink*. Hampshire: Ashgate.

Boyne, S., Hall, D. and Williams, F. (2003) Policy, support and promotion for food-related tourism initiatives: A marketing approach to regional development. *Journal of Travel and Tourism Marketing* 14 (3), 131–154.

Brown, H. (1974) The impact of the tourist industries on the agricultural sectors: The competition for resources and the market for food provided by tourism: The case of Jamaica. Proceedings of the 9th West Indies agricultural economics conference. New Kingston, 3–6 April.

Butler, R.W., Hall, C.M. and Jenkins, J. (eds) (1998) *Tourism and Recreation in Rural Areas.* Chichester: John Wiley and Sons Limited.

Chang, W.C. (2011) A taste of tourism: Visitors' motivations to attend a food festival. *Event Management* 15 (2), 151–161.

Cohen, E. and Avieli, N. (2004) Food in tourism: Attraction and impediment. *Annals of Tourism Research* 31 (4), 755–778.

Croce, E. and Perri, G. (2010) Supply operators in the food and wine tourism industry. In E. Croce and G. Perri (eds) *Food and Wine Tourism: Integrating Food, Travel and Territory* (pp. 137–156). Wallingford: CABI.

Enright, P., Morrissey, M. and Chisholm, N. (2003) Import substitution potential for the food sector in rural tourism: A case study. Proceedings of the WTO local food and tourism international conference (pp. 101–104). Larnaka, Cyprus.

Everett, S. (2008) Beyond the visual gaze? The pursuit of an embodied experience through food tourism. *Tourist Studies* 8 (3), 337–358.

Everett, S. and Aitchison, C. (2008) The role of food in sustaining regional identity: A case study of Cornwall, Southwest England. *Journal of Sustainable Tourism* 16 (2), 150–167.

Fields, K. (2002) Demand for the gastronomy tourism product: Motivational factors. In A.-M. Hjalager and G. Richards (eds) *Tourism and Gastronomy* (pp. 36–50). London: Routledge.

Frochot, I. (2003) An analysis of regional positioning and its associated food images in French tourism regional brochures. *Journal of Travel and Tourism Marketing* 14 (3–4), 77–96.

Gössling, S., Garrod, B., Aall, C., Hille, J. and Peeters, P. (2011) Food management in tourism: Reducing tourism's carbon 'footprint'. *Tourism Management* 32 (3), 534–543.

Hall, C.M. (2003) *Wine, Food and Tourism Marketing.* New York: Haworth Hospitality Press.

Hall, C.M. (2004) Small firms and wine and food tourism in New Zealand: Issues of collaboration, clusters and lifestyles. In R. Thomas (ed.) *Small Firms in Tourism: International Perspectives* (pp. 167–181). Amsterdam: Elsevier.

Hall, C.M. and Macionis, N. (1998) Wine tourism in Australia and New Zealand. In R.W. Butler, C.M. Hall and J. Jenkins (eds) *Tourism and Recreation in Rural Areas* (pp. 267–298). Chichester: John Wiley and Sons Limited.

Hall, C.M. and Mitchell, R. (2005) Gastronomic tourism: Comparing food and wine tourism experiences. In M. Novelli (ed.) *Niche Tourism: Contemporary Issues, Trends and Cases* (pp. 73–88). Oxford: Elsevier.

Hall, C.M. and Sharples, L. (2003) *Food and Wine Festivals and Events around the World.* Oxford: Butterworth-Heinemann.

Hall, C.M., Sharples, L., Mitchell, R., Macionis, N. and Cambourne, B. (2003) *Food Tourism around the World: Development, Management and Markets.* Oxford: Butterworth-Heinemann.

Haven-Tang, C. and Jones, E. (2005) Using local food and drink to differentiate tourism destinations through a sense of place: A story from Wales – Dining at Monmouthshire's great table. *Journal of Culinary Science and Technology* 4 (4), 69–86.

Henderson, J. (2004) Food as a tourism resource: A view from Singapore. *Tourism Recreation Research* 29 (3), 69–74.

Henderson, J. (2009) Food tourism reviewed. *British Food Journal* 111 (4), 317–326.

Himmelgreen, D.A., Daza, N.R., Vega, M., Cambronero, H.B. and Amador, E. (2006) 'The tourist season goes down but not the prices'. Tourism and food insecurity in Rural Costa Rica. *Ecology of Food and Nutrition* 45 (4), 295–321.

Hjalager, A.-M. (1996) Agricultural diversification into tourism: Evidence of a European community development programme. *Tourism Management* 17 (2), 103–111.

Hjalager, A.-M. and Richards, G. (2002) *Tourism and Gastronomy*. London: Routledge.

Hughes, G. and Leslie, D. (1995) Food, tourism and Scottish Heritage. In *Tourism and Leisure: Towards the Millennium*, Volume 1 Tourism and Leisure – Culture, Heritage and Participation (pp. 109–120). Eastbourne: Leisure Studies Association.

Lacy, J. and Douglas, W. (2002) Beyond authenticity: The meaning and uses of cultural tourism. *Tourists Studies* 2, 9–21.

Lin, Y., Pearson, T.E. and Cai, L.A. (2011) Food as a form of destination identity: A tourism destination brand perspective. *Tourism and Hospitality Research* 11 (1), 30–48.

Long, L.M. (2004) *Culinary Tourism*. Lexington: University of Kentucky Press.

Lothian, E. and Siler, P. (2003) Local food production and tourism: Scottish enterprise and the food and drink clusters. Proceedings of the WTO local food and tourism international conference (pp. 63–80). Larnaka, Cyprus.

Mak, A.H.N., Lumbers, M. and Eves, A. (2012) Globalisation and food consumption in tourism. *Annals of Tourism Research* 39 (1), 171–196.

McKercher, B., Okumus, F. and Okumus, B. (2008) Food tourism as a viable market segment: It's all how you cook the numbers! *Journal of Travel and Tourism Marketing* 25(2), 137–148.

Novelli, M. (2005) *Niche Tourism: Contemporary Issues, Trends and Cases*. Oxford: Elsevier.

Okumus, B., Okumus, F. and McKercher, B. (2007) Incorporating local and international cuisines in the marketing of tourism destinations: The cases of Hong Kong and Turkey. *Tourism Management* 20 (1), 253–261.

Pine, J. and Gilmore, J. (1999) *The Experience Economy*. Boston, MA: Harvard Business School Press.

Poon, A. (1993) *Tourism, Technology and Competitive Strategies*. Wallingford: CAB International.

Quan, S. and Wang, N. (2004) Towards a structural model of the tourist experience: An illustration from food experiences in tourism. *Tourism Management* 25 (3), 297–305.

Rand, G.E. du and Heath, E. (2006) Towards a framework for food tourism as an element of destination marketing. *Current Issues in Tourism* 9 (3), 206–234.

Reynolds, P. (1993) Food and tourism: Towards an understanding of sustainable culture. *Journal of Sustainable Tourism* 1 (1), 48–54.

Richards, G. (2002) Gastronomy: An essential ingredient in tourism production and consumption? In A.-M. Hjalager and G. Richards (eds) *Tourism and Gastronomy* (pp. 3–20). London: Routledge.

Sharpley, R. and Sharpley, A. (1997) *Rural Tourism: An Introduction*. Oxford: Alden Press.

Sims, R. (2009) Food, place and authenticity: Local food and the sustainable tourism experience. *Journal of Sustainable Tourism* 17 (3), 321–336.

Šimundić, B. and Stipetić, V. (1996) Health food and health tourism. *Tourism and Hospitality Management* 2 (2), 357 368.

Socher, K. and Tschurtschenthaler, P. (1994) Tourism and agriculture in Alpine regions. *The Tourist Review* 49 (3), 35–41.

Telfer, D. and Wall, G. (1996) Linkages between tourism and food production. *Annals of Tourism Research* 23 (3), 635–653.

Vitterso, G. and Amilien, V. (2011) From tourism product to ordinary food? The role of rural tourism in development of local food and food heritage in Norway. *Anthropology of Food* 8, 6833.

3   The Future of Food Tourism: The Star Trek Replicator and Exclusivity

Ian Yeoman and Una McMahon-Beattie

Highlights

- This chapter portrays two future states. The *Star Trek Replicator* recreates a future of food and science within which new experiences and cuisines are formed whereas *Exclusivity* is about the future of luxury dining.
- Six drivers of change are identified and explored: the advancement of science, scarcity of resources, quantified self, authenticity, affluence and social capital.
- The role of food tourism as an exclusive experience, supported by innovation and the continued desire for health and authenticity is discussed.
- A range of overlapping trends, ideas and circumstances provides foresight as to what the future of food tourism might be.

Introduction

Food has been seen as an important tourist attraction (Henderson, 2009) and gastronomy (defined as the style of cooking in a particular region or country) 'can be clearly considered as an indispensable part of the travel experience' (Sanchez-Canizares & Lopez-Guzman, 2013: 229). As such, food and tourism have a very close symbiotic relationship and 'local' food plays a central role in tourism products, destination promotion strategies, tourism decision-making and satisfaction (Nield *et al.*, 2000). Food is not only a basic necessity for human life but it serves a social purpose bringing pleasure and entertainment, helps the tourist to explore other cultures and provides insights into different ways of life (Bell & Valentine, 1997; Hegarty & O'Mahoney, 2001; Quan & Wang, 2004).

Henderson (2009) notes that a range of labels have been created for food-based tourism including:

- Culinary tourism (Wolf, 2002, cited in Kivela & Crotts, 2005);
- Gastronomy tourism (Hjalanger & Richards, 2002);
- Tasting tourism (Boniface, 2003);
- Food tourism (Hall *et al.*, 2003).

Notably an appreciation of both food and beverages is included in these types. Food tourism offers, therefore, a myriad of business opportunities in terms of, for example, restaurants and hotels, cookery schools, food and drink festivals, and farmers markets. The challenge for destinations, both now and in the future, is to develop or maintain an authentic food or gastronomy offer which draws on local distinctiveness and provenance.

Food is also integral to a destination's cultural heritage and heavily influences (and is influenced by) the farming landscape and other environments through its production. While this is true of every destination, these elements provide a means by which to differentiate destinations by shaping their own unique character, provenance and authenticity (Henderson, 2009).

The ancient Sicilian Greek poet and philosopher, Archestratus, is often referred to as the Father of Gastronomy. Writing what might be considered the world's first eating guide entitled *Gastronomia*, he noted that gastronomy was 'the pleasure of taste according code or set of rules' (cited in Santich, 1996). In 1825, the modern champion of gastronomy, Jean-Anthelme Brillat-Savarin, holistically defined gastronomy as the 'reasoned knowledge of everything pertaining to man, insofar as he nourishes himself'. Fundamentally, gastronomy is the heart of human life and allows for cultural adaption and reflection. Hence food tourism is a key area of focus and competitive advantage for many tourism policies and marketing campaigns (Yeoman, 2008).

But what is the future? Food prevails in almost every aspect of consumers' lives and can be seen as a necessity or a luxury indulgence. It reflects position and status. Indeed foods such as haggis, foic gras or dahl represent popular and/or national identity. But, food prices are currently rising, agricultural ground is becoming scarcer because of competition for land and urbanisation, the world's population is growing and diets are changing. This chapter presents two feasible scenarios about the future of food tourism. *Star Trek Replicator* explores the concepts of food and science within which new experiences and cuisines are formed whereas *Exclusivity* explores food as a luxury experience.

Looking to the Future: Tipping Points and Food

A tipping point is a stage at which the driving forces of change in relation to food tourism cannot be reversed. Examples of these forces may include how climate change is changing tourism products or the scarcity of oil for international travel (Gladwell, 2003; Hansen, 2008; Yeoman, 2012). The Food and Agriculture Organization of the United Nations (FAO) forecasts that global food consumption will nearly double between 2010 and 2050 (Future Foundation, 2013). A key driver behind food demand is the fact that millions of people's diets across the developing world are changing. As their incomes improve, wealthier cohorts in Asia, Latin America and Africa are adopting new diets (richer in salt, sugar and fat) that increasingly resemble the diets enjoyed by consumers in more advanced economies. The consumption of meat in particular is growing fast in developing markets (itself one of the most energy-hungry food types) and per capita meat consumption in East Asia is projected to double by 2050. As the trend towards energy-dense diets and sedentary lifestyles continues, it is likely that there will be a global convergence of diet-related health issues in the coming decades as levels of obesity and diabetes rise across the globe.

While undernourishment levels in non-Organisation for Economic Co-operation and Development developing countries are projected to fall from 16% in 2005 to 5% in 2050 (Yeoman, 2012), concerns remain about the ability in the future to feed a growing world population given the vulnerability of food resources to climate change and the extreme weather events it can cause. Other pressures include the growing constraints on resources such as land, water and energy which are crucial to food production; the growing output of biofuels; and the seemingly entrenched opposition in some parts of the world to agricultural innovation that could potentially alleviate some of the pressure on global food supplies.

Inevitably, as the world's population increases dramatically, food prices will rise as the new consumers of China and India demand a Western lifestyle and as land becomes scarcer due to continued urbanisation. From a tourism perspective, does this mean food will become the new luxury experience or will new scientific advancements produce innovative food products and fashions? The next section in this chapter explores these futures.

Why Study the Future?

The future is the indefinite time period after the present (Hastings et al., 1908). Whether it is less than a millisecond away or a billion years hence, its arrival is considered inevitable due to the existence of time and the laws of physics. Due to the nature of the reality and the unavoidability of the *future*, everything that currently exists and will exist is temporary and will come to an end. The *future* and the concept eternity have been major subjects of philosophy, religion and science and defining them non-controversially has consistently eluded the greatest of minds. Future studies, or futurology, is the science, art and practice of postulating possible futures, or more basically, the study of the future seeks to understand what is likely to continue, what is likely to change, and what is novel. Part of the discipline thus seeks a systematic and pattern-based understanding of past and present, and to determine the likelihood of future events and trends. So, in order to understand the future of food tourism it is important to understand how change is occurring, the fundamental driving forces and likely outcomes.

Scenario Planning

What are scenarios and scenario planning? There is no single, universal definition of either. For example, Michael Porter talks about scenarios as an 'internally consistent view of what the future might turn out to be' (Porter, 2004: 446), whereas Peter Schwartz describes 'scenario planning as a tool for ordering one's perception about alternative future environments' (Schwartz, 1991: 4). Scenario planning is one methodology applied within the field of futures studies.

The history of scenario planning lies in two worlds (Lindgren, 2009). The first was future studies, where scenario analysis became an important method for generating futures thinking and scenarios became an effective presentation format. The second was strategy, where strategists and managers since the 1970s have searched for new and more relevant tools to work with complex issues. Modern scenario planning is attributed to Herman Kahn (van der Heijden, 2002) and the RAND Corporation. Kahn developed a technique called 'future-now' thinking. The scenarios he developed were part of military strategy research conducted for the United States (US) government, and he coined the term 'thinking the unthinkable'. Walton (2008) places scenario planning in the paradigm of constructivist interpretation based on the underpinning criteria of emergent construction, development of alternatives, internalisation, localism and plausibility. However, Walton's arguments are undermined by the notion of plausibility in which he argues that any scenario should be possible, credible and relevant. Fahey and Randall (1998: 9) also use the argument, as 'Plausible evidence should indicate that the projected narrative could take place (it is possible), demonstrate how it could take place (it is credible) and illustrate its implications for the organisations (it is relevant).'

Scenarios and drivers

Two scenarios are used to demonstrate what the future could be. First, the *Star Trek Replicator* recreates a future of food and science within which new experiences and cuisines are formed, whereas *Exclusivity* concerns a future of luxury dining. Each scenario is constructed using three driving forces which are the trends shaping the scenarios. The driving forces identified and explored are the advancement of science, scarcity of resources, quantified self, authenticity, affluence and social capital.

Scenario 1: Wellington Food Festival: The Star Trek Replicator

The winner of this year's Wellington Food Festival award for innovation was The Whitehouse Restaurant Degustation Menu, combining the best of science, new tastes and food. In a world in which consumers are obsessed with food trends against a global background of food scarcity, the hospitality industry is facing new challenges in order to find new ideas. Inspired by the writings of chef come food scientist, Heston Blumenthal, the Whitehouse Restaurant is a three-star Michelin restaurant owned by Paul Hoather IV whose cuisine is based on healthy, novel and experiential food. The degustation menu was described by the judges as demonstrating inspirational insight into the future of food and dining. It consisted of Scottish Haggis grown in the laboratory at Victoria University of Wellington, the finest scallops poached in carrot broth (made by a robotic chef programmed by Honda), plant-based proteins which formed the basis of a fine Tournedos Rossini with Madeira sauce, and the finest patisseries made from subatomic particles produced by a replicator. The Whitehouse is showcasing the replicator, developed by the University of Otago's Institute of Food and Science. It has been one of New Zealand's success stories allowing for the mass production of food that is healthy, relatively cheap and sustainable.

This scenario represents on one level the food tourist's desire for innovation and novelty. On another level, it portrays how science could change the food production process from a traditional land-based system to a laboratory-based one.

Driver 1: The advancement of science

The advancement of food science is best represented by vitro meat (or test tube meat). According to Betti and Datar (2010) current meat production methods are a major source of pollution, deforestation and a major consumer of resources with, for example, the production of red meat requiring $15,500m^3$/ton of water. Given the world's growing population, urbanisation and competition for resources it no longer makes sense to produce meat in a natural way when each 1 kilogram (kg) of poultry, pork and beef requires 2 kg, 4 kg and 7 kg of grain respectively. An alternative is in vitro meat production (IMPS) which involves culturing muscle tissue in a liquid medium on a large scale.

Over the last 15 years, three technologies have emerged that make in vitro meat production possible in order to generate skeletal muscle and other mesenchymal tissues, namely stem cell isolation and identification, ex vivo cell culture and tissue engineering (Post, 2012). Most recently, Professor Mark Post demonstrated how the technology could be used, growing a beef burger in the laboratory, as reported in the following way as part of food tasting (Image 3.1):

The world's first lab-grown burger has been cooked and eaten at a news conference in London. Scientists took cells from a cow and, at an institute in the Netherlands, turned them into strips of muscle that they

Image 3.1 Vitro hamburger grown in the laboratory
Source: Permission: http://culturedbeef.net

combined to make a patty. One food expert said it was 'close to meat, but not that juicy' and another said it tasted like a real burger. Researchers say the technology could be a sustainable way of meeting what they say is a growing demand for meat. The burger was cooked by Schonwald. Upon tasting the burger, Austrian food researcher Ms Ruetzler said: 'I was expecting the texture to be more soft...there is quite some intense taste; it's close to meat, but it's not that juicy. The consistency is perfect, but I miss salt and pepper. (Ghosh, 2013)

Another field of science, linked to the advancement of food are genetically modified (GM) foods, which provide a realistic solution to feeding the world's population in 2050 (Chamberlain, 2004). GM foods are foods derived from genetically modified organisms where specific changes are introduced into their DNA by genetic engineering techniques, involving the insertion or deletion of genes. The potential contribution of GM foodstuffs towards the global malnutrition situation is through the capability to increase crop productivity and therefore the ability to feed more. Future envisaged applications of GM are diverse and include: drugs in food; bananas that produce human vaccines against infectious diseases such as Hepatitis B; metabolically engineered fish that mature more quickly; fruit and nut trees that yield years earlier; foods no longer containing properties associated with common intolerances; and plants that produce new plastics with unique properties.

Desponier (2010) argues that a future food supply could be based on vertical farming, an agricultural technique involving large-scale agriculture in urban high-rises or 'farmscrapers'. Using advanced greenhouse technology and methods such as hydroponics, these buildings would produce fruit, vegetables, edible mushrooms and algae year-round. Unlike traditional farming, vertical farming creates the multiplication of productivity of the farmed surface by a factor of four to six depending on the crop. Furthermore, these crops would be sold in the same infrastructures in which they are grown, thereby decreasing the need for transportation, resulting in less spoilage, infestations and energy required. This could significantly alleviate climate change as reduced energy for transportation will result in less atmospheric carbon produced. Desponier (2010) suggests that, if dwarf versions (i.e. smaller in size but richer in nutrients) of certain crops are used, year-round crops and 'stacker' plant holders are accounted for, a 30-story building with a base of a building block (five acres) would yield a yearly crop analogous to that of 2400 acres of traditional farming. Vertical farming provides a controlled, protective environment for crops, independent of weather and extreme weather events (apart from earthquakes and tornadoes), thereby significantly increasing agricultural productivity.

In science fiction literature, the *Star Trek Replicator* is the ultimate solution to the world's food crisis. A replicator can create any inanimate matter over and over again as long as the desired molecular structure is on file. Drum and Gordon (2003) argue that a replicator would work by rearranging subatomic particles, which are abundant everywhere in the universe, to form molecules and arrange those molecules to form the object. For example, to create a steak and French fries dinner, the replicator would first form atoms of carbon, hydrogen, nitrogen, etc., then arrange them into amino acids, proteins and cells, and put it all together into the form of a steak and French fries meal. Most recently, NASA has contracted Systems and Materials Research Corporation to build a 3D food printer to produce nutritious and flavourful mission supplies for astronauts (Dickinson, 2013). One of the first foods is expected to be pizza. The replicator works by first printing a layer of dough which is baked by a heated plate at the bottom of the printer. Then it prints a tomato layer made from a powder base mixed with water and oil, followed by a final protein layer.

Driver 2: Scarcity of resources

Rising affluence and growing access to resources will continue to fundamentally alter the lifestyles of consumers in developing economies; resources long taken for granted elsewhere in the world are fuelling significant changes to the behaviours, diets and expectations of these consumers. However, as demand for a finite supply of resources increases within ever-populous and prosperous emerging markets and as the disruptive impact of climate change on global supply continues, food and energy prices for the end-consumer are likely to be driven upwards (see Figure 3.1).

According to Evans (2008), there are four mains drivers for food inflation. First, the costs of agricultural inputs, and especially energy, are rising.

Today's global agricultural system is predicated on the availability of cheap, readily available energy, for use in every part of the value chain: both directly (e.g. cultivation, processing, refrigeration, shipping, distribution) and indirectly (e.g. manufacture of fertilisers, pesticides). World oil prices peaked in 2008 and will remain relatively high in the long term (Yeoman, 2012). In addition, since food can now be converted into fuel, there is effectively an arbitrage relationship between the two, implying an ongoing linkage between food and fuel prices. Second, water scarcity is likely to become a more pressing issue. Global demand for water has tripled in the last 50 years; 500 million people live in countries chronically short of water, and this number is likely to rise to 4 billion by 2050 (Yeoman, 2012). Third, there is the issue of land availability. Some commodities analysts argue that whereas historical increases in demand have been met through increasing yields, in future an expansion of acreage will also be required (Yeoman, 2012). However, this will be expensive, given the infrastructure investment involved. There may also be diminishing returns, since much of the best land is already under cultivation. Above all, there is simply increasing competition for what land there is. This is between food, feed, fibre (e.g. timber, paper), fuel, forest conservation, carbon sequestration and urbanisation, and is compounded by high rates of soil loss due to erosion and desertification. The fourth, and perhaps most fundamental, factor is climate change. The International Panel on Climate Change (IPCC) projects that global food production could rise if local average temperatures increase by between one and three degrees Celsius, but could decrease above this range (Parry *et al.*,

World food and oil price indices to 2030
Annual food and oil price indices (2005=100)

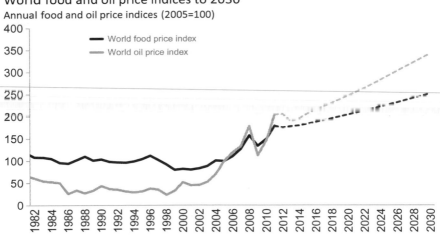

Figure 3.1 The future of resource prices
Source: Food and Agriculture Organization of the United Nations/International Monetary Fund/ Author Forecast.

2007). Crucially, however, this is before extreme weather events are taken into account and the IPCC judges that extreme weather, rather than temperature, is likely to make the biggest difference to food security.

Food security exists when all people, at all times, have physical, social and economic access to sufficient, safe and nutritious food to meet their dietary needs and food preferences for an active and healthy life. Food insecurity will mean a period of pronounced turbulence. Evans (2008) predicts an increased prevalence of *shocks*, sudden onset crises, such as extreme weather events driven by climate change, or sharp spikes in the price of energy. There will be *stresses* which are slower onset impacts such as land degradation or gradual price inflation that risk being overlooked by short-term policy or investment planning. Then there is the risk caused by human action through *ignorance or accident*: think of the positive feedback loop caused by one set of countries suspending exports while another attempts to build up imports. Finally, the food system could be disrupted by *malicious action*, for example, during conflicts or through intentional systems disruption by terrorists or insurgent groups. As such the food supply chain is threatened.

Driver 3: Quantified Self

Consumers' interest in food and health has spawned technological revolution in how people manage their health. Today, health can be monitored and tracked through smart phone applications (Future Foundation, 2013). Such applications mean consumers can exercise personal control over calories consumed, pulse rates and blood pressure, all via the smartphone. The real-time nature of tracking devices allows health conscious consumers to rectify poor or cost-ineffective choices almost immediately. Decision processes can be streamlined and behaviours modified *on-the-go*. As the consumer strives to attain health and weight targets and earn rewards, he or she will know the level of exercise needed to counteract the effect of eating a cream bun or the benefit of cycling rather than driving to work. Today, the smartphone is the new personal trainer.

Underpinning interest in such activity is concern about trying to stay fit and healthy, a concern that is widespread and growing (see Figure 3.2). It is clearly linked to food consumption and when combined with consumers' interest in 'staying younger longer', a trend emerges called the 'smart food revolution'. Here, consumers are using science through food to fight disease, to slow aging and even to improve their minds.

Crawford (1980) identified 'healthism' as a feature of modern society in the 1980s and health has continued to be a major preoccupation of people and governments. With the rise of neoliberalism, the creation of the health consumer and the promotion of personal responsibility for health have characterised contemporary health concerns. Since food is important for health, and vice versa, it is not surprising that food and health have

Usage of personal health tracking apps

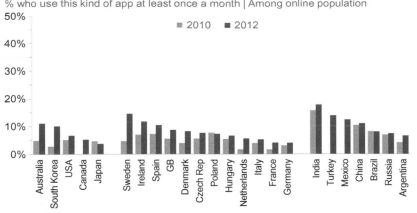

% who use this kind of app at least once a month | Among online population

Source: nVision Research | Base: 1,000-5,000 online respondents per country aged 16-64 (Mexico 16-54), 2012

Figure 3.2 Personal apps
Source: Future Foundation (2012).

become elided to a considerable degree in contemporary society. Many people have begun to engage in dietary supplementation, most commonly with vitamins and minerals, and frequently for health reasons. The benefits of supplementation remain unclear, and as Foote *et al.* (2003) have found, people who take dietary supplements regularly have healthier lifestyles (engage in more exercise, are less likely to smoke) and better dietary practices (lower fat, and higher fruit and fibre intakes) than people who do not take supplements, making the direct benefits of supplementation difficult to disentangle.

Supplementation products are commonly presented in drug-like forms, that is, pills and tablets, complete with dosage instructions and notes. Indeed, vitamin and mineral combinations are readily available in this form, alongside a huge range of special 'treatments' for various 'conditions', such as specific formulations for strengthening the immune system, for the prevention of prostate conditions in men or for the alleviation of menopausal symptoms for women. These products are becoming more widely available as they are increasingly sold through supermarkets, and no longer limited to pharmacies and specialist health food shops. Other specialist dietary supplements and food replacements are marketed specifically to bodybuilders and body-sculptors, many of whom have diets considerably removed from the ordinary.

Thus, through using technology and science the consumer is able to monitor and predict their health. They can collect and interpret real-time information about everyday food intake, count calories, monitor their heart rate and thus harness efficiencies to understand and shape their lifestyle.

Self-monitoring tools can be used to assess our lifestyles so that potentially damaging or inefficient patterns of consumption can be adjusted and bad decisions rectified on-the-spot.

Scenario 2: Exclusivity: The future of authentic dining

In 2050, 70 million people live in Shanghai, mostly in dilapidated and over-crowded apartments, along with the homeless who fill the streets and line the fire escapes of buildings. This world is suffering the effects of climate change, pollution, over population, dying seas and depleted resources. Food is scarce and expensive. Most consumers survive on rice and nutritional food supplements whereas the privileged in society can afford and have access to real meat, vegetables and fish. This is the story of Chen Kenichi (Peter) and Ching-He Haung (Mary) who live in a gated apartment in the suburb of Xinquia. Peter and Mary have booked an overnight stay at the Gordon Ramsay School of Rare Fine Cuisine @Shangrai-La. The cookery school is located in Shanghai's most famous and exclusive five star hotel. Students learn how to cook ancient and classic dishes from the famous French chef, Georges Escoffier, such as Baked Eggs Mirabeau, Beef Tenderloin Saint-German and Peaches Cardinal. Peter and Mary start off the cookery course hearing stories from 'Le Guide Culinaire' and the restaurants of the London Savoy and Ritz in Paris before sampling expensive foodstuffs to be used in the class. The class is taught by the great grandson of Gordon Ramsay, the famous Scottish celebrity chef and Michelin award winner. Throughout the day the students learn how to use kitchen knives, chop vegetables, cook steak and poach the finest peaches. All in all, a fine Escoffier experience.

The scenario represents a number of drivers of change in society, particularly food and its scarcity in society. As a consequence, real food becomes an exclusive experience for rich tourists. The ultimate experience focuses on authenticity and rare foods from the past. This is portrayed in the scenario with food tourists co-creating dishes from the *Le Guide Culinaire* (Escoffier, 1903), which is the culinary bible that first codified Escoffier's recipes.

Driver 1: Exclusivity and authenticity

According to Yeoman and McMahon-Beattie (2014) materialism is not dead but is at the centre of the concept of exclusivity. Goods such as luxury fast cars can be seen as a representation of a person's desire for what is exclusive, expensive, the best quality, self-indulgent, conspicuous and experiential. The Chinese middle-class consumer can be seen to exemplify this materialistic exclusivity. He/she wants *brands* and companies are placing importance on emphasising aspiration and status-building in their marketing communications. Yeoman (2012) identified food as an authentic, exclusive experience in the scenario entitled *Soylent Green*. This was based upon access to fresh food in a dystopian society akin to North Korea. Here only the wealthy have access to such food whereas the poor eat artificial and manufactured foodstuffs. Yeoman thus explores the concept of luxury, which means exclusive, rare and expensive. What distinguishes consumers that can access exclusive food experiences is authenticity.

Driver 2: Affluence

The weight of global economic activity is already shifting substantially from Western developed countries towards emerging economies in Asia and Latin America (Stancil & Dadush, 2010). This trend is expected to accelerate over the next 40 years. The economy of the G20 countries is expected to grow at an average annual rate of 3.5%, rising from $38.3 trillion in 2009 to $160 trillion in 2050 in real dollar terms (Stancil & Dadush, 2012). Over 60% of this $121 trillion dollar expansion will come from Brazil, Russia, India, China, Indonesia (the traditional 'Big Five' economies) and Mexico. In US$ GDP, these six economies will grow at an average rate of 6% per year; their share of G20 GDP will rise from 19.6% in 2009 to 50.6% in 2050. By contrast, GDP in the G7 (US, United Kingdom (UK), France, Germany, Italy, Canada and Japan) will grow by less than 2.1% annually, and their share of G20 GDP will decline from 72.3% to 40.5%. In China and India alone, GDP is predicted to increase by nearly $60 trillion, the current size of the world economy, and the US is projected to relinquish its title of the world's preeminent economic power to China in 2032 as rapid annual growth of 5.6% and a strengthening currency will drive China's US$ GDP up from $3.3 trillion in 2009 to $46.3 trillion in 2050. India is predicted to post the most rapid growth (5.9% annually) of all G20 countries. Its purchasing power parity GDP will be nearly 90% as large as that of the US. India is expected to become the world's most populous nation in 2031 eventually pushing US$ GDP to $15.4 trillion in 2050, over 14 times its current level. However, despite these dramatic increases in total GDP, US per capita GDP will be nearly three times that of China and over eight times that of India. US technological advantages will likely help the US maintain its position as a leader of the international community, but China's and India's much lower per capita income, combined with their very large size, may reinforce their authority in many forums as more representative of the vast majority of the world's peoples.

So, the world economy is shifting from the traditional Western economies to south and east, but Western consumers will still dominate. What does this mean? Rising income (and the wealth improvement connected) has been the driving agent of modern society. It is a key indicator of societal success, responsible for the empowerment of consumers and the growth of world tourism (Yeoman, 2012). Increased personal prosperity creates an emboldened consumer-citizen, a more demanding, sophisticated and informed actor with intensified expectations of quality innovation and premium choices in every market, efficient and ever-personalised customer service, and visible corporate commitment to tackling the environmental and ethical problems of the day. From a tourism perspective, according to the United Nations World Tourism Organisation (UNWTO, 2011):

> Tourism demand depends above all strongly on the economic conditions in major generating markets. When economies grow, levels of disposable income will usually also rise. A relatively large part of discretionary income will typically be spent on tourism, in particular in the case of emerging economies.

The UNWTO (2011) is projecting international arrivals to reach 1.8 billion by 2030, with the emerging economies of the world dominating this growth. However, income parity between emerging and developing countries in some way off (US GDP per capita in real terms, for instance, is over five times that of China). Personal prosperity in these emerging markets is rising, so millions more consumers will, as has traditionally been the case in the developed West, enjoy greater discretionary spend and a more varied consumption portfolio and travel will be a high priority (Yeoman, 2012).

Driver 3: Social capital and the experience economy

Previously the purchasing aspirations of millions of consumers were moulded most forcefully by the notion that *expensive material possessions plus conspicuous display equals social status*. Socially mobile consumers were continuously invited to *own more* whether that was a sports car, a designer watch, limited edition aftershave or vintage champagne. However, this proposition has been facing a significant challenge for some time now (Future Foundation, 2013). Many consumers still find capital in their ownership of the latest luxury item or experience but for many flaunting one's material possessions has lost much of the attraction it once had. Food and cooking as social capital can be seen as a representation of Bourdieu's (Swartz, 1998) forms of capital that reveal the dynamics of power relations in social life with food being a metaphor for social class divisions. Social capital is often associated with socially valued forms of art, music, fashion and indeed cuisine. Indeed food can be seen as the ultimate luxury experience, particularly with increased pressure on land due to population growth. As seen in the scenario above, demand is created for the food tourism experience since it supports cultural identification and social status. Accomplishments, talents and wider interests such as food have become the new form of currency by which degrees of personal success can be measured. For many consumers, cooking can be a way to fulfill core aspirations such as the achievement of self-actualisation and generating recognition from others. According to the Future Foundation (2012), four in five Britons agree that they are confident in their culinary skills – with one in five of them claiming to feel very confident, hence supporting the claim that food and cooking are important features of consumers' social capital and desire for experiences.

So What is the Significance about the Future for the Present?

The following section considers the significance of the scenarios and drivers from a 'so what' principle (Henderson, 2003) and establishes the importance and utility value of a number of issues including the trends and innovations that will be important for the future of tourism and the role of food tourism as an exclusive experience.

What are the trends and innovations that will be important for the future of food tourism?

One of the key drivers in *Exclusivity: The Future of Authentic Dining* is the desire for new experiences. Tourism and hospitality is one of the most competitive industries in the world and as a consequence of the global financial crisis (GFC) the out-of-home leisure market has been squeezed due to less disposable income being spent on discretionary items such as eating out. It has also been impacted by the growing role of the home as an entertainment space (Future Foundation, 2012). Simply, consumers are seeking better reasons and pretexts to spend their hard earned money. The industry in general has always been one of entrepreneurship and innovation given the presence of small to medium enterprises and low barriers to entry (Inwood *et al.*, 2009). As a consequence, it has sought to inject vibrancy and appeal into food tourism products and experiences. Here, some of those innovations are considered.

In a number of cities across the world, the early 2010s have heralded a growing number of restaurants which take choice *away* from the diner. While guests would normally expect to select their preferred dishes either à la carte or from a fixed menu, these establishments work on a very different proposition. Just one or two main options are available, with a strong emphasis being placed on the restaurant's gourmet or premium credentials. The anxiety of choice is thus removed from the selection process, with diners safe in the knowledge that their meal has been truly tried, tested and perfected by the chef. The restaurant experience is also injected with a sense of fun and adventure. For example, in *Chef's Table*, in New York (www.brooklynfare.com/pages/chefs-table) visitors have no idea what they are going to get from Chef Cesar Ramirez. The chef changes the menu for his 24-course meal every morning. All visitors can expect is 24 small plates. The *Le Relais de Venise* (www.relaisdevenise.com) offers only one starter (a green salad with walnuts dressed with mustard vinaigrette) and one main course (steak frites served with what the restaurant calls a secret recipe sauce). The steak dish is served in two stages, with 'one half held back to keep warm, so you can enjoy it at its best and is accompanied with more freshly prepared frites'.

While traditional fast-food offerings continue to thrive, several outlets have been attempting to give the concept a makeover by repositioning fast-food meals as a premium and yet affordable option to be enjoyed in restaurant style, out-of-home venues. Addressing consumers' desire to access high-quality food at cost-attractive prices, the provision of gourmet burgers has exemplified this trend. For example *Gourmet Burger Kitchen* (www.gbk.co.uk) was started by three Kiwis in London in 2001 and offered customers homemade burgers using only the freshest ingredients and best beef cuts.

In major cities and conurbations across the world, street vans and trucks have long since been inviting customers to sample authentic cuisine and *try something new*. Indeed street food is becoming more established. TV cookery shows like the *Food Truck* (http://tvnz.co.nz/the-food-truck/index-group-4174185) and the *Great Food Truck Race* (www.foodnetwork.com/the-great-food-truck-race/index.html) are examples of this trend. As food trucks continue to gain momentum, a similar but smaller and more mobile offshoot is also in the ascendancy. Food trikes and scooters are now able to zip between locations and thus follow (or indeed precede) the crowd. For example, *Tartines en Seine* (www.facebook.com/tartinesenseine) in Paris offers individuals walking along the banks of the river Seine the chance to buy freshly prepared sandwiches and coffee.

Although not a mainstream phenomenon, some leisure providers have sought to combine dining with art by providing interactive, sensory or simply unusual experiences where food takes centre stage. The *Preserve24* (www.preserve24.com) in New York is a restaurant that is also an art exhibition designed by sculptor Brian Goggin. Several venues and organisations have been utilising the idea of surprise by keeping diners in suspense and withholding details about their meal or venue until the last possible moment. *Diner en blanc* (dinerenblanc.info) reveals a secret location to its online followers who then descend upon a specially selected public location to have a mass, chic picnic, all dressed in white. At the time of writing, the service had online platforms operating in 12 countries, including the UK, US, Singapore, Spain, France and Italy.

Whether to improve speed of delivery, create a sense of novelty, or provide diners with entertaining distractions, in-store tablets and other digital devices are increasingly being used as ordering platforms. *Do* (www.theviewatkingplow.com/do/index.html) uses iPads for all aspects of the restaurant process. Customers can use the iPad at their table to look up the menu, send in their order to the kitchen, chat with other tables, call up their valet, split the check, and to pay with credit card. The restaurant even takes it a step further by also using iPads to replace the mirrors in their restrooms. The idea that meals out are to be enjoyed on separate tables remains the norm but it is a concept that has been challenged in some venues which have abandoned traditional seating arrangements in favour of large, shared tables where former strangers are seated next to each other. Elsewhere services are emerging which facilitate people dining out with groups of people they may not previously have met. *EatSocial* (http://letseatsocial.com/) for example is a website which encourages people to eat out socially with both friends and strangers, claiming that it facilitates 'interesting people meeting each other over delicious food without the usual disruptions like menus or splitting bills'.

For some time now many diners have been snapping and then sharing images of their meals. This trend is particularly prevalent within Generation Y (Yeoman *et al.*, 2010). But as the trend matures, there has been a reaction against this *over*-sharing culture and a sharpening sense that the activity must bring some sense of *value*. In the years ahead, the concept of *purposeful* sharing is one that is bound to gain further momentum. For example, *Burpple* (www.burpple.com) promotes itself as a smart and beautiful way to remember, organise and explore food moments with your friends.

In order to convey a sense of transparency, brands are finding new ways to open up conversation channels with customers, often by providing real-time, behind-the-scenes access. Almost inevitably, the idea that consumers should be able to scrutinise internal processes, speak directly to brands and receive near instantaneous responses will drive further innovation. In May 2013, *Domino's* pizza tested its Domino's Live system in Salt Lake City (http://dominoslive.com/). This is a platform that gave consumers live access to the pizza-making process. Five cameras installed in-store streamed a feed showing pizzas being made and cooked to a dedicated website, 12 hours a day.

Calls for more *responsible* forms of consumption can be heard elsewhere too, with wasteful behaviours of any type coming under scrutiny. Innovative uses for unwanted or unsold ingredients are thus growing in number as conspicuous or needless excess falls further from favour in many quarters. *Disco Soupe* (www.discosoupe.org) runs community events in France where food discarded by supermarkets and hotels is collected and then turned into meals. Typically, DJs or bands provide entertainment while the food is being prepared, with the meals then distributed to homeless individuals in the local area.

As consumers have looked for cost-effective and yet still enjoyable leisure experiences, the role of the home as an entertainment and socialising venue has been elevated. From renting the services of chefs to hosting gourmet supper clubs or 'event TV' parties, the rise of the professionalised home entertainment venue represents a serious challenge to the mechanics of how out-of-home leisure has traditionally been positioned. *KitchenSurfing* (www.kitchensurfing.com) allows chefs of all levels to offer their services, with users able to select an option which suits their event and/or budget.

Individuals can also rent out their kitchens. *Home Cooking For You* (http://homecookingforyou.com) is a platform that provides home-cooked meals made with fresh ingredients that are then delivered straight to your home. The meals are made to be frozen and reheated whenever is convenient for the customer. *Eat With* (www.eatwith.com) is a global community which allows tourists to dine in homes around the world. This experience allows people to connect with hosts and share culture and homemade cuisine.

What is the role of food tourism as an exclusive experience?

The extreme wealthy or high net worth individuals (HNWI) control a disproportionate amount of the world's assets and, according to the World Institute for Development Economics Research UN University, the richest 2% of adults own more than half of all of the world's household wealth (Davies, 2006). In many ways, the mega-rich are bound closely together as a niche of consumers isolated from the mainstream. They can afford the lifestyles, goods and services of the highest calibre and quality that are simply not accessible to the mass-market consumer. The high-profile spending activity of such people plus the daily gossip detailing the glamour of their celebrity lifestyles has brought the dealings and doings of the mega-rich into the heart of contemporary culture (Future Foundation, 2013). The activities of seriously wealthy and often very famous people directly affect the shape of markets. The mega-rich often own or influence very potent cultural objects and favour certain social causes. In this way they drive both expectation and behaviour on the part of the more ordinary citizen. Their direct impact on the market for luxury and style (what it is and where it is to be found) is immense. Their wealth and their tastes are a glorious incentivisation of the masses for anything designer, from handbags to Ferraris to restaurants and food destinations.

The words exclusive and materialism dominate an understanding of luxury (Yeoman, 2014). The conspicuous consumption displayed by food tourists in the *Exclusivity: The Future of Authentic Dining* scenario derives from the theory of economic capital based upon the work of sociologist Thorstein Veblen (1899). Within the scenario, the display and consumption of food has become the nouveau niche of social class and hierarchy. This scenario is being played out today through a number of manifestations. The *Marquis Los Cabos Beach Resort* (www.marquisloscabos.com) in Mexico offers popsicles made from 24-carat gold flakes and premium Clase Azul Ultra tequila. Available by its luxurious 'Infinity' pool, the ices are sold for a cool $1000 each which, the hotel claims, makes them the most expensive such popsicles in the world. Early 2012 saw *dougieDog* (dougiedog.com), a restaurant in Vancouver which specialises in 'all-natural' hot dogs, add what it calls the 'most expensive hot dog in the world' to its menu. Branded as the 'Dragon Dog' (in honour of the brand's appearance on the Canadian version of *Dragon's Den*), the snack comprises a foot-long bratwurst sausage infused with 100-year-old Louis XIII cognac (a drink which costs over $2000 per bottle). Today the consumer can get a $5,000 hamburger for lunch. The Fleur de Lys restaurant in Las Vegas at Mandalay Bay (http://mandalaybay.com/dining/fleur/) offers the 'Fleurburger 5000' for $5,000. The burger consists of a Kobe beef patty 'topped with a rich truffle sauce and served on a brioche truffle bun'. Moreover this burger comes with its own beverage, a bottle of 1990 Chateau Petrus that is served in Ichendorf Brunello stemware that you get to keep. In January 2012, travel brand *Kuoni* introduced a new range of *Limited Release Holidays* which is an assortment of five packages for different types of holidaymaker (www.kuoni. co.uk/). These include food tours, tailored, so the brand says, for those in search of a great value holiday, a trip away from everyday life, an adventure of discovery, an experience of serenity and luxury in natural surroundings and, finally, an attractive option for those with children.

The *Exclusivity: The Future of Authentic Dining* scenario portrays a divided society of haves and have-nots. This proposition is drawn from the present trend in society of income polarisation. Using the Gini coefficient, in countries such as Mexico, the US, the UK, Germany, Russia and China income inequality rose between the mid-late 1980s and the late 2000s. Whilst the causes for this vary and are difficult to generalise, it is clear that the fruits of recent economic growth have not been shared equally. The gap separating urban and rural populations has grown particularly wide, as has the gap separating the richest from the poorest *within* urban and rural areas. Governments here have been accused of doing little to tackle inequality (focusing instead on economic growth) with inadequate availability of social welfare systems to mitigate a poverty that is indeed relative but, for those victimised by it, all too real. Polarisation has given birth to a growing global community of super-wealthy individuals and dynasties. Yeoman (2012) highlights this trend as a reversal of fortunes, where food tourism is only available to the elite in society rather than the middle classes which dominate world tourism today. In *Tomorrow's Tourist* (Yeoman, 2008) the key drivers of food tourism are described as affluence, changing demographics, falling food prices, individualism, time pressures and the experience economy. But as *Exclusivity: The Future of Authentic Dining* portrays decreased disposal incomes, food inflation and scarcity may lead to the scenario becoming reality. Who knows!

Why an increased desire for health and authenticity?

The scenario *Wellington Food Festival: The Star Trek Replicator* is positioned against a background of increased demand for healthier foods, wellness and physical fitness. Fundamentally, whilst health declines gradually throughout a person's life this reduction does not cause problems until very old age. Fundamentally, consumers are trying to extend their healthy years and reduce the chronic illness years. This means from a food tourism perspective that key issues are health and authenticity. The global issue of obesity and its related conditions (diabetes, coronary disease, mobility problems, etc.) is placing pressure on hotels and catering establishments. According to the World Health Organisation (WHO), 346 million consumers suffer from diabetes (Yeoman, 2012). If current trends were to continue unabated, it predicts that this figure will more than double by the end of 2030. Restaurant brands will therefore be encouraged (or coerced) into proactively promoting good nutritional behaviour. Today, consumers already have low calorie alcohol drinks from *Skinny Girl* (http://skinnygirlcocktails.com), calorie-lite refresher drinks from *Starbucks* (www.starbucks.com) or raw haute cuisine from *M.A.K.E* (http://matthewkenneycuisine.com/). In the future, unhealthy eating may become a thing of the past as establishments are penalised for unhealthy offerings such as extra-large soft drinks or transient fats in food products.

Tourists will expect menus to tell them exactly where all the food they consume originates, not just for the products deemed to be premium. Tourists' expectations about meat being locally-reared, fruit being grown locally and food miles being minimised can only harden. Tracking apps on smartphones can already monitor calorie intake. *Foodscanner* (http://tracker.dailyburn.com/foodscanner) reads barcodes and tells the user their calorie intake. These apps go on to tell you how much exercise you must do to offset the calorie intake and detail how many calories are left in your daily allowance.

As much as global consumers continue to embrace the convenience and reliability delivered by globalised mass production, they also aspire to an alternative to the perceived *homogenisation* of contemporary culture, food and leisure experiences. To a certain extent, *Exclusivity: The Future of Authentic Dining* encompasses the search for real food as authenticity-seeking. Food and its connection to culture, place and provenance is important to the modern-day food tourist. Authenticity-seeking (Yeoman, 2008) has also become associated with the accumulation of knowledge. The food tourism experience is all part of the modern holidaymaker's wish to experience different cultures and to sample local foods particular to a region or country; they wish to immerse themselves in the local vernacular. Such collectible experiences in turn become rich sources of social and cultural capital and an important means of differentiating ourselves. *Authenticity-seeking* is also related to food experiences that offer a connection with the *natural* world as well as a return to some of the more traditional, honest and simple pleasures in life. In developing and rapidly urbanising countries, offers of this kind are likely to become increasingly appealing, especially as tourists manage the transition to urban lifestyles.

Will science fiction come true?

Science fiction involves systematically altering technological, social or biological conditions and then attempting to understand the possible consequences (Bergman *et al.*, 2010), thus making claims but not supplying a truthful explanation. Yeoman (2012) positions science fiction as fiction based on science, having elements of truthfulness which explains a future state. As scenario planning provides stories of a fictional nature, it could be propositioned that the future is fiction until it has happened. Bell *et al.* (2013) support the argument that science fiction is a prototype of the future in which businesses frame, test, experiment and explore innovations. Entrepreneurship and innovation are inherent within the tourism and hospitality industry given the presence of small to medium enterprises and low barriers to entry (Harrington & Kendall, 2007), and as such, science fiction plays an important part in the development of the future. In Warren Belasco's (2006: viii) book *Meals to Come: A History of the Future of Food* the author states, 'Food is important. In fact, nothing is more important.'

Humankind has a history of worrying about food, whether it is about the food supply chain, over and under eating, diets or food quality. This human trait is linked to the sustainability of life and population, which is portrayed in the film *Soylent Green* (Yeoman, 2012). Here countries face the issues of rising food costs and starvation and society is on the verge of collapse as climate change has produced falling water tables, eroded top soil and falling yields. However, innovations such as vertical farming and sea harvesting have brought about new forms of food. As Belasco (2006) observes, foods that are portrayed in popular culture such as the meal-in-a-pill, instant food and futuristic kitchens have all come true as they are based on technological advancement in society and changing cultural patterns. In the end science fiction becomes reality so the Star Trek replicator (in reality a 3D food printer) will create a *1787 Chateau Lafite*.

Concluding Thoughts: The Implications for the Future of Food Tourism

The implications for the future of food tourism portrayed in this chapter are important as the number of food tourism products is growing, represent ing a range of different experiences designed to satisfy the needs of gastronomists or consumers who want to gain social capital. Food tourism has become the symbol of new tourism within which culture has metamorphosed into a normalised experience. Food tourists experience both the physical and social aspects of food (and beverage), and the product is offered in a variety of forms, from tours, tasting and education.

Exclusivity: The Future of Authentic Dining maybe an extreme case but it presents an identifiable drive in destination politics where political and industry leaders are chasing and propositioning high-yielding tourists thereby creating a tourist world of haves and have-nots. The scenario portrays Shanghai in 2050 where authenticity, learning the ancient skills of cooking and having access to real food are an exclusive experience. Here impoverished local communities are kept away from rich – exclusive tourists who stay in gated compounds or resorts.

Wellington Food Festival: The Star Trek Replicator is a game shifter as science and technology are seen as drivers of innovation. It represents the competitiveness of the tourism and hospitality industry with tourists wanting new tastes and forms of food. Both scenarios represent symbols of change and key signals to industry leaders of what is coming next. They might sound scary, but scenarios do not claim to be the absolute truth but rather an explanation of the future.

At a macro level many other drivers and events could have been considered such as the emerging economy of China and new food consumption patterns, changes in demography, food tourism as a festival experience and emerging food destinations. However, the chapter has taken a meta-level approach in order for readers to understand the wider issues and provide a long-term perspective. For readers to make sense of the chapter from their own perspective, they are advised to identify key issues from their own perspective, discuss implications and simulate solutions.

References

Belasco, W. (2007) *Meals to Come: A History of the Future of Food*. Los Angeles: University of California.

Bell, D. and Valentine, G. (1997) *Geographies: We Are What We Eat*. London: Routledge.

Bell, F., Fletcher, G., Greenhill, A. and Griffiths, M. (2013) Science fiction prototypes: Visionary technology narratives between futures. *Futures* 50, 5–14.

Bergman, A., Karlsson, J. and Axelsson, J. (2010) Truth claims and explanatory claims: An ontology typology of future studies. *Futures* 42, 857–865.

Betti, M. and Datar, I. (2010) Possibilities for an vitro meat production system. *Innovation Food Science and Emerging Technologies* 11 (1), 13–22.

Boniface, P. (2003) *Tasting Tourism: Travelling for Food and Drink*. Aldershot: Ashgate.

Chamberlain, K. (2004) Food and health. Expanding the agenda for health psychology. *Journal of Health Psychology* 9 (4), 467–481.

Crawford, R. (1980) Healthism and the medicalisation of everyday life. *International Journal of Health Services* 10 (3), 365–388.

Davies, J. (2006) *The World Distribution of Household Wealth*. United Nations University. See www.wider.unu.edu/events/past-events/2006-events/en_GB/05-12-2006/ (accessed 11 August 2013).

Desponier, D. (2010) The vertical farm: Reducing the impact of agriculture on ecosystem functions and services. See www.verticalfarm.com/more?essay1 (accessed 10 March 2014).

Dickinson, D. (2013) NASA Looks at 3-D Food Printer for Star Trek like Replicator. See www.universetoday.com/102328/nasa-looks-at-3-d-food-printer-for-star-trek-like-replicator/ (accessed 10 November 2013).

Drum, R. and Gordon, R. (2003) Star trek replicators and diatom nanotechnology. *Trends in Biotechnology* 21 (3), 325–328.

Escoffier, G.A. (1903) *Le Guide Culinaire*. Paris: Flammarion.

Evans, A. (2008) Rising food prices: Drivers and implications for development. London: Chatham House, The Royal Institute of International Affairs. See www.chatham-house.org/publications/papers/view/108792

Fahey, L.R. and Randall, R. (1998) What is scenario learning. In L. Fahey and R. Randall (eds) *Learning from the Future: Competitive Foresight Scenarios* (pp. 3–43). New York: Wiley.

Foote, J., Murphy, S., Wilkens, L., Hankin, J., Henderson, B. and Kolonel, L. (2003) Factors associated with dietary supplement use among healthy adults of five ethnicities. *American Journal of Epidemiology* 157, 888–897.

Future Foundation (2012) *Social Capital and the Home*. See http://nvision.futurefoundation .net (accessed 14 September 2013).

Future Foundation (2013) *Resource Competition and Climate Change*. See http://nvision. futurefoundation.net (accessed 13 October 2013).

Ghosh, P. (2013) World's first lab-grown burger is eaten in London. See www.bbc.co.uk/ news/science-environment-23576143 (accessed 20 October 2013).

Gladwell, M. (2003) *Tipping Point: How Little Things Can Make a Big Difference*. London: Back Bay Books.

Hall, C.M., Sharples, L., Mitchell, R., Macionis, N., and Cambourne, B. (2003) *Food Tourism around the World: Development, Management and Markets*. Oxford; Butterworth-Heinemann.

Hansen, J. (2008) Tipping point: Perspective of climatologist. In W. Woods (ed.) *State of the Wild: A Global Portrait of Wildlife, Wildlands and Ocean*. Washington, DC: Island Press.

Harrington, R.J. and Kendall, K.W. (2007) Uncovering the interrelationships among firm size, organizational involvement, environmental uncertainty, and implementation success. *International Journal of Hospitality & Tourism Administration* 8 (2), 1–23.

Hastings, J., Selbie, J.A. and Gray, L.H. (1908) *Encyclopedia of Religion and Ethics*. Edinburgh: T. & T. Clark.

Hegarty, J.A. and O'Mahoney, G.B. (2001) Gastronomy: A phenomenon of cultural expressionism and an aesthetic for living. *International Journal of Hospitality Management* 20 (1), 3–13.

Henderson, J.C. (2009) Food tourism reviewed. *British Food Journal* 111 (4), 317–362.

Henderson, V. (2003) The urbanization process and economic growth: The so-what question. *Journal of Economic Growth* 8 (1), 47–71.

Hjalanger, A.M. and Richards, G. (2002) *Tourism and Gastronomy*. London: Routledge.

Inwood, S., Sharp, J., Moore, R. and Stinner, D. (2009) Restaurants, chefs and local foods: Insights drawn from application of a diffusion of innovation framework. *Agricultural and Human Values* 26 (3), 177–191.

Kivela, J. and Crotts, J. (2005) Gastronomy tourism: A meaningful travel market segment. *Journal of Culinary Science and Technology* 4 (2–3), 39–55.

Lindgren, M.B.H. (2009) *Scenario Planning: The Link Between Future and Strategy*. Basingstoke: Palgrave Macmillan.

Nield, K., Kozak, M. and LeGrys, G. (2000) The role of food service in tourist satisfaction. *International Journal of Hospitality Management* 19 (2), 375–384.

Parry, M., Canziani, J., Lindem, P. and Hanson, C. (2007) *Contribution of Working Group II to the Fourth Assessment Report of the Intergovernmental Panel on Climate Change*. Cambridge: Cambridge University Press.

Quan, S. and Wang, N. (2004) Towards a structural model of the tourist experience: An illustration from food experiences in tourism. *Tourism Management* 25, 297–305.

Porter, M.E. (2004) *Competitive Advantage*. New York: Free Press.

Post, M. (2012) Cultured meat from stem cells: Challenges and prospects. *Meat Science* 92 (3), 297–301.

Sanchez-Canizares, S.M. and Lopez-Guzman, T. (2012) Gastronomy as a tourism experience: Profile of the culinary product. *Current Issues in Tourism* 15 (3), 229–245.

Santich, B. (1996) *Looking for Flavour*. Adelaide: Wakefield Press.

Schwartz, P. (1991) *The Art of the Long View: Planning for the Future in an Uncertain World*. New York: Currency Books.

Stancil, B. and Dadush, U. (2010) The world order in 2050. See http://carnegieendowment.org/files/World_Order_in_2050.pdf (accessed 20 October 2013).

Swartz, D. (1998) *Culture and Power: The Sociology of Pierre Bourieu.* Chicago: University of Chicago Press.

UNWTO (2011) Tourism Towards 2030. See http://media.unwto.org/en/press-release/2011-10-11/international-tourists-hit-18-billion-2030 (accessed 20 October 2013).

van der Heijden, K.B., Burt, G., Cairns, G. and Wright, G. (2002) *The Sixth Sense: Accelerating Organisation.* Chichester: Wiley.

Veblen, T. (1899) *The Theory of the Leisure Classes: An Economic Study in the Evolution of Institutions.* New York: The Macmillan Company.

Walton, J. (2008) Scanning beyond the horizon: Exploring the ontological and epistemological basis for scenario planning. *Advances in Developing Human Resources* 10 (2), 147–165.

Yeoman, I. (2008) *Tomorrrow's Tourist.* Oxford: Routledge.

Yeoman, I. (2012) *2050 – Tomorrow's Tourism.* Bristol: Channel View Publications.

Yeoman, I. (2014) The Faberge Syndrome. *Journal of Revenue and Pricing Management* 13 (1), 61–63.

Yeoman, I. and McMahon-Beattie, U. (2014) Exclusivity: The future of luxury. *Journal of Revenue and Pricing Management* 13 (1), 12–22.

Yeoman, I., Hsu, C., Smith, K. and Watson, S. (2010) *Tourism and Demography.* Oxford: Goodfellows.

Part 2
Food Tourism

4 The Future Fault Lines of Food

Christine Hansen

Highlights

- This chapter examines the future of the globalised food industry.
- Flavour complexity is identified as a key marketing factor.
- Increasing food informational complexity will increase flavour complexity.
- Genetic monocultures, interchangeable raw materials and processed soils produce informationally depleted foods.
- The globalised food industry is contrasted with the food tourism sector.
- The food tourism industry should form important relationships with small organic farms and ecosystem-conscious restaurants.

Typology of the Forecast

We begin with a futures typology of the forecast, evoking truth claims and an explanation (Bergman *et al.*, 2010). A forecast for the future of food tourism can be made on the basis of a disjunction between two definitive mechanisms; that of a trend toward uniform food product as interchangeable parts of raw agricultural materials in the global food supply chain coupled with the fact that food tourism relies upon its opposite, the alluring uniqueness of chemical complexity in taste. The human palate derives from the interplay of thousands of millennia-old genes. At the same time, the system of industrial food delivery is increasingly constrained by a lack of flavour complexity, moving food in the opposite direction from the natural proclivities of the human palate. The clash between these two directions will create significant opportunities for food tourism.

The tourism industry is by nature aligned with a desire for novelty. Travellers want to break out of routines and experience something new and memorable. A robust food tourism industry has developed around the search for novel food experiences. Not all of these relate to flavour. Some, for example, may relate more to the consumption of food in a novel setting. But at home, the industrialised food supply is becoming increasingly bland. Although supermarket shelves burst with a variety of alluring packaging, colours, shapes and gimmicks, these products are not actually novel in terms of their basic composition or complexity. The products are actually built from an increasingly small number of 'food commodity' ingredients as basic building blocks within the globalised industrial food chain. This managed system is designed to control the novelty of nature, and in some ways could be compared to a machine designed to input the lowest cost, and output the maximum possible quantity of food. The globalised industrial food system is managed according to a few very simple economic principles, almost all of which undermine food novelty. Within this system, basic food commodity building blocks are shipped around the industrialised world. Raw materials are grown wherever food can be grown cheaply, then mass processed to create the basic food commodities (e.g. corn syrup, for example), and afterward, these food commodities are recombined in various ways to make the processed foods which are sold throughout the industrialised world. All of this is possible due to relatively cheap fuel, because otherwise long supply chains in the food industry would be prohibitively expensive (Heinberg, 2005).

Uniformity in the building blocks of processed food can be tasted, because the creation of many superficially diverse food products via packaging and visuals is completely different from the taste of the underlying food chemistry. And so, because food chemistry can be tasted, corporate uniformity can also be tasted in its food products. Indeed, this is the reason for the thriving parallel industry in flavourings and colouring additives. In an attempt to address the problem of industrial taste blandness, artificial flavours have been added back into industrialised food, to try to mask the underlying uniformity. However, this has proved difficult to do convincingly, because of the sensitivity of the human sense of taste. Indeed, it has recently been discovered that human beings can distinguish over a trillion different smells (Williams, 2014), with smell being an integral part of the human taste system.

Put simply, industrialisation of the food supply has led to a diminution of authentic taste novelty in the daily lives of people living in industrialised countries. It has become a luxury to experience genuine taste novelty. This is largely because food additives are cheaper than genuine food novelty. And the result of all this blandness at home is a potentially growing market for food tourism in the future. The chemical complexity of local soils can actually be marketed in the food tourism industry.

Halweil (2000: 121) describes how a few corporations like ConAgra and Cargill have come to increasingly dominate the food industry. Just as Wal-Marts proliferate across the industrialised landscape, so too the bland taste of food becomes the equivalent of the suburban strip mall. As a general rule, not only is the taste of food itself becoming blander, but actual food is also increasingly 'cut' with non-food filler ingredients like cellulose

(Reimer, 2011) to stretch the total supply and increase profits. In the United States, for example, the rich eat organic meats and produce, while the fare of the poor or powerless may be 'pink slime'. On the other hand, food will increasingly become a site of tourism, creativity, colour, culture, pleasure and adventure for those who can afford it, as flavourful, healthful food increasingly takes on the trappings of an adventure. The stage is also set for the quest of the food tourist to embark upon a quest for flavour. And this trend can only be expected to continue and accelerate.

Yet, as the supply-chain arteries of trade pulse ever faster with the flow of trucks, container ships and planes transporting the standardised industrial food, local reactions of farmers' markets and small organic farms will continue. In fact, as control over the food supply is increasingly consolidated by transnational agribusiness, encounters with complex, flavourful food will even become museum-like and rare. Food tourists of the future will seek out the rare food places of the world, and will be willing to pay for these novel experiences just as the tourist of today pays to visit the Roman Colosseum or the Louvre or to see the Terracotta Warriors. The charm of the farmers' market is a prelude to what will come.

In more detailed terms, what are these food tourists seeking? Essentially, they seek to taste the nuances of informational complexity. More on this later, but one could think of such a tourist as tasting the complexity of whatever ecosystem that produced it, and of the food tourist as increasingly challenged to obtain this experience within a food system of increasing uniformity and blandness. Yes, a food grown while richly embedded in a complex ecosystem tastes complex. It partakes of 'food personality' (World Food Travel Association, 2013). There is no adventure in the taste of industrially produced fare.

Of course, the existence of a straightjacket of industrialised food may be questioned by some on the basis of the wide range of choice as you enter any grocery store in the developed world. The fruits, vegetables, meats and packaged goods are colourful and alluring to the eye, and the range of choice at first seems impressive. But what do you really see? The orderly rows of cosmetically perfect food, beaming up as if to speak of the efficacy of scientific agricultural methods, and delivered to their destinations by the sheer brute strength and determination of machines, scientific planning, diesels trucking product through long supply chains regardless of weather or geographic obstacle. The very uniformity of these foods is a testament to the predictability of industrialised food methods. The yield itself is stunning, and is surely better than would hunger. And if this 'trophy yield' displayed in grocery stores throughout the industrialised world is not mirrored in the food outlets in the developing world, this is known to be not a problem of yields, but a problem of politics. The world produces adequate food to feed everyone on the planet, but the poor and the powerless lack access to the food (Sale, 1980: 239). Though important to mention, the problem of uneven development and food access cannot be fully considered here.

Background of Industrial Agriculture Methods

Industrial agriculture was introduced after World War II. World population on the eve of World War II stood at about 2 billion (Taylor, 2011), while today it stands at more than 7 billion, and is still growing, particularly in developing nations. Just 50 years before, the so-called American frontier had closed, along with a belief in unlimited expansion. Across the world, famines of the 20th century had killed 70 million people (Meng *et al.*, 2013). The solution to these problems, apparently, was the spread of Fordist industrial agricultural methods, the development of new types of seed, and above all the intensive infusion of external energy into the physical systems of the farms, all leading to the so-called Green Revolution. It is no exaggeration to say that the age of petrochemicals allowed for the age of transnational corporations, and certainly for the rise of industrialised agriculture. It is fairly obvious that the form of a society's physical energy prescribes the length of its possible economic supply chains. According to Smil (2001: 4), 'Since 1900 the world's cultivated area increased by only about one third, but because of more than a fourfold increase of average yields the total crop harvest rose almost six-fold. This gain has been largely due to a more than eightyfold increase of external energy inputs, mostly fossil fuels, to crop cultivation.' Some writers (Pfeiffer, 2006) even predict catastrophe in the wake of these predicted changes, although further consideration of this issue is beyond the scope of this chapter. Pfeiffer argues (2006: 25), 'The increase in food miles is, of course, made possible by an increase in fossil fuel consumption. So the globalization of food production and the atrophying of localized food infrastructure are subsidized by cheap and abundant fossil fuels.'

It was almost like a new corporate commandment: Food would henceforth be a commodity, an industrial product mass-produced and distributed on a supply chain assembly line.

Nor was this the only parallel between industrialised agriculture and other forms of mass production. For example, Henry Ford grew up on a farm and was arguably as concerned with the application of mechanical methods of power farming and agricultural efficiency as he was with the automobile. In 1922 he wrote,

> Farming in the old style is rapidly fading into a picturesque memory. This does not mean that work is going to remove from the farm. Work cannot be removed from any life that is productive. But power-farming does mean this – drudgery is going to be removed from the farm. Power-farming is simply taking the burden from flesh and blood and putting it

on steel. We are in the opening years of power-farming. The motor car wrought a revolution in modern farm life, not because it was a vehicle, but because it had power. Farming ought to be something more than a rural occupation. It ought to be the business of raising food.

He foresaw the rise of industrial food production as a business, and noted that 'farming will justify itself as a business if it raises food in sufficient quantity and distributes it under such conditions as will enable every family to have enough food for its reasonable needs'. Yet, while it may seem that today's interchangeable food products and methods of agricultural efficiency are pure outgrowths of Fordism, this would be untrue.

One problem is long supply chains for industrialised food's raw commodities. An analogy could be made to a gigantic amoeba, with its nucleus located in the headquarters of a few transnational agricultural corporations, and arm-like pseudopodia structures stretching out into the world to sense economic gain, then to move towards it, and then to suck the nutrients of those gains back into the nucleus. The nucleus controls the actions of the vast corporate body. The body draws in raw materials from various points within its reach, processes them, and the paramount need within this body is always to feed the nucleus of the body as efficiently as possible. This is done by ignoring anything in nature or culture that does not further the overall goal. The inputs function like Ford-style assembly line parts, imposing a schematic discipline on the range of possible variations (Scott, 1998).

The interchangeable raw material food commodity arose from this system, with all of its nondescript, uniform flavour, almost the analog of Ford's interchangeable industrial parts (Vanclay & Lawrence, 1993). The authors quote Friedmann's (1991: 74) declaration that 'What is wanted is not sugar, but sweeteners; not flour or cornstarch, but thickeners; not palm oil or butter, but fats; not beef or cod, but proteins.' Although the external appearance and name of the final consumer food product may look superficially the same as before, this is due mainly to accidental limitations of the human senses and to flavourings and colourings added. Ford's reliance on interchangeable parts (Public Broadcasting System (PSB), 1998), uniformity, just-in-time pacing of the tasks, and mechanised processes driven by inputs of fossil fuel energy are the same as those that drive today's assembly line of industrial food. This food is essentially moving along a gigantic conveyor belt, all of which is made possible by relatively low-cost fossil fuels used in transportation.

Links Between Agricultural Soils and Flavour Complexity

Perhaps it will be questioned whether uniform agricultural methods lead to uniform taste. A visit to a Western supermarket may seem like a visit to the horn of plenty: violet blueberries plump and succulent; rangy pineapple fruits spearing the air with their indomitable and improbable cactus-like spikes; buoyant dark green leaves of mustard and collards bunched and ready to lift gently and collectively into the basket or cart. There are fresh fruits and vegetables from all around the world. Out of season, some can be pricey, but the idea of shortage or unavailability would be unthinkable to the Western middle class. In today's globalised world, we are the beneficiaries of long supply chains that exist in the background almost unnoticed (unless you happen to unload container ships or to be a long-distance trucker), even though such accomplishments in food transportation would have seemed like a miracle to our forebears. This fine bounty comes to us without much consumer reflection, despite the occasional mention of 'locally grown' products. For the most part, locally grown products are a luxury, and the palette of colours of the far-flung choices of the more mainstream marketplace in the large chain grocery stores is the norm. Bounty of choice and bounty of quantity are ours but not always the subtleties of individual taste. Predictable uniformity may exist. Sometimes you will even hear people mention how different the food in the supermarket tastes from food grown in a family garden. And sometimes you will also notice the proliferation of artificial flavourings and colourings in 'value added' packaged food, designed to artificially put the flavour and colour back into food whose raw ingredients have been stripped of their natural complexity.

This complexity is not always detectable by our eyes or describable by our food-related vocabulary. Pollan (2006: 269) has written, 'The fact that the nutritional quality of a given food (and of that food's food) can vary not just in degree but in kind throws a big wrench into an industrial food chain, the very premise of which is that beef is beef and salmon.' In other words, the Fordist interchangeability of raw agricultural ingredients ignores changes in the informational complexity of food (no matter how great), treating (at best) beef as beef or salmon as salmon (or at worst, protein as protein), even though Pollan (2006: 269) points out that the informational content of the beef or salmon is actually more important nutritionally than the appearance or name. He writes,

> Conventional nutritional wisdom holds that salmon is automatically better for us than beef, but that judgment assumes the beef has been grain fed and the salmon krill fed; if the steer is fattened on grass and the salmon on grain, we might actually be better off eating the beef. (Grass-finished beef has a two-to-one ration of omega-6 to -3 compared to more than ten to one in corn-fed beef.) The species of animal you eat may matter less than what the animal you're eating has itself eaten. (Pollen, 2006: 269)

He points out that grass-fed beef can have a two-to-one ratio of omega-6 to omega-3, versus more than ten-to-one in corn-fed beef. Through these examples we have begun to see that there is a disjunction between the actual chemical variability of food, and the supposed equivalence of food products through corporate eyes. Today's version of Gertrude Stein's 'a rose is a rose is a rose' is 'a soybean is a soybean is a soybean', whether that soybean was produced by agricultural forcing of a chemical system (e.g. by the application of large amounts of nitrogen-based fertiliser to force the system of nitrogen-fixing), and by forcing of its physical system (e.g. the use of oil and natural gas in transportation and farm equipment), by monocultured fields, or by non-rotated, depleted soils. The methods used to accomplish this were adaptations of the same principles that drove Henry Ford in his automobile assembly lines. Ford's reliance on interchangeable parts (Public Broadcasting System, 1998), uniformity, just-in-time pacing of the tasks and mechanised processes driven by inputs of fossil fuel energy are the same as those that drive today's assembly line of industrial agriculture. Our inability to tell the difference in microstructures with our eyes has allowed the actual food to be 'cut' with other non-food substances, while still being considered the same food. A bewildering host of artificial flavours and colours has been developed (Schlosser, 2002) to trick the eye and to some extent the palate. To give an example, Schlosser discusses the actual chemicals that can be used to try to fool the palate into believing it is encountering a strawberry. According to Schlosser (2002: 125–126),

> The phrase 'artificial strawberry flavor' gives little hint of the chemical wizardry and manufacturing skill that can make a highly processed food taste like strawberries. A typical artificial strawberry flavor, like the kind found in a Burger King strawberry milk shake, contains the following ingredients: amyl acetate, amyl butyrate, amyl valerate, anethol, anisyl formate, benzyl acetate, benzyl isobutyrate, butyric acid, cinnamyl isobutyrate, cinnamyl valerate, cognac essential oil, diacetyl, dipropyl ketone, ethyl acetate, ethyl amyl ketone, ethyl butyrate, ethyl cinnamate, ethyl heptanoate, ethyl heptylate, ethyl lactate, ethyl ethylphenylglycidate, ethyl nitrate, ethyl propionate, ethyl valerate, heliotropin, hydroxyphenyl-2-butanone (10 percent solution in alcohol), a-ionone, isobutyl anthranilate, isobutyl butyrate, lemon essential oil, maltol, 4-methylacetophenone, methyl anthranilate, methyl benzoate, methyl cinnamate, methyl heptine carbonate, methyl naphthyl ketone, methyl salicylate, mint essential oil, neroli essential oil, nerolin, neryl isobutyrate, orris butter, phenethyl alcohol, rose, rum ether, g-undecalactone, vanillin, and solvent.

It could be argued, however, that the palate would not really be fooled if it were given a comparison test between the flavouring and an actual strawberry. In general, the eye is easier to trick than the palate.

The ability of the human palate to discern 'flavour' as a conscious construct of perception is a combination of both taste and odour (Danker, 1968: 32), with the entire perception of the palate being actually a construct of not only these but also sensations in the tissues of the mouth, throat and nasal cavity (Danker, 1968: 31). In this sense, the pleasure associated with certain flavours or gastronomical experiences – and in general the ability of human flavour detectors to discern thousands of different nuances of flavor – is based in the sensing of soluble substances in food and its subtle play and stimulation of those senses (Danker, 1968: 10). Schlosser (2002: 124) explains that these artificial flavours tend to be inexpensive. Certainly they are inexpensive compared to the cost of growing food in environments with natural informational complexity. Thus, industrial agriculture has been systematically removing this natural informational complexity and replacing it with a cheaper manufactured version of complexity. This manufactured variety may be based on chemicals that are not ordinarily considered food or even consumable. This switch can be tasted. Although a consumer may purchase a processed food with artificial strawberry flavouring, they are also aware that the artificial flavouring is not really to be confused with the taste of 'real' strawberries.

On the one hand, agriculture based in uniformity of soil, fertiliser, genetic strains and methodology is likely to produce food products with greater uniformity of soluble substances within the food product. On the other hand, any food with a memorable taste usually acquired these nuances of taste from the complex information absorbed as a result of the food crop being embedded as part of a complex, interdependent ecosystem. In other words, the industrial food system can trick the eye, but not always the palate. Artificial colours are part of this trompe-l'œil. Yet the palate often knows. There is a subtlety to the palate that leaves it less vulnerable to the powers of illusion. And it is this fact that is important for the food tourism industry. There will always be a demand for tastes that are 'real'.

Thus, the food that is the output of industrial food systems cannot constitute a sound basis of the future of food tourism. This is because the monocultures that often characterise industrial produce become depleted of the very forms of complex information that make for an extraordinary gastronomical experience. For example, it is well known in the wine industry that certain types of soil produce distinct types of taste in the grapes. According to Lamy (2011),

> The French have an expression that relates the taste of a wine to the place in which it was grown: gout de terroir. It is loosely translated to taste of the earth or sense of place. Winemakers in every country try to identify such relationships for two reasons. First, it may help them understand their wines. And second, the concept can be used to differentiate their product from the competition.

Considering the soil alone, there are a tremendous number of variables that can impact taste, and these do not exist in isolation, but rather in relation to many other systems and variables. Lamy (2011) further explains that,

Soils are not homogeneous throughout. The 'A horizon' (topsoil) may only be 6–12 inches. Some soils have 'A', 'B', 'C', and deeper horizons. It depends on how the soil was built up over millions of years. Typically, about 85% of a vine's root system is located in the first 18 inches of soil depth. The remaining 15% will go deeper, depending on the vine's need to access water in the dry months, and the soil's composition which may, or may not, permit the roots to grow through it. In some soils, the root system can reach down 40–60 feet in search of water…

Grapevines take up nutrients and minerals from the soil entirely by ion exchange at the root hairs. Hydrogen ions (H+) are given up by the root in exchange for nutrient and mineral ions from the soil. So, the mix of ions entering the vine is different within each soil layer, and is strongly influenced by the soil's pH (electron bonds may be strong or weak).

Thus we see that when it comes to wine, the taste of the grapes is strongly influenced by the surrounding environment in which the grapes are grown. The final set of information taken up into the grape is a product of previous ion exchange of the plant, etc. They are responsible for much of the chemical conversion that takes place in an ecosystem. Looked at in this way, a food ecosystem is a kind of systemic computer, with myriad possible informational combinations and reactions that can produce possible taste nuances detectable by the palate, even though the same reactions may be invisible to the eye. Anyone interested in cheese or beer knows that taste can be connected to the metabolism of microorganisms. Moreover, microbes (along with small invertebrates) are incredibly diverse and prolific in soil. For example, Ponting (1992: 15) notes that there was no soil before the earliest life emerged from the sea, and, 'Just one acre of good soil from a temperate region will contain about 125 million small invertebrates and thirty grams of that soil will contain 1 million bacteria of just one type, 100,000 yeast cells and 50,000 fungus mycelium.' Soil is the legacy of the prior lives of countless creatures interacting, and thus its chemistry is incredibly complex. Indeed, the chemistry of many things on the earth (not just soil) is 'living engineered' and microbes have been dubbed the tiny 'chemical engineers' of the environment (Public Broadcasting System, 1999) because they convert myriad forms of substances into other substances. There are iron-eating bacteria, caffeine-eating bacteria, arsenic-eating bacteria, sulfur-eating bacteria and bacteria that eat certain types of nuclear waste (Veronese, 2012). We begin to see the possible richness of information that can potentially be detected by the human palate. In the case of 'a beer is a beer is a beer', we also see that microbial reactions are one reason why this is not true.

According to Pfeiffer (2006: 11), 'topsoil is built up by decaying plant matter and weathering rock' and it takes 500 years for nature to produce an inch of topsoil. All of the chemical nuances of the decaying plant matter and rock are present in that soil on a non-industrialised farm. But arable land in an industrial system is depleted and degraded, having lost much of this chemical complexity. And so, fertilisers have to be forced back into the system, but if they are products of the industrial system, the chemicals that are forced back in do not possess the local chemical complexity. They are much more uniform batches of chemicals produced on a large scale. So the produce of such farms does not taste as good, because we have failed to coax out the system's local chemical bounty and the palate can taste this through what we may call somewhat whimsically the 'still small voice of food'. It is the personality of the food. In contrast, the food produced by industrial farming is mute food.

According to Scott (1998: 294–295),

> Modern agricultural research commonly proceeds as if yields, per unit of scarce inputs, were the central concern of the farmer. The assumption is enormously convenient; like the commercial wood of scientific forestry, the generic, homologous, uniform commodities thus derived create the possibility both of quantitative comparisons between the yield of different cultivation techniques and of aggregate statistics. The familiar tabulations of acres planted, yields per acre, and total production from year to year are usually the decisive measure of success in a development program. But the premise that all rice, all corn, and all millet are 'equal', however useful, is simply not a plausible assumption about any crop unless it is *purely* a commodity for sale in the market. Each subspecies of grain has distinctive properties, not just in how it grows but in its qualities as a grain once harvested.

This is what Scott also describes a 'straightjacket' of current food production techniques. We force each kernel of grain into the shape of our economic and administrative vision, but in doing so, we remove the rich potential range of our trillion-plus possible chemical taste experiences, making our food experiences boring and impoverished.

We are intent on 'telling food what to do'. The methods described by Scott (1998: 294) of industrial agriculture are almost diametrically opposed to the methods needed to allow food to express its personality and to form the basis of a thriving food tourism sector. The more the food is forced from a field according to a rigid paradigm, the less it can be unique. Thus, the future of food tourism will be the legacy of the food whisperer, and the ability to appreciate the market for this style of farming that sings to the mulberry and dances with the pear, instead of ordering the fields and orchards of the earth to be quiet.

Links Between Crop Genetics and Flavour Complexity

The informational complexity of food is not just tied to the complexity of the soils and environment, but depends on crop genetics; it may be true to say 'the more things are sprayed, the more they remain the same'. According to Pringle (2003: 39),

> A 1983 survey of American publicly available fruits and vegetables showed that 97 percent of the varieties being sold by commercial U.S. seed houses had disappeared since the beginning of the century. In that period, the varieties of cabbage in the U.S. Department of Agriculture's seed storage bank dropped from 544 to 28, carrots from 287 to 21, cauliflower from 158 to 9, tomatoes from 408 to 79, cucumbers from 285 to 16, and Mendel's garden peas from 408 to 25. Of the 7,089 varieties of apple in use during the same period, 6,211 had been lost, and of the 2,683 pears, 2,354 no longer existed.

Here we can see uniformity rather unequivocally. Returning to Henry Ford's idea of interchangeable basic parts, the planners of industrialised food believe the industry needs to be designed around a limited number of basic parts. In fact, Ford himself said that his Model T automobile was less complex than any other. In agri-business, this drive towards simplicity of overall system management has meant the elimination of most natural genetic complexity in food crops, and instead a reliance on a few basic sets of more-or-less interchangeable repeated genetic codes. The curtailing of this genetic code in diet is a huge change, and one that impoverishes our encounters. One could think of it as a kind of untested experiment. Pringle (2003: 43) notes that this handful of genetic codes has 'squeezed out the local traditional varieties that had fed, housed, clothed, and cured people throughout history'. It is possible to think of our genetic inheritance on the earth as a kind of library. If so, then this narrowing of our encounters with the volumes of the great library is like the burning of a Library of Alexandria.

The question perhaps arises as to whether this type of informational diversity can be tasted. The answer is rather obviously yes. Anyone who can taste the difference between a beefsteak tomato and a Roma tomato can attest to the ability of the human palate to taste differences in genetic information in food. Moreover, because of the human tendency to become bored by eating the same foods over and over, monoculture can also be said to be linked to dreary food experiences. Not only will the food tourist seek food experiences from informationally diverse and complex soils, but also from informationally diverse genetic crops.

Concluding Remarks: The Implications for the Future of Food Tourism

Successful food tourism requires exactly the opposite view to that of industrial farming. Tourists seek novelty. According to Scarpato (2002: 4), food tourists are giving expression to disruptions of the dominant food narrative. If we think about the dominant food narrative as being corporate, and of its industialised food as being built up of Ford-like interchangeable food commodity parts – with this masked by a host of artificial flavourings and colourings – then we can imagine the food tourist as seeking a novel experience outside the scope of this dominant narrative. Food that incorporates the nuances of local complexity is outside this narrative, and so the drive towards complex food is linked to the drive to tourism destinations with local uniqueness. Just as an area can be marketed for its unique history or unique crafts, so too it can be marketed for the unique chemical complexity of its lands, giving rise to unique food tastes that can only be experienced in that local area. This is already done to some extent in enotourism, but seldom in the area of food tourism.

As the future of the food tourism industry lies outside mainstream food production, so the food tourism industry should form important relationships with small organic farms and ecosystem-conscious restaurants that produce food in informationally rich ways that lead to complex flavours. We should begin looking beyond an outward 'apple' or a 'tomato' to the underlying, much more diverse, chemical complexity that can reside in variations of these, depending on the local conditions under which they are grown. We can taste the differences in chemistry, registering delight or disappointment, and so the palate can be as exciting a guide to local uniqueness in tourism as our eyes or ears. If gastronomy is becoming an important source of local identity within globalised industrial homogeneity (Richards, 2002), the palate is a vehicle into these disruptions of industrial uniformity, and an entry point into an experience of local uniqueness. We have seen that the palate can detect differences in 'local versus global' far more easily than can the eye. It is therefore recommended that the food tourism industry market more than just the cultural and visual aspects of unique local foods but also the unique local chemistry of the soil and how it can be tasted in the local bounty. So the chemistry of local soils can become an important part of the branding of a local tourism destination. In marketing a local tourism destination, actual experiences of eating can be linked to excursions to the growing areas, colourful local food markets and an emphasis on achieving good health through experiences of local food chemistry. Just as Hungary markets the unique chemistry of healthful local baths, so local growing areas can also market the unique chemistry of their healthful local soils. As novel flavour experiences become increasingly scarce, exciting and 'real tasting' food will take on mythical proportions, and the experience of complex, flavourful food will be sought out as avidly as today's museums. Food tourism can become an excursion outside uniform industrialised fare. Let them eat complexity!

References

Bergman, A., Karlsson, J.C. and Axelsson, J. (2010) Truth claims and explanatory claims: An ontological typology of futures studies. *Futures* 42, 857–865.

Danker, W.H. (1968) *Basic Principles of Sensory Evaluation*. Philadelphia: American Society for Testing and Materials.

Ford, H. (1922) *My Life and Work*. See www.gutenberg.org/dirs/etext05/hnfrd10.txt (accessed 28 November 2013).

Friedmann, H. (1991) Changes in the industrial division of labor: Agrifood complexes and export agriculture. In W. Friedland, L. Busch, F. Buttel and A. Rudy (eds) *Toward a New Political Economy of Agriculture* (pp. 65–93). Boulder: Westview.

Halweil, B. (2000) Where have all the farmers gone? In *Global Issues 2001/2* (pp. 115–126). Guilford, CT: HarperCollins.

Heinberg, R. (2005) *The Party's Over*, 2nd ed. Gabriola Island, BC: New Society.

Lamy, J.L. (2011) *Wine Soils I; Gout de Terroir and the Dirteaters*, blog. See http://enobytes. com/2011/09/21/gout-de-terroir-dirteaters/ (accessed 21 April 2013).

Meng, X., Qian, N. and Yared, P. (2013) The institutional causes of China's Great Famine, 1959–1961. See http://isites.harvard.edu/fs/docs/icb.topic1314442.files/Qian%20 famines_20130731_final.pdf (accessed 29 November 2013).

Pfeiffer, D.A. (2006) *Eating Fossil Fuels*. Gabriola Island, BC: New Society.

Pollan, M. (2006) *The Omnivore's Dilemma*. New York: Penguin.

Ponting, C. (1992) *A Green History of the World*. New York: Penguin.

Pringle, P. (2003) *Food, Inc*. New York: Simon & Schuster.

Public Broadcasting System (1998) Ford installs first moving assembly line 1913. *A Science Odyssey: People and Discoveries*. See www.pbs.org/wgbh/aso/databank/entries/dt13as. html (accessed 29 November 2013).

Public Broadcasting System (1999) Keepers of the biosphere. *Intimate Strangers: Unseen Life on Earth*. DVD. See www.pbs.org/opb/intimatestrangers/ (accessed 29 November 2013).

Reimer, M. (2011) Fifteen food companies that serve you 'wood'. *The Street*. See www. thestreet.com/story/11012915/1/cellulose-wood-pulp-never-tasted-so-good.html (accessed 29 November 2013).

Richards, G. (2002) Gastronomy: An essential ingredient in tourism production and consumption. In A. Hjalager and G. Richards (eds) *Tourism and Gastronomy* (pp. 1–20). London: Routledge.

Sale, K. (1980) *Human Scale*. New York: Perigee.

Scarpato, R. (2002) Sustainable gastronomy as a tourism product: The perspective of gastronomy studies. In A. Hjalager and G. Richards (eds) *Tourism and Gastronomy* (pp. 131–151). London: Routledge.

Schlosser, E. (2002) *Fast Food Nation*. New York: Perennial.

Scott, J.C. (1998) *Seeing Like a State*. New Haven, CT: Yale University Press.

Smil, V. (2001) *Feeding the World: A Challenge for the Twenty-First Century*. Cambridge, MA: MIT Press.

Taylor, A. (2013) In focus: World War II: After the war. *The Atlantic*. See www.theatlantic. com/infocus/2011/10/world-war-ii-after-the-war/100180/ (accessed 28 November 2013).

Vanclay, F. and Lawrence, G. (1993) Environmental and social consequences of economic restructuring. *International Journal of Sociology of Agriculture and Food* 3, 97–118.

Veronese, K. (2012) Ten surprising things that bacteria like to eat. See http://io9.com/ 5908318/10-surprising-things-that-bacteria-like-to-eat (accessed 29 November 2013).

Williams, S.C.P. (2014) Human nose can detect a trillion smells. See news.sciencemag.org/ biology/2014/03/human-nose-can-detect-trillion-smells

World Food Travel Association (2013) Food personality. See www.worldfoodtravel.org/ food-personality/ (accessed 20 April 2013).

5 The Impact of Future Food Supply on Food and Drink Tourism

Harvey Ells

Highlights

This chapter aims to highlight and discuss the following key areas in relation to food tourism:

- The ongoing effects of historical trade agreements and food policy on future food security.
- Future impacts of agrifood supply chain concentration and distribution on food tourism.
- The progressive reduction of global food and water resources.
- How traditional models of food and gastronomic tourism will need to adapt looking forward.

In doing so, it will provide the reader with a prognosis of how emerging food supply trends and considerations will potentially shape future food and drink tourism activities.

Introduction

The previous chapter has highlighted our established over-reliance on fossil fuels as a natural resource and the recognition that all the time supplies are available, challenges to the accepted status quo are less likely due to the concentration of power resting with key, high-volume global oil producers who ultimately control both trade in this commodity and the resultant consumer energy price tariffs. This is not a new problem. Many of the interdependencies between oil consumption (in a variety of derivatives, e.g. fertilisers) and food production were initially highlighted and well documented as a result of a range of observed energy crises in the 1970s. The work of Wilson (1974), Stock (1978) and most notably Tarrant (1980) centred on food and energy policies at the time raised a number of concerns from an agrifood supply chain perspective. These earlier writings, with others, clearly differentiated between the then developed, principally northern, nations and the relatively under-developed global south. Over 30 years later these concerns are not only more acute as global food production levels off, but increasingly affect many more nations, not just those with low gross domestic product (GDP) and limited service sectors.

The early work of the United Nations World Food Programme (UNWFP), conceived in 1961 and established in 1963, presented a solution centred on the essential global (re)distribution of food at a time when the world's population was estimated at just over 3 billion (UN Population Division, 2013) and there was the agricultural capacity to produce considerably more food. However, in 2010 the UN estimated that the world population increased to nearly 7 billion (UN Population Division, 2013) and that WFP support will have reached 90 million global citizens at the time of writing (World Food Programme, 2013). This raises two immediate questions: first, how sustainable are such aid programmes in the medium to long term? And second, with the global population index gradient exceeding that of the global food supply index (Defra, 2013: 38) is there now enough affordable food to feed everybody on the planet (subject to an optimised global agrifood supply chain)? The reality is now clear in that high volume food aid schemes might not be sustainable, are open to an ongoing ethical debate (Thompson, 2010) and if we continue to consume food, in particular meat, at current levels in the developed world there will inevitably be ongoing food shortages. Uncertainty in supply has already seen significant surges in basic food commodity prices with spikes on global markets in both 2008 and 2011 (FAO, 2013). This has not only made southern country food aid schemes more costly, but it has also increased dependency on these schemes. Furthermore, developed urban areas are also witnessing more food poverty interventions in the form of food banks (Trussell Trust, 2013; Feeding America, 2013), with the International Red Cross highlighting that food aid in Europe is now at its highest level since the end of the World War II.

The above themes highlight major concerns for *all* food supply chains whether they be international, regional and, for the purposes of this chapter, more localised and tourism-centric. Future considerations need to move away from established productionist attitudes to food and consider a significant shift in thinking and more sustainable alternatives. Lang and Heasman (2004: 20) have commented that post-war farming technologies have run their course and that they are now 'showing up major limitations'. The consequences of this observation are wide ranging, even when considering more traditional tourist destinations. For example, Spain currently has 3 million citizens dependent on food aid and Greece has recently witnessed a number of food riots as the global economic crisis continues.

The Effect of Historical Trade Agreements and Food Policies on Food Security

It is important to understand from a global perspective how we arrived at today's observed agrifood global supply chains. At the end of the 19th century most of the world's staple food supply was both regional and indigenous. The then established colonies provided a range of higher value specialist products which contributed some variety to the early industrial nations' food tables. Because much of this production was commodity-based (tea, sugar, coffee, cocoa) and had a price premium it was economically viable to transport these (longer life) ambient foods long distances. This food supply chain model became significant for a number of reasons. First, it highlighted the benefits of specialised production from a producer/supplier perspective; second, it enhanced food choices for more aspirational consumers in industrialised nations; and third, from a policy perspective it established the beginnings of the previously mentioned productionist (high yield, big scale) farming mind-set. While it is recognised that this model of farming had a number of unethical labour issues associated with it (as exist in many tropical regions today) it continued to grow beyond those original colonies and develop to embrace a wider range of lower value food commodities and products. As a result, at the commencement of the 20th century the global upper and emerging middle classes had become increasingly enthusiastic about the importing of non-indigenous novel food products for regular consumption, with clear evidence in the 1930s of protectionism mechanisms in place for the large-scale producers of many staple food commodities.

Global Agrifood Supply Chains and Distribution

It was not until the outbreak of World War II in 1939 that it became acutely apparent to all how dependent some countries were on others to provide for their daily staples. The disruption caused to global food supply chains as a result of war in the 1940s continued into the early 1950s but most significantly acted as a catalyst to initiate a significant series of events aimed at securing global food supplies, boosting production and creating a fairer (food) trade environment through policy initiatives. The most significant of these was the GATT agreement of 1947 which despite good intentions has not always produced an equitable, liberal trade environment and which has as a result often left the poor (particularly in regions of traditional subsistence agriculture) significantly disadvantaged. This was often a result of direct foreign investment in, and control of, agricultural technologies and the practice of 'dumping' agricultural excess production from other parts of the world. One only has to look at a series of databases, e.g. FAO Agromaps

(2013), or the work of Millstone and Lang (2008) to observe where the regional variation and concentration of supply and cultivation occurs and dominant agricultural practices exist. Of particular note are the newly emerging global players in the form of the BRIC (Brazil, Russia, India, China) countries as they have increasing influence on patterns of global food supply (e.g. mass soya bean production in Brazil) as they develop their agrifood practices (Gagnon, 2012) and more westernised patterns of food consumption (IFPRI, 2012), with increasing red meat consumption in China being of particular note (Liu *et al.*, 2009.) Globally there has been a clear shift away from local and seasonal supply chains and diets to guarantee year-round availability from multinationally controlled global food companies and retailers. The consequences of this are that the number of small-scale producers face increasing challenges in getting their products to market because of both lack of economies of scale and the fact that much of the decision-making in global supply chains rests in the hands of a very low number of buyers in major food manufacturing companies and retailers. This supply chain 'funnelling' effect results in a significant concentration of power. An example is highlighted by the work of Grievink (2003) who estimated that 160 million consumers in six European Union countries were having their food choices controlled by 70 supermarket buyers negotiating with 160,000 suppliers through an increasingly large system of centralised distribution networks. Practices such as this can remove opportunities for the diversification of food production by suppliers as they are often forced to produce fewer products in larger quantities to satisfy dictated and generic (often processed) product specifications. As a consequence, the availability of unique foods at tourism destinations might gradually be eroded or alternatively might not be made available for visitors as they are exclusively consumed by locals from their small market gardens and allotments. It is also important to note that there has been considerable vertical integration by global food retailers in an attempt to increase profits, for example Morrisons in the UK now has its own farms and abattoirs (Morrisons, 2013), influencing other areas of the supply chain. A recent report by Eagleton (2005) highlights that five transnational companies (TNCs) control 90% of the global grain trade with similar monopolies existing in other markets, with one company reportedly controlling 80% of Peru's milk production (Eagleton, 2005).

Potential Impacts of Supply Chain Concentration on Food Tourism

From reading the above it might at first appear that the niche food producer, essential to food and gastronomic tourism, is suffering as a result of food market concentration, but from a consumer perspective there is evidence to suggest that domestic interest in sustainable: artisan and specialist food production is flourishing, as are many of the leisure industries (including tourism) associated with it. Despite difficulties and inequalities within the supply chain, the activities of a growing number of food policy activists, networks and non-governmental organisations are becoming increasingly important in facilitating and maintaining alternative foodscapes and cultures. One of the highest profile being the Slow Food Movement as discussed by Andrews (2008), or perhaps the more recent emergence of the Locavore culture (Blue, 2009) originating in San Francisco, which aims to source all foods within a 100-mile radius of the city centre. Although it can be argued that this lifestyle is only possible near agricultural regions, the benefits are clearly tangible, for example residents near the poorer Tenderloin District benefit from cheap food and the associated food aid scheme at the Heart of the City Farmers Market (2013) whereas more affluent locals, tourists and celebrity chefs frequent the more upmarket Ferry Plaza Farmers Market (2013). Elsewhere, awareness of small-scale producers has increased in prominence through a number of accredited labelling schemes (De Boer, 2003; Ilbery *et al.*, 2005) and most notably Fair Trade (Dubuisson-Quellier & Lamine, 2008), which in addition to guaranteeing income to predominantly subsistence farmers has equally importantly allowed traditional cultivars and cultivation techniques not to become either marginalised or to disappear from local agricultural practices. Geographical indication (GI) schemes are also essential from a food tourism and supply chain perspective, e.g. the EU Protected Designation of Origin (PDO) mechanism (EU, 2013) that not only offers protectionism for the producers of small-scale niche food products but which also has the benefit of preserving many traditional food production techniques of relevance to many gastronomic tourists. Armesto López and Martin (2006) discuss the benefits of these schemes to the Spanish rural economy, with Canoves and Morais (2011) stressing the importance of new and authentic niche tourism products including food and wine. Chaney and Ryan (2012: 316), in their recently developed model of gastronomic tourism, highlight both the importance of the tourist experience and authenticity as a motivation. Although not explicit within their model it can be argued that more focus on the alised food supply chains is integral in the ongoing understanding and development of gastronomic destinations. Increasingly, the tourist needs to look beyond the immediate hospitality offer and work back down the food supply and value chains at tourism destinations and their localities to fully understand components of the foodscape. Looking forward, the supply chain will need to be more clearly defined from both experiential and marketing perspectives. This might be assisted by the inclusion of food 'badging' schemes, examples include the Rainforest Alliance (2013) and Bees for Development (2013), both of which help to draw indirect attention to the food sovereignty movement which is increasingly for to the global food tourist and other related, mobilised food supply chain actors. The international peasants movement, La Via Campesina (2013) also campaigns for food supply chain-related social justice, with the ethics of food supply chains starting to be more closely scrutinised along with other elements of the product mix. This is discussed by Kline *et al.* in Weeden and Boluk (2014: 105), who highlight that 'Tourism experiences occur at each stage of the food supply chain, thereby providing opportunities for identifying ways to improve the sustainability and ethical nature of the food tourism experience', with the future significance of broader tourism ethics being more fully considered by Weeden (2013).

Limitation of Food and Water Resources

When combined, the above supply chain considerations assist in preserving food sovereignty and sustainable food production practices which in turn will make a significant ongoing contribution to supporting activities aligned to food tourism in the future. It can be argued that a focus on more sustainable agrifood practises provide some resilience to the influences of globalisation on local food supplies, particularly where tourists actively seek out these as part of a slower lifestyle (Parkins & Craig, 2006: 35). Further resistance is provided as tourists seek alternatives to the corporate control of the supply chain, as highlighted by Yeoman (2012: 178). This may in part be a reason for the re-emergence of less formal, less structured and cheaper ways of experiencing local foods as part of the tourism experience. Given the increasing price of commodities this might also alleviate some of the concerns expressed by Sonnenfield (2001) regarding issues with the (higher) pricing structure of artisan foods if consumers wish to adopt slower lifestyles.

However, the pricing of food is not the only issue that needs to be borne in mind. One significant, but less obvious consideration is that of water availability and how it affects food production and food tourism-associated industries. At the same time that food miles began to be analysed, considerations were also being made for 'virtual water' (Allan, 1997). The work of Allan, and later others, started to consider water as not just a natural resource featuring in physical geography cycles but also a commodity that could be measured in relation to food supply chains (Allan, 2003). This enabled more widespread consideration of exporting water, water-related land degradation and potential desertification as a result of a lack of water conservation. For example Velázquez (2007), in her consideration of Andalucia, highlights that more consideration is required regarding the mix of crops grown to achieve a balance between those used for domestic consumption versus export. If this changes significantly in the future, what are the implications of a Spanish interior devoid of citrus groves? How will a food tourist perceive this given the importance of that image in terms of destination analysis (Pike, 2002)? The future food tourist needs to be open to shifting their expectations of image in line with changing patterns of food production. There are also possibilities that established agrifood-related industries will begin to shrink as water becomes in short supply in the production as well as the growing process. Recent calculations indicate that a number of crops that are associated with niche tourism, e.g. tea (Jolliffe, 2007), coffee (Jolliffe, 2010) and wine (Mitchell *et al.*, 2012), consume variable but significant amounts of water. In 2009 *The Economist* highlighted the research work of The Pacific Institute and revealed that coffee production was the greatest consumer with approximately 20,000 litres of water required to ultimately produce 1 kg of goods. While this is not significant in terms of tourism volumes, if the more significant wine industry is considered, it has been estimated that nearly 1000 litres of water is required to produce one litre of wine. The latest ongoing biennial overviews provided by Gleick (2012) provide some very sobering reading indeed on a range of agrifood-related water issues, including the implications for the Colorado River and Californian agricultural region, amongst others.

If we therefore continue to assume that food and water resources are to become scarcer it is next reasonable to ask how existing models of food tourism (and their related supply chains) might be re-worked. Key to this consideration is how sustainable ongoing food sourcing and practices are? Leat *et al.* (2011), in their discussion of Scotland's food and drink policy, highlight the dimensions of sustainability based on the work of the Forestry Commission in which consideration is given to economic, social and environmental dimensions. They argue that when these areas are fully considered and overlap, sustainable development exists, with the caveat that this is informed by a viable economic model which benefits the local community without depleting natural resources. This implies that the carrying capacity of local food resources is not overstretched and also that food supply chains are kept as short as possible. The South West of England's food tourism is considered one of the reasons for its ongoing success (in addition to region-based government investment). A number of high-profile food actors, particularly celebrity chefs, have increased the awareness and importance of food suppliers in the region, for example Rick Stein's *Food Heroes* (2002) and more recently the campaigning work of Hugh Fearnley-Whittingstall (2013) centred on the UK fishing industry. Regardless of sympathies for or against celebrity chefs, it needs to be recognised that they have acted as ambassadors for a supply chain rethink as a result of adhering to four key principles:

- Being enthusiastic and open to creating added-value within emerging local food supply chains.
- Redistributing the wealth created from ongoing food tourism in their local communities.
- Supporting new, sustainable culinary and food sourcing initiatives within their locality.
- Reaching audiences who would otherwise not be aware of non-retail actors in the food supply chain.

These principles have proved critical in establishing new food tourism initiatives and events elsewhere, with chef-writers such as Anthony Bourdain (2013) frequently reflecting on the global food scene through his 'No Reservations' travelogue. Interestingly, the final series of this programme closes with an episode centred on the food haunts of Brooklyn and the established food cultures within the city. The location is also nearby one of the most successful developed country urban agriculture (UA) initiatives: Brooklyn Grange Farm (2013) in Queens. This rooftop urban farm grows approximately 40,000 lbs of organic food each year and, having recently become fully economically viable (although partially dependent on food volunteers), champions a new model of food supply chain for New York City dwellers. This development is significant as it not only provides a food retail, hospitality and event destination but also indicates a possible next step in urban food tourism, providing both alternative skyline vistas and food experiences while at the same time extending the existing culinary trails within the city. Other such initiatives are discussed at length by Viljoen et al. (2005), building on their previous architecturally centric work on continuous productive urban landscapes (CPULs). However, within this model the role of the volunteer needs further consideration and it could be argued it is increasingly important for two reasons. First, because the services provided by the volunteer might provide the difference between viability within a sustainable economy, and second, because the food tourist might actively seek out a food 'pilgrimage' (Mustonen, 2006) or more altruistic driver for engaging with a local food supply chain. Alternatively, volunteering might manifest itself as a form of contribution to a gastronomic experience where educational parallels with wine tourism are acted out when foraging for ingredients and then instruction is received and skills transferred on the best way to prepare foods before dining. Hall (2013) notes some of the links between these practices and more fully appreciating the supply chain with a number of high-profile restaurants establishing part of their reputation and brand image based on foraging expertise in rediscovering local cuisine (as in the case of Michelin-starred Noma in Denmark).

How Traditional Models of Food and Gastronomic Tourism Will Need to Adapt

If established models of food tourism are reviewed based on Hall and Mitchell's (2001) highlighting of the visitations of tourists to food actors there are a range of perspectives that can be viewed. Tikkanen's (2007) focus on Maslow's hierarchy, Kim et al.'s (2009) use of grounded theory and Mak et al.'s (2012b) identification of dimensions of motivational factors offer insights into a range of destination, food and environmental factors, but more specific discourse centred on the food supply chain is sometimes lacking critical analysis. For example, Tikkanen mentions picking tourism, but coverage of the range of considerations is limited (2007: 731). Similarly Kim *et al.* (2009: 429) in their proposed model indicate learning knowledge as being important but do not highlight how this can be fully considered from a production and primary processing perspective. More recently, attention has been directed at the concept of culinary supply, see Smith and Xiao (2008) and Deale *et al.* (2008), with recognition of the links to theories of globalisation through the work of Mak *et al.* (2012a: 173) who highlight that 'culinary supply may include production, processing, wholesaling, retailing and food services'. This said, within this essentially linear system, future thinking will need to embrace a wider range of actions outside of traditional food supply chains. Examples of these future considerations for inclusion are highlighted below.

Emerging Considerations within Food Tourism

Table 5.1 summarises the emerging considerations within food tourism.

Table 5.1 Emerging considerations within food tourism

Fads	Where new trends in food tourism supply chains are more quickly introduced into elements of the localised marketing mix.
Farms	Where diversification of specialist food production and primary processing enables a new niche food tourism offer.
Fatigue	Where tired food tourism concepts are replaced with more sustainable alternatives.
Festivals	Where newly established food supply chains are highlighted to food tourists through newly conceptualised events.
Fisheries	Where sustainable inshore fish stocks are recognised, protected and re-marketed to food tourists through local retail and hospitality providers.
Food heroes	Where a clearly identifiable food actor or celebrity champions the best local ingredients to food tourists.
Food policy	Where a wider range of supply chain actors become actively involved in policy networks associated with food tourism.
Foraging	Where indigenous wild ingredients are actively sourced and incorporated into local gastronomy and food tourism.
Free labour	Where unpaid volunteering is rewarded with specialist culinary knowledge within the wider food tourism offer.
Front rooms	Where local food consumers showcase their combined culinary skills and knowledge of local suppliers in a domestic setting.

Concluding Remarks: The Implications for the Future of Food Tourism

This chapter has offered some insights into a range of important emerging food supply chain considerations. Historically, the food tourist has had a relatively free choice of where (and more importantly) what to eat when traveling but the diversity of influences is undergoing a period of considerable change involving a wider range of policy paradigms. The food offered at tourism destinations will soon start to evolve more rapidly as a result of increasing demand pressures on the available food, water and land resources. Sustainable food systems and localised protectionism mechanisms will offer some safeguards for the stability of niche food and hospitality offers, but conversely, a disregard for the supply chain, its food actors and the way that it consumes finite renewable natural resources will significantly reduce the more exclusive components of the food tourism product mix. In future, the food tourist will have to more actively investigate, seek out and source authentic foods and gastronomic offers. This might in turn expose them to a new range of associated experiences and more detailed interactions with food producers, suppliers, processors and other food consumers. Alternatively, we may see a re-focusing on more localised exploration of traditional food cultures with less international travel and a continued resurgence or expansion of the 'staycation' model's food components. Academics will also have to more frequently rethink the food supply chain element of the tourism product mix and destination brand, potentially making fewer assumptions and generalisations when developing conceptual models. Food supply chains and networks will have to take a more central position in the full spectrum of local tourism-centric foodscape components. The change in food supply chain dynamics will also present a range of opportunities for future research looking at both food logistics and patterns of food consumption as the balance between physiological versus psychological food tourist needs potentially shifts.

References

Allan, J.A. (1997) *Virtual Water: A Long-term Solution for Water Short Middle Eastern Economies?* School of Oriental and African Studies (SOAS) Water Issues Study Group, University of London, Occasional Papers (pp. 24–29). London: School of Oriental and African Studies, University of London.

Allan, J.A. (2003) Virtual water – The water, food, and trade nexus. Useful concept or misleading metaphor? *Water International* 28 (1), 106–113.

Andrews, G. (2008) *The Slow Food Story: Politics and Pleasure.* London: Pluto Press.

Armesto López, X.A. and Martin, B.G. (2006) Tourism and quality agro-food products: An opportunity for the Spanish countryside. *Tijdschrift voor Economische en Sociale Geografie* 97 (2), 166–177.

Bees for Development (2013) See www.beesfordevelopment.org/what-we-do (accessed 1 April 2013).

Blue, G. (2009) On the politics and possibilities of locavores: Situating food sovereignty in the turn from government to governance. *Politics and Culture 9*, 68–79.

Brooklyn Grange Farm (2013) See www.brooklyngrangefarm.com/aboutthegrange/ (accessed 29 March 2013).

Bourdain, A. (2013) *No Reservations.* The Travel Channel. See www.travelchannel.com/tv-shows/anthony-bourdain (accessed 1 April 2013).

Canoves, G. and de Morais, R.S. (2011) New forms of tourism in Spain: Wine, gastronomic and rural tourism. In R.M. Torres and J. Henshall Momsen (eds) *Tourism and Agriculture: New Geographies of Consumption, Productions and Rural Structuring* (pp. 205–219). New York: Routledge.

Chaney, S. and Ryan, C. (2012) Analyzing the evolution of Singapore's World Gourmet Summit: An example of gastronomic tourism. *International Journal of Hospitality Management* 31 (2), 309–318.

Deale, C., Norman, W.C. and Jodice, L.W. (2008) Marketing locally harvested shrimp to South Carolina coastal visitors: The development of a culinary tourism supply chain. *Journal of Culinary Science & Technology* 6 (1), 5–23.

De Boer, J. (2003) Sustainability labelling schemes: The logic of their claims and their functions for stakeholders. *Business Strategy and the Environment* 12 (4), 254–264.

Defra (2013) *2012 Food Statistics Pocketbook.* See www.defra.gov.uk/statistics/foodfarm/food/pocketstats/ (accessed 29 March 2013).

Dubuisson-Quellier, S. and Lamine, C. (2008) Consumer involvement in fair trade and local food systems: Delegation and empowerment regimes. *GeoJournal* 73 (1), 55–65.

Eagleton, D. (2005) *Power Hungry: Six Reasons to Regulate Global Food Companies.* London: Action Aid.

EU (2013) Geographical indications and traditional specialities database. See http://ec.europa.eu/agriculture/quality/schemes/index_en.htm (accessed 29 March 2013).

FAO (2013) FAO Food Price Index. See www.fao.org/worldfoodsituation/wfs-home/foodpricesindex/en/ (accessed 29 March 2013).

FAO Agromaps (2013) See http://kids.fao.org/agromaps/ (accessed 29 March 2013).

Fearnley-Whittingstall, H. (2013) Hugh's Fish Fight. See www.fishfight.net (accessed 29 March 2013).

Feeding America (2013) See http://feedingamerica.org/ (accessed 29 March 2013).

Ferry Plaza Farmers Market San Francisco (2013) See www.ferrybuildingmarketplace.com/farmers_market.php (accessed 29 March 2013).

Gagnon, N. (2012) Introduction to the global agri-food system. In I. Joyce and Y. Arcane (eds) *Green Technologies in Food Production and Processing* (pp. 3–22). New York: Springer.

Gleick, P.H. (2012) *World's Water 2011–2012.* Washington, DC: Island Press.

Grievink, J.W. (2003) The changing face of the global food industry. OECD Conference on Changing Dimensions of the Food Economy. See http://rstb.royalsocietypublishing.org/content/360/1463/2139.full (accessed 15 April 2010).

Hall, C.M. (2013) Why forage when you don't have to? Personal and cultural meaning in recreational foraging: A New Zealand study. *Journal of Heritage Tourism* 8 (2–3), 224–233.

Hall, C.M. and Mitchell, R. (2001) Wine and food tourism. In N. Douglas, N. Douglas and R. Derrett (eds) *Special Interest Tourism: Context and Cases* (pp. 307–329). Brisbane, Australia: John Wiley & Sons.

Heart of the City Farmers Market (2013) See www.hocfarmersmarket.org/ (accessed 29 March 2013).

IFPRI (2012) The meat of the issue. See http://insights.ifpri.info/2012/10/the-meat-of-the-issue-2/ (accessed 29 March 2013).

Ilbery, B., Morris, C., Buller, H., Maye, D. and Kneafsey, M. (2005) Product, process and place: An examination of food marketing and labelling schemes in Europe and North America. *European Urban and Regional Studies* 12 (2), 116–132.

Jolliffe, L. (2007) *Tea and Tourism: Tourists, Traditions and Transformations*. Clevedon: Channel View Publications.

Jolliffe, L. (ed.) (2010) *Coffee Culture, Destination and Tourism*. Bristol: Channel View Publications.

Kim, Y.G., Eves, A. and Scarles, C. (2009) Building a model of local food consumption on trips and holidays: A grounded theory approach. *International Journal of Hospitality Management* 28 (3), 423–431.

Kline, C., Knollenberg, W. and Deale, C.S. (2014) Tourism's relationship with ethical food systems. In C. Weeden and K. Boluk (eds) *Managing Ethical Consumption in Tourism* (pp. 104–121). London: Routledge.

La Via Campesina (2013) http://viacampesina.org/en/ (accessed 29 March 2013).

Lang, T. and Heasman, M. (2004) *Food Wars: The Global Battle for Mouths, Minds and Markets*. London: Earthscan.

Leat, P., Revoredo-Giha, C. and Lamprinopoulou, C. (2011) Scotland's food and drink policy discussion: Sustainability issues in the food supply chain. *Sustainability* 3 (4), 605–631.

Liu, H., Parton, K.A., Zhou, Z.-Y. and Cox, R. (2009) At-home meat consumption in China: An empirical study. *Australian Journal of Agricultural and Resource Economics* 53, 485–501.

Mak, A.H., Lumbers, M. and Eves, A. (2012a) Globalisation and food consumption in tourism. *Annals of Tourism Research* 39 (1), 171–196.

Mak, A.H., Lumbers, M., Eves, A. and Chang, R.C. (2012b) Factors influencing tourist food consumption. *International Journal of Hospitality Management* 31 (3), 928–936.

Millstone, E. and Lang T. (2008) *The Atlas of Food*. London: Earthscan.

Mitchell, R., Charters, S. and Albrecht, J.N. (2012) Cultural systems and the wine tourism product. *Annals of Tourism Research* 39 (1), 311–335.

Morrisons (2013) Media Centre briefing. See www.morrisons-corporate.com/Media-centre/Corporate-news/Morrisons-sets-out-to-be-UKs-biggest-fresh-food-maker/ (accessed 29 March 2013).

Mustonen, P. (2006) Volunteer tourism: Postmodern pilgrimage? *Journal of Tourism and Cultural Change* 3 (3), 160–177.

Parkins, W. and Craig, G. (2006) *Slow Living*. London: Berg.

Pike, S. (2002) Destination image analysis – A review of 142 papers from 1973 to 2000. *Tourism Management* 23 (5), 541–549.

Rainforest Alliance (2013) See www.rainforest-alliance.org.uk/ (accessed 29 March 2013).

Smith, S.L. and Xiao, H. (2008) Culinary tourism supply chains: A preliminary examination. *Journal of Travel Research* 46 (3), 289–299.

Sonnenfield, A. (2001) Series editor's introduction. In C. Petrini *Slow Food: The Case for Taste* (p. xi). New York: Columbia University Press.

Stein, R. (2002) *Rick Stein's Food Heroes*. London: BBC Consumer Publishing.

Stock, J.R. (1978) The energy/ecology impacts on distribution. *International Journal of Physical Distribution and Logistics Management* (8) 5, 247–283.

Tarrant, J.R. (1980) *Food Policies*. Chichester: John Wiley and Sons.

The Economist (2009) Thirsty work: The water needed to produce everyday goods and beverages, 25 February. See www.economist.com/node/13176056 (accessed 1 April 2013).

Thompson, P.B. (2010) Food aid and the famine relief argument (brief return). *Journal of Agricultural and Environmental Ethics* 23 (3), 209–227.

Tikkanen, I. (2007) Maslow's hierarchy and food tourism in Finland: Five cases. *British Food Journal* 109 (9), 721–734.

Trussell Trust (2013) See www.trusselltrust.org/ (accessed 29 March 2013).

UN Population Division (2013) See http://esa.un.org/unpd/wpp/index.htm (accessed 29 March 2013).

Velázquez, E. (2007) Water trade in Andalusia. Virtual water: An alternative way to manage water use. *Ecological Economics* 63 (1), 201–208.

Viljoen, A., Bohn, K. and Howe, J. (2005) *Continuous Productive Urban Landscapes: Designing Urban Agriculture for Sustainable Cities.* Oxford: Architectural Press.

Weeden, C. (2013) *Responsible Tourist Behaviour.* Advances in Tourism series. Abingdon: Routledge.

Weeden, C. and Boluk, K. (2014) *Managing Ethical Consumption in Tourism.* Abingdon: Routledge.

Wilson, C. (1974) Energy budgets and rational planning. *Energy Policy* 2 (2), 90.

World Food Programme (2013) See www.wfp.org/ (accessed 29 March 2013).

Yeoman, I. (2012) *2050 – Tomorrow's Tourism.* Bristol: Channel View Publications.

6 Future Consumption: Gastronomy and Public Policy

John D. Mulcahy

Highlights

- Jointly, gastronomy and tourism create competitive advantage which is difficult to imitate.
- Case studies demonstrate possibilities and benefits that accrue from gastronomy.
- Gastronomy will benefit economic, social and environmental aspects of destinations.
- Gastronomy will be a very effective argument in policy-making as it adds value.
- Deep collaboration between government, business and civil society is desirable.

Introduction

Increasingly, a ubiquitous aspect of human life, gastronomy, will be leveraged by government, utilising existing structures, to benefit not only the tourism industry and the visitor, but also economic, social and environmental aspects of a destination. Why? When combined with tourism, gastronomy has natural competitive advantage, not easily replicated when specific to both a location and a culture. Public/private collaboration will be important if gastronomy is to truly reflect local and regional food, particularly in rural tourism where scale and volume are success factors.

The evidence for this is assembled by looking at the symbiotic nature of tourism and gastronomy, as gastronomy can be utilised to boost tourism, while tourism depends on the quality of its gastronomic offering to maintain business. Then, by evaluating five broadly similar jurisdictions, a future framework for gastronomy from a public policy perspective emerges. This approach utilises an ontological typology of future studies suggested by Bergman *et al.* (2010) in which the forecasts here could be considered to be a prognosis, where empirical trends are being extrapolated into the future. The implication for the future is that gastronomy has a sustainable role in the public policy forum.

The Symbiosis of Tourism and Gastronomy

Global tourism is a significant economic sector experiencing increasing competition. The United Nations World Tourism Organization (UNWTO) (2008) estimated that in 1950 the top 15 destinations received 98% of all international arrivals and in 2007 this fell to 57%, reflecting the emergence of new destinations, mostly in developing countries. Looking to the future, the UNWTO forecasts that annual international tourism visits, currently growing at 4% per annum, will reach 1.6 billion by 2020 (from 903 million in 2007) even allowing for unexpected crises. Given this scenario, Nunes and Spelman (2008) anticipate that tourism-related prices will escalate as demand outstrips supply in the face of that demand level and that governments will seek to control demand on high-intensity sites and cities.

That future demand, according to Chambers (2009: 354), will be driven by tourists from emerging economies, in addition to the increasing numbers of the retired in developing countries. Furthermore, analysis of the UNWTO figures by Aramberri (2009) suggests that 80% of international tourism is domestic, 20% is within the same continent, and only 5% is long-haul business travel, thus reducing cultural dissonance (e.g. language and food) between travellers and locals. Think of Asian tourism in Western countries, where Asian tourists are more dependent (than Western tourists in a similar situation) on establishments providing their own national cuisines. Cohen and Avieli (2004: 775) show that it is entirely possible that Asian tourists will not visit a given destination in volume unless it features outlets serving their national cuisine.

However, perspective is important. Heldke (2003: xx–xxiv) refers to culinary tourists as 'food adventurers', but defines them as 'Euro-American, Christian, white, middleclass, well educated people' for her purposes and suggests that such food adventurers unwittingly participate in a cultural colonialism through the pursuit of exotic experiences in authenticity. Still, she does clarify that any culture or nation can be culinary tourists. This observation is important as it highlights and helps to explain the fundamental flaws in a singular, parochial interpretation of tourism and the inherent danger of a sort of intellectual fascism. The mistake would be to assume that the experience is the same thing for each culture, nation or person; it cannot be, as the reference points are so diverse. At this point, it is worth noting that, as Andersson (2007) observes, each individual tourist experience is a distinct moment, connecting production and consumption, unlike other types of consumer transactions when production and consumption are likely to have occurred at different times and places. It is the tourist who organises their time and skills, and acquires goods and services to create the experiences that satisfy their own basic, social and intellectual needs, and these vary over time, according to Tikkanen (2007). Furthermore, Urry (2002) observes that these needs also vary between individuals, so anticipating and meeting those needs are a challenge for any tourist enterprise. Yet, the perceived value of the experience to the tourist depends on the individual's mix of those needs at that moment in time.

Not only that, but a person's food preferences and their ability to discriminate aesthetically is deeply ingrained and socially embedded, according to Mennell (2005), hence it seems natural, although it has been learned rather than being innate. As a result, Mennell explains, gastronomy, its discourse and its evolution act as a highly sensitive marker for much broader social, political and economic changes in society. Gastronomy therefore becomes a very effective argument in policy-making, and the multi-disciplinarity of gastronomy suggests that not only is gastronomy related to reflectively sourcing, preparing, cooking and eating, it is also a broad-based discipline that incorporates everything that food is a part of, including tourism.

From a business perspective, gastronomic tourism's primary advantage, according to Richards (2002), is its ability to adapt to and react to the effects of phenomena such as globalisation, localisation or creolisation, mostly because the adjacent living culture changes. Currently, destinations are responding to dramatic economic change by investing in food tourism, motivated by the fact that food and beverages command one-third of tourism revenue which is substantial enough to interest both enterprise and government. However, this could be considered low (Boyne et al., 2002; Hashimoto & Telfer, 2006). As a tourism product which expresses identity and culture, Hall and Sharples (2003) argue that food can encourage people to travel and experience it, and it is therefore a critical component of cultural and heritage tourism (Bessiére, 1998). They point out that if food tourism is considered as special interest tourism, where food is the motivation for travel, then the level of engagement or interest matters, ranging from no interest (eating for fuel) through the interested (rural/urban tourism), the curious (culinary tourism), to high interest (cuisine, gastronomic or gourmet tourism). In their view, Hall and Sharples (2003) see the 'spatial fixity' of the food tourism product as being a critical factor as the tourists must arrive at the production site to consume the food (both physically and metaphorically) and become food tourists. Therefore, they contend, food tourism is the consumption of the local, and the consumption and production of place. If this is true, food issues caused by globalisation, such as homogenisation and the effects on regional cuisines, become less acute. Arguably, globalisation has increased a focus on, and interest in, regional identities and cultural roots, so that regional foods rather than international versions of ethnic cuisines will be emphasised.

Gastronomic tourism, at several levels, has the capacity to create interdependencies that influence the development and acceptability of both a destination and its gastronomy to a visitor. In struggling destinations or those without the benefit of sun, sea and sand, gastronomy has been shown by Scarpato (2002) to be a cost-effective, profitable option, and is usually associated with quality tourism by adding value to the tourist experience (e.g. short breaks and wine tourism), which attracts a premium. Thus gastronomy is a viable tourist product, as it is an enduring part of a holiday experience due to the symbiotic relationship between gastronomy and a tourist destination (Kivela & Crotts, 2009).

From a policymaker's or a commercial perspective, gastronomic tourism offers a means of enhancing and extending the tourist spend without compromising the environmental, social or cultural fabric of a region. It also has a role in securing the 'triple bottom line' of economic, social and environmental sustainability, but in order to do so, notes Everett and Aitchison (2008: 150), 'a better understanding of the "food tourist" in relation to typologies of tourist motivation, characteristics and behaviour, should enable the development of more informed policymaking'.

Public Policy Role in Gastronomic Tourism – Case Studies

The case studies are drawn from countries which are broadly similar in terms of size, population and tourism industry structure, and they are intended to plainly demonstrate the diversity of what is possible and the range of benefits that can accrue from gastronomic tourism.

Austria

Government policy seeks to ensure that small farming communities are provided with relevant support in order to make a living. Marketing and selling local produce is seen as a central feature of that policy, and the vast majority of hotels in ski and hiking resorts work closely with local farmers and use their products. The emergence of several Michelin and Gault-Millau rated restaurants in the Salzburg province is evidence provided by Lonsgood (2004: 11) of the popularity and quality of the local ingredients available.

Gastronomic trails and routes

Described as networks of regional attractions, Austria's first was opened in 1955, and over 70 themed trails now exist. Usually established in economically weak areas, most have evolved from producer and marketing associations, and two-thirds are based on farm products of the region in which the trail is located. Originally intended to improve access for the farmers, the trails also improved accessibility for tourists.

An example of a trail is the regional development initiative brand 'Via Iulia Augusta', a Roman trade route coming north from Italy into Austria, offering several experiences involving typical foods. There are also examples of interactions between trails such as the complimentary match between the Bregenzerwald cheese walking trail and a wine road in Lower Austria where the products are offered together in both regions. According to Meyer-Cech (2005), this project comprises a 200-member network including 30 different cheeses, 24 municipalities, 50 restaurants and 50 alpine diaries, as well as supermarkets and handicraft enterprises. Its existence ensures continued farming of alpine pastures in addition to the added value of tourism, transport, increased economic confidence and regional pride.

The trails are good examples of cooperation between agriculture and tourism at sectoral, local, regional and national levels, of collaborative agreements with service providers such as accommodation, hospitality and artisan producers, and for direct marketing and quality assurance mechanisms. Meyer-Cech (2003) notes that the level of member cooperation is sometimes graded; there might be a core team, supported by an extended network, and buttressed by a group of associated partners, but the level of cooperation can be impressive. Led by the tourist board, one exceptional consortium of eight wine regions and their ten sub-organisations, involving 1200 businesses and 150 municipalities, developed its own criteria for each member category in a concerted effort to harmonise and professionalise the offer of the trails to visitors.

Success seems to depend more on an effective management structure to capitalise on a range of strong personal friendships and business relationships rather than on raw resources. It is clear from Meyer-Cech's work that distinct social and emotional benefits are important along with tangible outputs, well-structured meetings, effective communication, active cooperation, a sense of community in a globalised world and contributions to a common goal.

Rural tourism

A sectoral organisation, the Austrian Farm Holidays Association (AFHA), offers tourists, writes Loverseed (2007: 26), a 'natural, authentic and reasonably priced' holiday through its network of 3400 members, which between them have 44,800 beds, mostly located in the mountain regions. Association membership criteria require that at least five agricultural products (usually food and made on the premises) be offered to guests. Recognising that tourists expect to find rural landscapes of communities farming local breeds producing local products and local culture, some Austrian villages and businesses subsidise farmers to ensure that these desired features do not decline, thereby attributing a market value to local breeds.

Norway

Norway has primarily been concentrating its policies on restructuring of agricultural production and rural development, and the establishment of a local food system, with the intention of linking that work to tourism later on.

Norway is party to 'New Nordic Food', a programme of the Nordic Council of Ministers and one of a number of cooperation programmes initiated by Nordic governments such as Iceland, Denmark, Finland, Norway and Sweden in 2006. The initiative combines Nordic food culture with the strengths and developments in the fields of gastronomy, business, raw materials, tourism and regional partnership.

Norway seems to be able to maintain food traditions without a commercial prop to ensure the survival of those traditions. This may be explained by food relocalisation, characterised by the persistence of strong local food cultures and small farms. For example, Fonte (2008) describes how making half-fermented trout has been a food tradition in Valdres since the 16th century or earlier. Its establishment as a local brand has motivated local authorities to set up initiatives in favour of family farms that would not have ordinarily been included in development efforts at local and national levels.

In their examination of 'scary food' (a sheep's head meal), Mykletun and Gyimóthy (2009: 11) make some apt and relevant observations; 'the sheep's head meal renaissance is a creation achieved by individual entrepreneurs and entrepreneurial networks which has contributed to growth and distinctiveness of the area and its branding as a tourist destination. Moreover, they have inspired and accelerated other entrepreneurs within farming and the supply of other products and services.'

This is echoed by Fonte (2008: 219), who shows how working among peers in the regions is important, that is, local stakeholders working as equals to rebuild local knowledge through networking, shared experiences, discussions and observation, while avoiding the risk of valuable local knowledge being hijacked by external or non-local consultants.

New Zealand

New Zealand has demonstrated some leadership in the gastronomy tourism niche, and is seen by Kivela and Crotts (2006: 373) as being particularly innovative in creating wine and food tourism networks through champions and individual innovators who have created local interest and involvement. Termed 'lifestyle entrepreneurship' by Hall et al. (2003: 57), it is seen as a major factor in the development of new food and tourism-related developments. A neighbourhood in Auckland is emblematic of what many outsiders see as New Zealand's approach to hospitality and tourism. As described by Bell (2007: 14), the hospitality entrepreneurs took a crucial role in defining the 'feel' of the neighbourhood, and in consciously shaping their businesses to promote a distinctive conviviality and informality attractive to locals and tourists alike.

Hawke's Bay Wine and Food Group

Formed in 2000, the Hawke's Bay Wine and Food Group developed a food and wine trail, brochures, effective signage, a joint promotion strategy and a regional brand through its website. As part of that strategy, the region hosted the second New Zealand Wine and Food Tourism Conference in 2001. Hall (2005) notes that, due to the success of the initiative, especially the national conference, local government felt that it had to respond through increased involvement. Hall also notes how critical 'knowledge brokers' were at the initial public meetings to set up the initiative. These brokers were perceived as independent and helped to establish a climate of trust between potential members of the cluster group, while also allowing the work of the champions to be seen as wider than self-interest in the creation of the cluster. Hall (2005) found that the regular stakeholder meetings, usually over a long period of time, were most significant in the development of a group by creating new forms of social capital through webs of relationships where none existed previously. Hall (2005) also describes how the social capital of the brokers/champions was converted into the social and economic capital of others by virtue of multilevel networks of local firms. These networks extended beyond tourism to include a broader range of sectoral linkages between businesses that had previously seen themselves as having little in common to form clusters. Therefore, he argues, a cluster champion to initiate those meetings is also critical, providing that the champion has a long-term commitment to cluster and network development, so that the benefits of increased intellectual capital, innovation capacity and economic growth would be realised.

Scotland

Traditionally, Scotland has successfully established its food credentials with whisky, haggis, shortbread and salmon, principally as standalone products (Jones & Jenkins, 2002). More recently, Yeoman et al. (2009: 393) demonstrate how the authenticity of Scotland's regional food and whisky is being used to reposition Scotland using the 'Taste of Scotland' initiative, which constructed a food heritage for Scotland as a means of engaging with local communities and then used it as a marketing tool.

In November of 2006, VisitScotland published a briefing paper by Yeoman and Greenwood (2006) that examined the potential roles for food tourism in Scotland and how food tourism could contribute to Scotland's ambition to grow tourism revenue by 50% by 2015. The issues were addressed by discussing what is driving the role of food and beverage in society, by examining the concept of food tourism and forecasting the future of the eating-out market in Scotland. Finally, informed by the discussion, and using two food tourism scenarios, prospects for food tourism in the future were examined. The trading-up scenario shows that, as tourists trade up, food tourism gains 'cultural capital and social cachet', while in the food commodity scenario, food tourism loses differentiation and profit margins become unstable. The conclusions point out that while food is not the main driver for visiting Scotland, over 50% of visitors have an interest in food, highlighting how food tourism is becoming an important aspect of an overall tourism experience, especially where culinary heritage is not obvious. Their key point is that food tourism must be a first-class experience at all levels, from fast food to pubs to slow food, and that food tourism can contribute to the ambition of the 'Tourism Framework for Change' strategy of the Scottish Executive (2006) as tourists trade up.

The Orkney Islands

The Orkney Islands are identified by Williams and Copus (2005: 314) as being innovative and as having strong networks and linkages. In 1999, the local community created an Orkney brand, which is leveraged by Orkney Quality Food and Drink, a membership organisation responsible for bringing mutual benefits to the Orkney food and drink industry. The range of products is impressive and not entirely what one would expect: they include Orkney herring, cheeses, fudge, chocolates, wine, whiskey, ale, beef and lamb. Visitors are encouraged to nominate their favourite restaurant or coffee shop, product or shop for the Taste of Orkney Food Awards, in order to reward the businesses that have excelled in quality and customer service, thus creating a symbiotic relationship between production and providers.

Opportunities for Policymakers from the Case Studies

A common theme throughout has been the leadership role of local, regional or national government either by way of collaborative marketing across sectors (New Zealand), setting a specific target after utilising scenario planning (Scotland), or by facilitating and recognising innovation by responding favourably when local initiatives have early success (Norway). In the majority of cases, though, collaborative community action, with or without state assistance, led by those who can demonstrate social and cultural capital, is critical to success. While these champions of gastronomy might have economic capital as well, instinctively they are aware that others in the community will think differently, and that for any one project to work, it must benefit the entire community in multiple ways through sharing, communication, openness and good management. This approach also identifies and protects local food assets and exploits them appropriately (Norway's 'Scary Food', and Orkney's lamb). Such is the level of enthusiasm currently evident for gastronomic tourism experiences, the capacity to handle demand from visitors is implicit in all examples. If gastronomic tourism is to truly reflect local and regional food, collaboration is a vital theme (chiefly between agriculture and tourism), particularly in the gastronomy and economics of rural tourism where scale and volume are factors of success.

Concluding Remarks: The Implications for the Future of Food Tourism

The implications for the future of food tourism are that there is a substantial economic, social and developmental rationale to argue for the viability and sustainability of gastronomic tourism in the public policy forum. From a business perspective, gastronomic tourism's primary advantage is its ability to adapt and react to the effects of phenomena such as globalisation, localisation or creolisation. This because gastronomy is close to changes in local culture, especially cuisines where culinary vitality depends on adaptability and flexibility, and has been shown to be a highly sensitive marker for much broader social, political and economic changes in society. It therefore becomes a very effective argument in policy-making as it is a cost-effective, profitable option for all stakeholders. Similarly a symbiotic relationship exists between gastronomy and a tourist destination as gastronomic tourism has the capacity to create interdependencies that influence the development and acceptability of both a destination and its gastronomy to a visitor. Importantly, 'spatial fixity' is a critical factor, as tourists on location initiate a range of other opportunities. Food in tourism, therefore, is not only an instrument of destination development, but also general economic development. Spatial fixity has also created one of the 'new' forms of independent and sustainable tourism that enables tourists to enhance their cultural capital while providers increase their social and economic capital. Enterprises can 'out local' global competition by leveraging and sustaining, maintaining, developing/constructing that local cultural capital. The evidently supple nature of capital and its crucial role in gastronomic tourism suggests greater potential for that role to be developed. This perspective should inspire public administrators, policymakers, research institutions and businesses to collaboratively focus on cultivating local cultural capital and resources.

Collaborative community action led by those who can demonstrate social and cultural capital has been critical to success in multiple locations. While these champions of gastronomy might have economic capital as well, they seem to be instinctively aware that some in the community will think differently, and that for any one project to work, it must benefit the entire community in multiple ways through sharing, communication, openness and good management.

Policymakers could learn from Scotland's scenario planning experience by assessing the effects of the process and its applicability to their locality Clearly, the role of a state tourism agency will be as a proactive, holistic, element of a local innovation system, cluster or network, primarily working alongside local businesses, but also their suppliers, customers, government and other agencies. Key support features will include the provision of information (technical, marketing, product, etc.), frequent systematic contact, coordinating and leading the interrelationships between agencies. As the UN general assembly heard in 2005, 'the very best solutions come when business, governments and civil society work together' (Blanke & Chiesa, 2008: 98).

Policymakers must find ways to protect the intellectual property embedded in gastronomic culture in order to maintain competitive advantage and the distinctiveness of products in the face of increasing competition from other destinations. For example, producers of food and tourism products could be stimulated to take an interest in gastronomic heritage and intellectual property rights as suggested by Ravenscroft and van Westering (2002). Assets could be identified elsewhere in the economy with the potential to create new tourist market segments, and to collaborate with the various actors in that sphere for mutual advantage. This could include the preservation of indigenous food types and varieties (such as breeds of cattle or varieties of apples), recipes, food combinations and local life and traditions related to eating and drinking (opening hours, working days, festivals, fetes), all of which knit together to become a unique local, regional or national gastronomic culture. An additional desirable outcome would be an inventory of all the features that make up that area's identity and it would help to profile, contrast, distinguish and emphasise its uniqueness. This implies concentrating on local capacity building, i.e. strengthen the knowledge, skills and attitudes of local people for establishing and sustaining food tourism within an area.

Some tourism destinations have been shown to be particularly well placed to provide an authentic experience and are ripe for this type of capacity building. The gastronomic tourism business case could do much to convince these sectors of the benefits of tourists to a business and, consequently, the surrounding area. Food diminishes the cultural gap between the visitor and a local resident as it forms a nexus of common ground to share experience – a relation of regard, which gastronomic tourism can exploit. Gastronomic tourism is a potent intermediary between visitor and resident, as gastronomy has been shown to be highly personal, individualistic and made more complex. Each individual tourist experience is key as it is the element connecting production and consumption, visitor and resident, needs and gratification.

From a business case perspective, the most compelling and logical argument is this. Gastronomic tourism is a people business – both in terms of those who provide and consume the experience. The possession of economic capital allows and facilitates the investment in cultural capital through allowing the investment of time needed to accumulate cultural capital. A transaction can take place. Yet built into that transaction and because of it are other transactions of cultural capital (on the part of the tourist, acquiring and displaying it) and social capital (on the part of the service provider in assembling and providing the experience), all of which generate further capital, especially economic capital, thus creating a virtuous circle for all. Gastronomy's existential tourist experience is therefore a credible driver of tourism and, by implication, the wider economy.

References

Andersson, T.D. (2007) The tourist in the experience economy. *Scandinavian Journal of Hospitality & Tourism* 7, 46–58.

Aramberri, J. (2009) The future of tourism and globalization: Some critical remarks. *Futures* 41 (6), 367–376.

Bell, D. (2007) The hospitable city: Social relations in commercial spaces. *Progress in Human Geography* 31 (1), 7–22.

Bergman, A., Karlsson, J.C. and Axelsson, J. (2010) Truth claims and explanatory claims: An ontological typology of futures studies. *Futures* 42 (8), 857–865.

Bessiére, J. (1998) Local development and heritage: Traditional food and cuisine as tourist attractions in rural areas. *Sociologia Ruralis* 38 (1), 21–35.

Blanke, J. and Chiesa, T. (2000) *The Travel and Tourism Competitiveness Report 2008.* Geneva. World Economic Forum.

Boyne, S., Williams, F. and Hall, D. (2002) On the trail of regional success: Tourism, food production, and the Isle of Arran taste trail. In A.-M. Hjalager and G. Richards (eds) *Tourism and Gastronomy* (pp. 91–114). London: Routledge.

Chambers, E. (2009) From authenticity to significance: Tourism on the frontier of culture and place. *Futures* 41 (6), 353–359.

Cohen, E. and Avieli, N. (2004) Food in tourism: Attraction and impediment. *Annals of Tourism Research* 31 (4), 755–778.

Everett, S. and Aitchison, C. (2008) The role of food tourism in sustaining regional identity: A case study of Cornwall, South West England. *Journal of Sustainable Tourism* 16, 150–167.

Fonte, M. (2008) Knowledge, food and place. A way of producing, a way of knowing. *Sociologia Ruralis* 48 (3), 200–222.

Hall, C.M. (2005) Rural wine and food tourism cluster and network development. In D. Hall, I. Kirkpatrick and M. Mitchell (eds) *Rural Tourism and Sustainable Business* (pp. 149–164). Clevedon: Channel View Publications.

Hall, C.M. and Sharples, L. (2003) The consumption of experiences or the experience of consumption? An introduction to the tourism of taste. In C.M. Hall, L. Sharples, R. Mitchell, N. Macionis and B. Cambourne (eds) *Food Tourism Around the World: Development, Management and Markets* (pp. 1–24). Boston, MA: Butterworth-Heinemann.

Hall, C.M., Sharples, L., Mitchell, R., Macionis, N. and Cambourne, B. (2003) *Food Tourism Around the World: Development, Management, and Markets.* Oxford: Butterworth-Heinemann.

Hashimoto, A. and Telfer, D.J. (2006) Selling Canadian culinary tourism: Branding the global and the regional product. *Tourism Geographies* 8 (1), 31–55.

Heldke, L.M. (2003) *Exotic Appetites: Ruminations of a Food Adventurer.* New York: Routledge.

Jones, A. and Jenkins, I. (2002) A taste of Wales – Blas ar Gymru: Institutional malaise in promoting Welsh food tourism products. In A.-M. Hjalager and G. Richards (eds) *Tourism and Gastronomy* (pp. 115–131). London: Routledge.

Kivela, J. and Crotts, J.C. (2006) Tourism and gastronomy: Gastronomy's influence on how tourists experience a destination. *Journal of Hospitality & Tourism Research* 30 (3), 354–377.

Kivela, J. and Crotts, J.C. (2009) Understanding travellers' experiences of gastronomy through etymology and narration. *Journal of Hospitality & Tourism Research* 33 (2), 161–192.

Loverseed, H. (2004) Gastronomic tourism – Europe. In *Travel & Tourism Analyst.* Mintel International Group Ltd.

Loverseed, H. (2007) Rural tourism. In *Travel & Tourism Analyst.* Mintel International Group Ltd.

Mennell, S. (2005) Conclusions, culinary transitions in Europe: An overview. In D. Goldstein and K. Merkle (eds) *Culinary Cultures of Europe: Identity, Diversity and Dialogue*, (p. 469). Strasbourg: Council of Europe Pub.

Meyer-Czech, K. (2003) Food trails in Austria. In C.M. Hall, L. Sharples, R. Mitchell, N. Macionis and B. Cambourne (eds) *Food Tourism Around the World: Development, Management and Markets* (pp. 149–157). Oxford: Butterworth-Heinemann.

Meyer-Cech, K. (2005) Regional cooperation in rural theme trails. In D. Hall, I. Kirkpatrick and M. Mitchell (eds) *Rural Tourism and Sustainable Business* (pp.137–148). Clevedon: Channel View Publications.

Mykletun, R.J. and Gyimóthy, S. (2009) Beyond the renaissance of the traditional Voss sheep's-head meal: Tradition, culinary art, scariness and entrepreneurship. *Tourism Management* 30 (6), 1–13.

Nunes, P.F. and Spelman, M. (2008) The tourism time bomb. *Harvard Business Review* 86 (4), 20–22.

Ravenscroft, N. and van Westering, J. (2002) Gastronomy and intellectual property. In A.-M. Hjalager and G. Richards (eds) *Tourism and Gastronomy* (pp. 153–165). London: Routledge.

Richards, G. (2002) Gastronomy: An essential ingredient in tourism production and consumption? In A.-M. Hjalager and G. Richards (eds) *Tourism and Gastronomy* (pp. 3–20). London: Routledge.

Scarpato, R. (2002) Gastronomy as a tourist product: The perspective of gastronomy studies. In A.-M. Hjalager and G. Richards (eds) *Tourism and Gastronomy* (pp. 51–70). London: Routledge.

Scottish Executive (2006) *Scottish Tourism: The Next Decade – A Framework for Change*. See www.scotland.gov.uk/Resource/Doc/95406/0023096.pdf (accessed 1 November 2013).

Tikkanen, I. (2007) Maslow's hierarchy and food tourism in Finland: Five cases. *British Food Journal* 109 (9), 721–734.

United Nations World Tourism Organization (UNWTO) (2008) *Tourism Highlights*. Madrid: UNWTO Publishing.

Urry, J. (2002) *The Tourist Gaze* (2nd edn). London: Sage Publications.

Williams, F. and Copus, A. (2005) Business development, rural tourism, and the implications of milieu. In D. Hall, I. Kirkpatrick and M. Mitchell (eds) *Rural Tourism and Sustainable Business* (pp. 305–322). Clevedon: Channel View Publications.

Yeoman, I. and Greenwood, C. (2006) From fast food to slow food: The prospects for Scotland's cuisine to 2015. In *Tomorrows World: Consumer and Tourist*. Edinburgh: Visit Scotland.

Yeoman, I., Greenwood, C. and McMahon-Beattie, U. (2009) The future of Scotland's international tourism markets. *Futures* 41 (6), 387–395.

7 Architecture and Future Food and Wine Experiences

Tobias Danielmeier and Julia N. Albrecht

Highlights

- Economic and societal changes (related to wealth distribution, education, individualism, marketing scepticism, the increasing importance of experience economies, among others) will alter representational means of the tourism and hospitality industries.
- Specifically, place and the narration of place will increase in importance as they are used to convey uniqueness and points of difference to consumers.
- Experiences and place performances will thus take precedence over the mere consumption of wine or food products.
- Architecture as a place-making activity will be employed to address consumer desires. These developments will occur almost independently from localised wine and food production.

Introduction

Winery operators have increasingly recognised the potential value of merging the hospitality and wine industries. Incentives are perceived as business diversification and, consequently, increased revenue (Hall & Mitchell, 2008). For this reason, contemporary wineries often combine wine, food and complementary visitor experiences (Mitchell et al., 2000, 2012). More recently, the performative turn in tourism suggests an additional significant aspect: the visitor's desire for a collaborative enactment of values associated with wine and food production (e.g. rurality, authenticity). The literatures on food and wine tourism as well as consumer behaviour explain how consumers increasingly seek opportunities for performative

behaviour when visiting wineries and food tasting facilities. They illumi-
nate how experiencing and performing place can take precedence over the
mere consumption of wine or food (e.g. Leatherbarrow, 2004).

Architecture is identified as an important driver and narrator of place, a
role in which it is currently vastly underestimated (Haldrup & Bærenholdt,
2010; Hodgson & Toyka, 2007; Horwitz & Singley, 2004; Lansansky &
McLaren, 2004). The chapter argues that architecture will become a key
factor in winery visitor experiences as well as in the creation of food and
wine tourism experiences more generally. Design practice is in most cases an
evolutionary process. By analysing two key architectural designs that are in
use today, evaluations are made and design trajectories and design potentials
for future winery architecture projects identified.

As such, this is one of the few contributions in the tourism literature that
identifies and explains the relevance of the built environment for tourism.
Ontologically speaking, this chapter aims to predict the future state of
winery (tourism) experiences; it offers both descriptions of future winery
experiences as well as an explanatory dimension that explains how these
experiences are shaped (Bergman *et al.*, 2010).

Emphasising a futures perspective, the chapter further identifies trends
and drivers that fuel consumers' desire to increase their relationship with
place rather than product. It is built on the following assumptions:

- The wine industry seeks to engage consumers in multiple ways.
- Consumers of the future are highly individualised and seek authentic
  experiences.
- The performative turn in tourism and visitor experiences is gaining in
  importance.
- Architecture holds sign values that help to convey and narrate
  experiences.
- Architecture can render experiences more performative.

The chapter thus links notions of future consumers and the increased emphasis of performativity whilst drawing out aspects of current architectural
design for visitor experiences that will be relevant for future consumers
(Clark *et al.*, 2008). It shows how and why wine and food as produce decrease
in importance whilst experiential aspects become paramount.

Literature and Context

Place, subjects and objects

Place is of particular importance to the wine industry. Vintners and
winemakers use the term 'terroir' synonymously for place (Smart, 2002;

Wilson, 1998). It refers to differences in soil characteristics, microclimates, cultural meanings and applications, individual winemaking practices as well as specific technologies used that impact on the taste, quality and experience of wine. When it comes to marketing, most wine producers use terroir as a concept of exclusion that differentiates individual businesses from their competition (Danielmeier, 2014).

In the context of this chapter, place is understood as a construct as well as a framework that acknowledges time-space dependent variables that are actively practised, experienced and felt. Places, as argued by Agnew and Duncan (1989), depend on the 'local' and 'locality' and are subject to frequent and dynamic transformation processes (Massey, 2005). For Eisenman (in Iblings, 1998) places consist of two key defining components: objects and subjects. All objects carry the potential to enable and foster emotional interactions between subjects and matter and can potentially trigger behavioural changes of individuals to and within place. Conscious and unconscious changes of place parameters can hence not only impact on physical appearances, they can also alter reactions and emotional attachments of people to place.

Of particular interest for the future of wine and food tourism within consumer culture is Baudrillard's observation on object specific characteristics (discussed in Proto, 2006). He argues that objects hold sign values that can be expressed though images, logos and styles. Following this ethos, architectures can be seen as products of environmental needs and societal demands that are subject to manipulations of images, logos and styles. Venturi et al. (1977) analyse urban and architectural potentials and threats. Aiming at the identification of potential design challenges and opportunities, the Las Vegas strip is used as an urban laboratory to describe phenomena of consumer culture expressed through architectural imagery and sign language. The authors conclude that consumers of place, such as tourists, participate in the consumption of place as well as place-based sign values.

In the past, expressive shapes or precious materials have been used to highlight significance of (touristic) places through the medium of architecture. Well-known examples include Wright's famous Guggenheim Museum in New York, Utzon's Opera House in Sydney or Gehry's Guggenheim museum in Bilbao. These buildings are examples of architectures capable of lifting the reputation of surrounding streetscapes or destinations. Indeed, the 'Bilbao effect' is as well-known in architecture as it is in tourism (Foster, 2011; Ockman, 2004).

Architecture's capability to portray company and product values is well-established. Behrens' AEG Turbinenhalle (built in 1908-1909) is considered one of the most powerful examples of design-led thinking that incorporates product as well as building design. Subsequently, commissioning renowned architects has become a status symbol for many manufacturers and sales outlets. Technology companies IBM, Olivetti and Apple, fashion label Prada, as well as many Western car manufacturers (e.g. Daimler Chrysler, BMW) use 'star architects' to design their representative buildings. Over time, the medium of design has also proved to mirror changing consumer cultures and values.

The tourism industry adopted the strategic employment of imagery and sign values in the early days of photography and photomontage. This promotion of places and attractions aimed at increasing awareness and visitation. The use of imagery within purpose-built structures has been employed since the mid-1950s. An early and powerful example is the Hilton Hotel Istanbul designed by Skidmore, Owings and Merrill, which offers an 'all American experience'. The key concept is that visitors can experience commodities and conveniences common within American hotels in the US, but in the context of a foreign setting. All services, products as well as visual language, including the architectural appearance of the building, promote this ethos (Danielmeier, 2011).

Many holiday resort accommodations in Polynesia adopt the opposite approach. Tourists are provided with the opportunity to stay in proximity to the ocean in *fale*. Today's circular-shaped skeleton frame structures are modified to suit expectations of foreign travellers. While not assembling traditional storehouses in communal settings anymore, these buildings have become a synonym for holiday accommodations on the islands. Both examples showcase how architecture can be employed to display values of familiarity and contribute to communicate location values.

Comparable to other producing industries, winery businesses focus on optimisation of production qualities and quantities. Aiming to utilise additional revenue streams and to be less reliant on seasonal cycles, some winery businesses have diversified. Hospitality and tourism functions have since become a widely implemented strategy for wine producers around the world. The display of corporate values is not exclusively limited to bottle labels anymore. Agricultural businesses that used to focus on production started interacting with customers, to host as well as to entertain people in new ways. Front-of-house operations quickly became common and architectural representation became a consideration. Besides attracting connoisseurs and architecture enthusiasts, some wineries benefitted from the additional media attention. The visual display of terroir through architecture opened up opportunities for the narration of business values and locality (Danielmeier, 2014).

Different from multinational corporations or cultural institutions of international significance, wineries have much smaller operating budgets. Another challenge is that adjacent businesses often convey similar key values about local grape varieties, microclimates, winemaking traditions and glorification of almost similar produce. Consequentially, during the last decade many world-class producers have focused on the creation of unique and memorable visitor experiences. Through that the industry has shifted gradually from what you do, to how you do it, how you celebrate it, and how you communicate every single one of your actions.

As a result, the inclusion of hospitality and tourism functions changed existing business structures and forced winemakers to rethink established wine practises and modes of operation. The design of front-of-house operations required an overarching brand and corporate identity. The industry thus turned from a purely performance-oriented approach into the realm of performative acts and spatial performativity. While traditional winery models coexist, tourism and hospitality functions are increasingly expected, and performative acts and spatial performativity become deciding factors: people, produce and place turn wineries into stages.

Performative visitor experiences

The design and provision of visitor experiences lies in the hands of a number of distinctive professions. Curators of museums and galleries may have backgrounds in history, art history, ethnology or even palaeontology. Fields like landscape design, planning and even engineering are undoubtedly important in the establishment and development of an attraction or a destination. Destination managers also tend to have eclectic backgrounds and do not always have previous experience in tourism or hospitality. The only common trait of these providers and managers of visitor experiences is that they aim to create a 'positive' tourist experience. This is a highly subjective notion, yet typical for a field where reflective practice is common.

Another level of complexity lies in the sites of tourism consumption. Places associated with accommodation or retail are commonly purpose-built, but many of today's attractions (such as historic sites, religious or cultural sites, picturesque villages, sites in peripheral areas more generally) have not been conceptualised for tourist consumption. The places that tourists visit will inevitably be altered by their presence, rendering true Hultman and Hall's (2012) suggestion that place-making is a social process.

The performative turn in tourism proposes, among other things, that today's and tomorrow's tourism experiences transcend authenticity (Yeoman et al., 2007) and turn towards the performative. Following Edensor (2001) and Perkins and Thorns (2001), performativity is here understood as the continuous enactment of values and norms. The (en)actors are the hosts and guests who act according to a mutually (yet silently) agreed set of values seen fit in said situation. This results in three conclusions:

(1) Performative visitor experiences involve most if not all actors in a situation. This adds complexity to the provision of such experiences: everybody needs to share similar values and norms for a given situation (or, at least, to appear to do so).
(2) Visitor experiences are commonly described as intangible, and Haldrup and Larsen (2006) have enquired whether they can be deliberately

designed at all. Aside from being a conceptual conundrum, there is also the question of how many and what stakeholders are involved.

(3) Performativity is indeed 'place-making in action' (Hultman & Hall, 2012: 561). This assertion results from a paper exploring governance rather than product development or visitor management; it nevertheless applies here.

Further to these more conceptual considerations, the internal and external trends outlined in Table 7.1 shape the performative tourist and related experiences.

Performativity in food and wine tourism

Hall *et al.* (2003) suggest that food is a signifier of identity. Clearly, where an everyday commodity is thus elevated, food tourism must be even more of

Table 7.1 Trends shaping the performative tourist

Trend 1	**Affluence in some parts of the global population** Wealth will increase in importance as a driver of tourism and travel behaviour (Yeoman, 2008; Yeoman, 2012).
Trend 2	**Experience economy** Following Maslow's argument, the satisfaction of our material needs means that cultural, social and emotional needs become more central in both offerings and marketing. Perceived benefits for the consumer include prestige and status-enhancement, stress-alleviation and potentially deeper, escapist experiences.
Trend 3	**(Higher) education** Education standards will continue to rise, in particular in Asian countries and countries in the global south. Educated consumers will demand more sophisticated products. Changing economic structures will grant access to these products and goods.
Trend 4	**Individualism** Global capitalism is the normal state for younger generations. Instead of rebelling, they show little interest in politics. Increased prosperity means that fulfilment and excitement are at hand; holidays are associated with various forms of escapism. Self-actualisation is a priority. Individuals' fluid identities (Yeoman, 2012) mean decreased homogeneity in recreational activities.
Trend 5	**Scepticism towards marketing** Criticism of the capitalist global order and related marketing policies have become mainstream.
Trend 6	**Prioritising how spare time is spent** Unlike baby-boomers and, to a degree, Generation X, Generation Y and the following place high emphasis on work–life balance.

a signifier and display of identities. Finkelstein (1989) argues that dining out involves the 'commodification' of our emotions and is 'a means by which personal desires find their shape and satisfaction through the prescribed forms of social conduct' (Finkelstein, 1989: 4). Interactive modes of engagement between visitors, produce and winemakers reach far beyond conspicuous consumption. Not only what, but also increasingly how and where you consume is gaining importance.

In addition to its roots in tourism and architectural considerations as explained above, this work also incorporates ideas that transcend geography and material culture. Haldrup and Larsen (2006: 276) suggest that tourism provides 'multi-sensuous and technologized [sic] performances through which people are actively involved in the world, imaginatively and physically'. This is relevant for this chapter in so far as the built structure where a tourism experience takes place essentially constitutes a vehicle for both aesthetic and physical performance.

Examples

Mondavi, Napa Valley, California, USA

In the early 1960s, wine entrepreneur Robert Mondavi developed the idea of opening wineries to the public. Until this point, wineries had been solely perceived as agricultural production facilities. Designer Cliff May, neither trained nor registered as an architect, was commissioned to design a winery with an initial capacity of 25,000 cases (Mondavi, 1999). May designed the building in the California mission style that incorporates architectural elements of Spanish monasteries, haciendas, as well as an Italian-style campanile. At the time the winery opened to the public, New World wine countries were perceived to produce wine of inferior quality. The Spanish-inspired design elements recall California's historic linkages with the Iberian Peninsula, a region known for its enduring winemaking history. The architectural elements provide visual cues to countries with well-established wine cultures. The sacral shape of a monastery also helps the perception that this is not an agricultural or even an industrial building, but a place of meditation, culture and sophistication. The earthy colours of the facades underline the connectivity of building and land. Architecture in this instance is clearly used in the fabrication and narration of values and identity.

Since Mondavi's family has an Italian migration background (Mondavi, 1999), the Italian tower can also be considered part of the family's very own cultural heritage. The Italian and Spanish architectural influences, while being geographically inaccurate, obviously provide linkages to the location's colonial past and to its present due to many of the harvest helpers in California having a Central American background. Mondavi certainly influenced many of the following winery renovations, upgrades and new development projects around the world. To this day, historic linkages are a common theme within the architecture of winescapes. And while people generally appreciate that the provided backdrop is an imaginative one, people's fluid identities (Yeoman, 2012) acknowledge other complex cultural backgrounds and family histories and accordingly are less irritated by imprecisely represented design languages.

Loisium Weinwelt ('World of Wine'), Langenlois, Austria

American architect Steven Holl recently created a combination of wellness hotel with restaurant, wine information centre, and access to a 900-year-old cellar system situated underneath a sloping hillside covered with vines. He describes the architecture as a result of 'a moment of intuitive thinking [sic] and immediate inspiration'. The visitor experience consists of a walk through the main wine centre, the cellars and the gardens. Notably, instead of explicitly including a wine tasting, sensory experiences such as touching loess loam, experiencing the reflection of the rays of the sun, wine-related music and smells are at the core of the experience. The brochure uses slogans such as 'All senses engaged' and 'Become wine' (Loisium Weinwelt, 2012). Besides utilisation of a renowned architecture practice that guaranties to draw in architects and architecture enthusiasts alike, this approach describes an innovative design and exhibition concept. The focus has shifted from the provision of tasting facilities to narrated stories that enable individuals to have individualised sensory experiences. Furthermore, the interactive part of the experience provides wine novices access to wine knowledge without the common patronising attitude. Learning, showcasing, experiencing and use of the facilities as a working winery are blurred. In a world full of stimulus sensations, visitors can rely on their individual tastes and preferences. Choice and curiousness counteract scepticism towards targeted marketing. Thus Loisium Weinwelt offers experiences that are non-descriptive, cater for individualism and a satisfactory experience economy.

Drivers of Future Food and Wine Tourism

Eight drivers that explain the growing significance of architecture in wine and food tourism are identified:

Driver 1: Food as cultural capital

Even in today's world, where a wide variety of local and non-local food is available to large parts of the global population, certain foods are charged with cultural capital. In order for food to possess this characteristic, it needs to be perceived as a special or luxury experience. Indeed, food is used as a form of differentiation: Most crudely, food may serve as a distinguishing factor where one can afford a larger amount than another person. More subtle ways in which food is used to distinguish oneself are through the appreciation of unusual food, knowledge about where and how to obtain it, and how to prepare and eat it. Yeoman (2012) suggests that food will be scarcer and thus more expensive in the future. If that is the case, it will elevate the status and prestige associated with food, and the cultural capital associated with it will increase. Wine, its appreciation, purchase, collection and related knowledge in particular are associated with cultural capital. Current wine purchasing behaviour in emerging economies in Asia suggests that this is unlikely to change in the future.

Driver 2: The social significance of food

Food is not only sustenance. Instead, it is charged with social as well as emotional values. The cultural capital of food is commonly acknowledged (see above, also Counihan & Van Esterik, 2007), but social implications of current developments around commensality (the practice of sharing food and eating together in a social group such as a family) are not well known. An important social development related to food is the disappearance of the family meal. Up to the 1980s, families would share at least one meal around the dining table. Herbst and Stanton (2007: 649) state that,

> In the fairly recent past, families gathered on a nightly basis to dine together and chat. [...] One area in which families are multi-tasking in an effort to get all finished in a day's time is eating. The unfortunate result has been that family members eat together less often now than they do individually.

This development is usually associated with longer and more irregular work times that do not allow for a communal meal at a certain time of the day. Additional factors include commitments outside of work and school, constant availability and diversions such as television or online gaming.

This chapter posits that food and wine tourism provide an opportunity for a backlash to the above development. Where people cannot obtain the social benefits of food during their everyday lives, they will crave its benefits during holidays or short breaks. Food tourism providers will need to accommodate this need by providing spaces that allow for social experiences involving food and wine.

Driver 3: Food tourism as a luxury experience

As has been discussed elsewhere, there is no doubt that income and cultural capital shape tourism consumption (Bourdieu, 1984; Urry, 1995). This chapter emphasises the role that architecture may have in the perception of food and wine tourism experiences as 'luxury'. It is important to note the difference between something being truly 'luxury' and something that merely creates the impression of luxury (Atwal & Williams, 2009).

For the context of architecture, this is made evident through the following quote that mentions 'the appearance of luxury' rather than true luxury. From a paper that looks at urban development: 'For non[sic]architects however, the appearance of luxury and prestige and the sensation of a peaceful, friendly area are more important' (Llinares *et al.*, 2011: 10).

For architecture for food and wine tourism this means that an impression of luxury can help and may be important. It is therefore included as a driver here.

Driver 4: Continuum of valuing technology and natural environmental aspects

The roles of technology and nature in humans' lives will continue to change dramatically. Technology will further increase in significance and continue to take over previously human functions and tasks. On the one hand, it will thus continue to fascinate and entice, but on the other hand it will become second nature. At the same time, the ubiquity of technology will result in a backlash – the natural world will be valued by those who can afford not to exploit or obliterate it. While this continuum strongly influences everyday aspects of our lives, its impact on recreational behaviour is also immense. It is one of the commonplaces in tourism research that one seeks what is lacking in the everyday. This is reflected in our selection of holiday places, activities and travel behaviour.

This is relevant for future architecture for food and wine tourism because the space it needs to provide will also be influenced by the polar ends of this continuum. Technology provides the possibilities to offer certain things while food and wine are essentially natural experiences, so there is opportunity to exploit that. Exactly how architecture reacts will depend on individual sites, clients and types of experiences that will be provided.

Driver 5: Urbanisation and population density

Two developments shape this driver of architecture in food and wine tourism. First, the exponential increase in world population. By the time this book is published, the world population will have reached about 7.3 billion. Second, urbanisation and increases in population density. In 44 countries, including most Latin-American countries (e.g. Brazil, Venezuela) and many European countries (e.g. France, Belgium), more than 90% of the population will live in urbanised areas.

Aside from the many issues that this development will cause in terms of urban planning and related fields, the implications for tourism and increases in travel are immense (and discussed elsewhere: Yeoman, 2008). One impact that is highly relevant for food and wine tourism experiences relates to the increased appreciation of space that the above developments are likely to bring about. Indeed, as space will become scarcer, people will pay more attention to its appearance, design, use and the experience. This may not be possible for large parts of the population in everyday life so it may be extremely relevant during travel and leisure activities.

Driver 6: Globalisation and glocalisation

Food and wine and place are the topic of much debate in the tourism literature. Despite many potential issues regarding health or eating habits, wine and food of other locales is generally a desired part of many visitor experiences (Cohen & Avieli, 2004). Globalisation and glocalisation are buzz-words accompanying these discussions (Inglis & Gimlin, 2009). Globalisation in trade and commerce on the one hand, and in consumer behaviour on the other hand, is the force that enables the availability of non local products in many (often developed) places. Glocalisation, the process by which a product is adapted to suit a specific locality or culture, is a side-effect of globalisation and consumer demands. Burgundy-style wines grown in India or China where they are not traditional is a case in point.

What are the implications for food and wine tourism? These products will be consumed in many non-traditional places. This allows for a new interpretation of places offering food and wine. As the quality of production (at least in the foreseeable future) will not match that of more traditional locales for food and wine production, the focus will likely need to be more experience-focused. This comes with chances for food and wine tourism for the mass market, but the implications for the market of true connoisseurs of these products are more difficult to anticipate.

The next driver, climate change, is closely related to this point as it also involves changes in production areas, and hence place.

Driver 7: Climate change

Climate change, increasing temperatures and changes to the average amount of precipitation in many regions will severely influence where wine can be grown. For example, most central and southern European wine regions are expected to become much drier (with the notable exception of Tuscany which is expected to become too moist for growing grapes). This is expected to result in a low quality of grapes and, eventually, the selection of different varieties. At the same time, new wine regions are expected to emerge in northern Europe or at high altitude (Fraga et al., 2013). New World wine regions such as Australia (Hall & Jones, 2009) or parts of Napa Valley may become unsuitable for growing wine or face severe declines in quality (Lechmere, 2011). It is predicted that Australia will lose the majority of its growing regions due to droughts (Allen, 2010). The industry will need to adapt, but in many cases relocation of wine-growing businesses will occur.

Driver 8: Competition among attractions and destinations

Competition between destinations will increase as (due to technology and loss of natural environments) destinations' possibilities are only restricted by their financial means. Architecture can serve not only as a distinguishing factor but can also be actively employed to strategically outdo competing destinations by offering more desirable experiences. This is yet another driver that may take wineries and related food outlets away from the original produce, away even from place, and into the realm of constructed visitor experiences.

Concluding Remarks: Implications for the Future of Food Tourism

Using architecturally designed wineries as examples, the chapter shows how transformations in winery visitor experiences will coincide with spatial changes in the physical layout, organisational structure and appearance of wineries. Indeed, architectural interventions will act as vehicles for spatial experiences, user interactivity will increase and both visually and sensually experiences will be provided. The chapter further shows how societal engagement with produce and places of origin will increase further; as the last driver suggests, eventually even up to the point where performative places become more significant and decisive than the actual place of food and wine production. Both examples address trends related to the performative traveller, and they are likely within the framework set by the drivers in the previous section. Opening wineries to the public was only a first step, and current tasting rooms are still mainly about provision of basic amenities. An important implication for the future of food tourism is that increasing expectations of consumers will see a rising demand in personalised sensory and bodily place experiences. It is reasonable to assume that the level of consumers' wine knowledge will continue to increase. Patronising behaviour will be less tolerated. These consumer expectations will lead to highly interactive enactments of place, people and produce. But the future of food tourism in so far as it relates to wineries is also ambiguous: Performativity within winescapes is seeking to achieve 'unstaged authenticity' too. This can be accomplished through designed experiences that engage visitors to create their very own, meaningful, connections and experiences. In the context of food and wine tourism, architecture will be crucial in providing spaces that allow for either (a) keeping up an illusion of times gone by and previous better days, or (b) it will provide an experience that caters for the performative visitor of the future by providing unique experiences. Remarkably, none of these developments need to specifically relate to the products in question: wine and food.

References

Agnew, J.A. and Duncan, J.S. (eds) (1989) *The Power of Place*. Boston, MA: Unwin Hyman.
Allen, M. (2010) *The Future Makers: Australian Wines for the 21st Century*. Melbourne; London: Hardie Grant.

Atwal, G. and Williams, A. (2009) Luxury brand marketing: The experience is everything. *Brand Management* 16 (5–6), 338–346.

Bergman, A., Karlsson, J.C. and Axelsson, J. (2010) Truth claims and explanatory claims: An ontological typology of futures studies. *Futures* 42, 857–865.

Bourdieu, P. (1984) *Distinction: A Social Critique of the Judgement of Taste.* London: Routledge.

Clark, N., Massey, D. and Sarre, P. (eds) (2008) *Material Geographies: A World in the Making.* London: Sage Publications.

Cohen, E. and Avieli, N. (2004) Food in tourism: Attraction and impediment. *Annals of Tourism Research* 31 (4), 755–778.

Counihan, C. and Van Esterik, P. (2007) *Food and Culture.* London: Routledge.

Danielmeier, T. (2011) The architecture of post-consumerism. In *Die Architektur der neuen Weltordnung – Architecture in the Age of Empire.* Symposium Reader (pp. 520–527). Weimar. Bauhaus Universität Weimar.

Danielmeier, T. (2014) Winery architecture: Creating a sense of place. In *Wine and Identity: Branding, Heritage, Terroir.* London & New York: Routledge.

Edensor, T. (2001) Performing tourism, staging tourism – (Re)producing tourist space and practice. *Tourist Studies* 1 (1), 59–81.

Finkelstein, J. (1989) *Dining Out: A Sociology of Modern Manners.* Cambridge: Polity Press.

Foster, H. (2011) *The Art-Architecture Complex.* London; New York: Verso.

Fraga, H., Malheiro, A.C., Moutinho-Pereira, J. and Santos, J.A. (2013) Future scenarios for viticultural zoning in Europe: Ensemble projections and uncertainties. *International Journal of Biometeorology.* See doi:10.1007/s00484-012-0617-8.

Haldrup, M. and Bærenholdt, J.O. (2010) Tourist experience design. In J. Simonson, J.O. Bærenholdt, M. Büscher and J.D. Scheuer (eds) *Design Research – Synergies from Interdisciplinary Perspectives* (pp. 187–200). London: Routledge.

Haldrup, M. and Larsen, J. (2006) Material cultures of tourism. *Leisure Studies* 25, 275–289.

Hall, A. and Jones, G.V. (2009) Effect of potential atmospheric warming on temperature-based indices describing Australian winegrape growing conditions. *Australian Journal of Grape and Wine Research* 15, 97–119.

Hall, C.M. and Mitchell, R.D. (2008) *Wine Marketing: A Practical Guide.* Amsterdam: Elsevier/Butterworth-Heinemann.

Hall, C.M., Sharples, E., Mitchell, R., Cambourne, B. and Macionis, N. (eds) (2003) *Food Tourism Around the World.* Oxford: Butterworth-Heinemann.

Herbst, K.C. and Stanton, J.L. (2007) Changes in family dynamics predict purchase and consumption. *British Food Journal* 109 (8), 648–655.

Hodgson, P.H. and Toyka, R. (2007) *The Architect, the Cook and Good Taste.* Basel, Boston, Berlin: Birkhäuser.

Horwitz, J. and Singley, P. (eds) (2004) *Eating Architecture.* Cambridge, MA: MIT Press.

Hultman, J. and Hall, C.M. (2012) Tourism place-making – Governance of locality in Sweden. *Annals of Tourism Research* 39 (2), 547–570.

Iblings, H. (1998) *Supermodernism: Architecture in the Age of Globalization.* Rotterdam: NAi Publishers.

Inglis, D. and Gimlin, D. (eds) (2009) *The Globalization of Food.* Oxford; New York: Berg.

Lansansky, D.M. and McLaren, B. (eds) (2004) *Architecture and Tourism.* Oxford: Berg.

Leatherbarrow, D. (2004) Table talk. In J. Horwitz and P. Singley (eds) *Eating Architecture* (pp. 211–220). Cambridge, MA: MIT Press.

Lechmere, A. (2011) Napa 'unsuitable' for premium wine in 30 years: Study. *Decanter,* 7 July 2012.

Llinares, C., Montanana, A. and Navarro, E. (2011) Differences in architects and nonarchitects' perception of urban design. *Urban Studies Research.* See doi: 10.1155/2011/736307.

Loisium Weinwelt (2012) Alle Sinne bezaubernd – All senses engaged. See www.loisium-weinwelt.at/architektur/index.php (accessed 8 March 2013).

Massey, D. (2005) *For Space*. Thousand Oaks: Sage Publications.

Mitchell, R., Charters, S. and Albrecht, J.N. (2012) Cultural systems and the wine tourism Product. *Annals of Tourism Research* 39 (1), 311–325.

Mitchell, R., Hall, C.M. and McIntosh, A. (2000) Wine tourism and consumer behaviour. In M. Hall, L. Sharples, B. Cambourne and N. Macionis (eds) *Wine Tourism Around The World* (pp. 115–135). Oxford: Elsevier Science.

Mondavi, R. (1999) *Harvest of Joy: How the Good Life Became Great Business*. Boston, MA: Mariner Books.

Ockman, J. (2004) New politics of the spectacle: 'Bilbao' and the global imagination. In D.M. Lansansky and B. McLaren (eds) (2004) *Architecture and Tourism* (pp. 227–240). Oxford; New York: Berg.

Perkins, H. and Thorns, D. (2001) Gazing or performing? Reflections on Urry's tourist gaze in the context of contemporary experience in the Antipodes. *International Sociology* 16 (2), 185–204.

Proto, F. (2006) *Mass Identity Architecture: Architectural Writings of Jean Baudrillard*. Chichester: Wiley.

Smart, R.E. (2002) New world response to old world terroir. *Australian and New Zealand Wine Industry Journal* 17, 65–67.

Urry, J. (1995) *Consuming Places*. London: Routledge.

Venturi, R., Scott Brown, D. and Izenour, S. (1977) *Learning from Las Vegas*. Cambridge: MIT Press.

Wilson, J.E. (1998) *Terroir: The Role of Geology, Climate, and Culture in the Making of French Wines*. London: Octopus Publishing.

Yeoman, I. (2008) *Tomorrow's Tourists: Scenarios and Trends*. Oxford: Elsevier.

Yeoman, I., Brass, D. and McMahon-Beattie, U. (2007) Current issue in tourism: The authentic tourist. *Tourism Management* 28 (4), 1128–1138.

Yeoman, I. (with Tan, R., Mars, M. and Wouters, M.) (2012) *2050 – Tomorrow's Tourism*. Bristol: Channel View Publications.

8 Envisioning AgriTourism 2115: Organic Food, Convivial Meals, Hands in the Soil and No Flying Cars

Karen Hurley

Highlights

- The chapter is based on a preferred future/desired vision of the world and for agritourism in 2115.
- It explores the possible contribution of agritourism in creating sustainable and just localised economies.
- The discussion is focused on why we need positive visions of diverse futures to guide and inspire action in the present.
- It aims to be a demonstration of collaborative work between tourism and futures studies researchers.

Introduction

A sustainable world can never come into being if it cannot be envisioned. (Meadows *et al.*, 1992: 225)

This chapter centres on a preferred future/vision of agritourism in 2115 as told from a voice in future time. AgriTourism 2115 takes place within a vision of a world that is healthy and compassionate, where human actions are ecologically sound and socially just. Within this vision, tourism, and especially agritourism, has reached the hopeful tourism research principles of care and respect for people and the environment (Pritchard *et al.*, 2011). Creating this vision 100 years in the future has not been a Pollyanna-ish exercise. Futures studies' *preferred futures* methodology and hopeful tourism researchers, in their hopes for change to positive futures, include either an implied or an explicit critical assessment of present time as well as an insistence on transformation. Many of the details of the future in AgriTourism 2115 emerged as a solution to an issue that was identified in scholarly research in the present. For example, Hashimoto and Telfer, in 2011, identified an issue related to women doing an unfair amount of the work in attending to guests on the farm; in response, in AgriTourism 2115 the hospitality work is shared amongst many and across genders, and women have leadership roles on the farm and in the community. In addition, I have used Joanna Macy's (Macy, 2007; Macy & Brown, 1998) research on how change happens within the Great Turning (sustainability revolution) as *holding actions, alternative structures* or shifts in *new consciousness* to theorise the transformational acts within the vision of AgriTourism 2115. In this way, issues and problems in present time are reframed as positive change that *has* happened in future time.

Agritourism (agrotourism) in Europe is generally considered to involve on-farm accommodation with varying levels of active participation with farming operations (Greif *et al.*, 2011; Ohe & Ciani, 2012). Whereas in North America, notably California, Australia, and New Zealand agritourism 'includes any income-generating activity conducted on a working farm or ranch for the enjoyment and education of visitors' (Rilla, 2011: 173). These other income-generating activities may include: dining on local foods; horseback riding, garden/farm tours, farm-gate or vineyard sales; u-pick operations; or special events such as weddings and dances as well as hiking in nearby nature (Agapito *et al.*, 2012; Eckert, 2013; Ohe & Ciani, 2012; Oredegbe & Fadeyibi, 2009; Rilla, 2011).

Agritourism is strongly connected to place. Visitors to rural operations value both cultural and environmental assets; therefore, agritourism often results in environmental and landscape protection and activities that support local cultural practices (Aikaterini *et al.*, 2001). Growing concern about the impacts of pesticides, chemical fertilisers and genetically modified organisms (GMOs) on the environment and human health have lead to a global awareness of the benefits of organic agriculture. This awareness is providing a significantly increasing market for agritourism on organic farms (ORGANIC, 2011). It is these beginnings of care for the environment, humans and non-human animals that inspire preferred futures, one of which is found in this chapter.

Futures studies that is dedicated to an exploration of alternative futures within the categories of 'what can or could be (the possible), what is likely to be (the probable), and what ought to be (the preferable)' (Bell, 2000: 73). The development of possible or probable futures is based strongly on how things are today and is often crafted in response to a problem, which will 'result in the realisation of a merely less awful future, not a magnificent one' (Ellyard, 2011: 177). Whereas a preferred future, or vision, comes from our heart's desire, treasured dreams, values and love and such visions have the power to guide us instead towards sustainable, just and joyful futures (Meadows, 1999). This fits well with Pritchard *et al.*'s (2011: 942) description of '*hopeful tourism* as a values-based, unfolding transformative perspective (imbued by principles of partnership, reciprocity and respect)'. An aim of this chapter, as a preferred future, is to explore how agritourism could be part of sustainable and just futures. This vision of agritourism takes place in the year 2115, a time far enough in the future for the completion of societal-level transformation. When I refer to this specific vision it will be as 'AgriTourism 2115'. As compared to my use of 'agritourism' in present time discussions.

Visioning is best done in community – resulting in a vision that is widely shared and supported. In writing this vision I cannot claim the involvement of the wider community – this is *my* preferred future for the world and AgriTourism in 2115. It comes out of my life experiences as a scholar, food security activist, restaurateur, organic community farm founder and ecological futures specialist. I have envisioned a future as guided by Donella Meadows (1999: 110) that 'come[s] from commitment, responsibility, confidence, values, longing, love, treasured dreams, our innate sense of what is right and good'. Bergman *et al.* (2010) would characterise preferred futures and visions as utopian, but in our cynical present time *utopias* are associated with the unachievable. True, this is my desired vision of the future, which comes from my loving dreams for my community and the world, but it is inspired by the work of many who are dedicated to transforming our food and tourism systems into localised, compassionate and healthy economies. Perhaps more accurately then, AgriTourism 2115 is a *practical utopia*, as coined by Ivana Milojevic (2013: 18), because it is a strategic vision and 'has a solid chance of becoming reality'. I look forward to others joining me in expanding and refining this vision until it is realised.

Why a Vision of Agritourism?

Creating a vision helps us become clear about what we desire for our futures, and for future generations, as well as guide actions in the present. In creating a vision of agritourism, love is important because sustainability will depend upon societal transformation that is based on the best of human nature (Meadows *et al.*, 1992). A love for nature and community 'that empowers us to go beyond ourselves by imagining and creating a world worthy of love' will create great hope (Delio, 2013: 198). Hopeful tourism research also shares this commitment to love and hope as well as to 'a vision of human possibilities' (Pritchard *et al.*, 2011: 953). Meadows (1996, 1999) acknowledges how difficult visioning is because it involves a heart-centred departure form rational thinking and encourages us to move past cynicism and physical constraints so we can envision the kind of world we truly want – not what we would merely settle for.

In addition, it is not easy to envision beyond the hegemonic images of the future because those who create them have succeeded in convincing us about the inevitability of their dominant vision (Milojevic, 2005). For example, in film, advertising and much professional futures work there is a dominant and ceaselessly repeated image of a singular future – as hyper urban and high-tech – high-rises, elevated highways, computer technology everywhere and flying cars (Hurley, 2008b). Envisioning flourishing agricultural communities with healthy landscapes, therefore, becomes an act of resistance to the hegemonic images of the future (Hurley, 2008a).

The most effective visions of the future are written in futures-tense and are full of detail. According to Meadows (1999) the most profound visions include visual descriptions, other senses (taste, hearing) and societal details. What follows is my envisioned future of the state of the world from the perspective and voice of 100 years into the future. Please enjoy this journey into future time.

The Global Vision Supporting Agritourism 2115

It is the year 2115 and the world is a place much changed from 100 years ago. The sustainability revolution (Meadows *et al.*, 1992), also known as the Great Turning (Macy & Brown, 1998; Macy, 2007; Korten, 2006) is complete and humans now conduct their lives and economies in ways that are sustainable and just. The human species learned in our hearts and minds that we do not have rights to the lands and waters of the world more than any other species – we now deeply understand our interconnectedness with all life on earth, and indeed with the earth itself. We now live our lives, and structure our communities and organisations, based on compassion and care for all peoples and all species. This has changed how we work, learn, raise children, build homes, grow our food and how we take our holidays.

The single-minded push into cities was acknowledged as a failed experiment in human settlement and we now support a diverse range of settlement types, including very active and cultured villages, towns and small cities as well as many people living in extended families and friendships on farms. There are still a few large cities in the world, as some people enjoy urban life, but these cities do not have the vast areas of slums that accompanied megacities in the previous century. Every person on earth has adequate water, sanitation, housing and food. Every child has a family, whether or not they are their biological relations. Everyone feels safe.

A major turning point in the Great Turning was the removal of the rights of personhood and limited liability from corporations, who previously were legally bound to care only about shareholder profits at the expense of social and ecological well-being (Balkan, 2004). This change began with the smaller countries, like Iceland, and then spread around the world. Many countries were led by their indigenous peoples to remove power from corporations and to legally protect their land, water and seeds. Around the world communities came together to stop corporate control of their lives. Commerce became localised and ethical. Happiness and relationships with others, including nature, became more important in people's lives than money. In 2115, people and entire societies are no longer in service to *the* economy; now we have diverse economies that are in service to communities (De Graaf & Batker, 2011).

Governments in 2115 now freer from corporate control are also localised and have returned to serving the people. Governments have evolved into basing policies and decision-making on compassion and care for all beings and the earth. This has resulted in societies that are peaceful and equitable.

Twentieth-century notions of power and greed caused great inequality amongst people. This economic and power disparity was a primary factor in massive amounts of money being spent on war and militarised security, but change began – slowly – in the beginning of the 21st century as violence began to decline (Ashford & Dauncey, 2006). And then around 2030 significant global reductions in war and military expenditures became evident as the world relatively quickly moved towards peace. We now live in a world that has attained Elise Boulding's (1988) vision of a *World Without Weapons*. The $1.74 trillion that was once spent globally on armaments (SIPRI, 2012) is now dedicated to education, housing, agriculture, arts and culture, environmental restoration, creating beautiful public spaces, taking care of those who are unwell and raising happy children.

Our world without weapons was built upon the efforts of millions of people around the world saying 'no' to war (*holding actions*) but the most significant change resulted from a *shift in consciousness* where humans saw their oneness with others, including non-humans (Macy, 2007). It is now unthinkable to want to harm another person, especially because of cultural, racial or gender difference. This shift in consciousness came as a result of collaborations across neurobiology, quantum physics, cosmology, mindfulness and spirituality that made it clear that we are all part of the same consciousness and the same holistic ecological system, and that in hurting others we were hurting ourselves and our beloveds (Brach, 2012; Cannato, 2006; Capra, 2000; Delio, 2013; Siegel, 2007, 2011; Swimme & Berry, 1992; Wheatley, 2006). So the violence stopped. We still have conflict, but we solve it with dialogue and rituals, not weapons.

Donella Meadows' (1999), Vandana Shiva's (2004), and Frances Moore Lappé's and Anna Lappé's (2002) visions of a *World without Hunger* have also been reached. The great disparity between those who had too much food and those who did not have enough food has been erased. All peoples have *food sovereignty*; sufficient culturally appropriate food that is mostly grown locally. Farmers, researchers, consumers and, eventually, local and national governments, challenged the myths about organic farming by showing that it can feed the world (A. Lappé, 2012; F.M. Lappé, 2011; Rodale, 2010). All agriculture is now organic, biodynamic and/or permaculture (Greer, 2009). The soil, waters and farmers' bodies are now free from contamination by pesticides, chemical fertilisers and GMO. And farmers are freed of the corporate control of their livelihoods. In addition, the global shift to organic agriculture, with its superior carbon sequestration, provided a significant contribution to reduction in climate change so the world is more stable and resilient (Gattinger *et al.*, 2012; Lappé, 2010; Scialabba & Müller-Lindenlauf, 2010).

Our compassion and care extends to all beings, therefore no animals, including fish, suffer in factory-like environments or from inhumane treatment. There are still people who eat meat, fish and dairy products, but in much smaller amounts than in previous times, and now only from ecological and compassionate farmers, producers and ranchers.

In AgriTourism 2115, at least four weeks of holidays are available to everyone, supported by law. And because we now have an equitable system of wealth everyone can take a vacation of their choice, and many people choose to spend part of their holidays in agritourism.

AgriTourism 2115

In AgriTourism 2115, agritourism is a vibrant, flourishing sector of community-based, rural economies. AgriTourism 2115 visitors often come from nearby communities or countries because they can travel by train and because people have discovered the pleasure of simplicity in a rural vacation not too far from home (Ohe & Ciani, 2012; Yeoman, 2012). Tourists now choose to eat locally grown/gathered, raised and produced foods while on holiday out of the spirit of adventure as well as in support of the local culture, environment and economy that they are visiting (DeMotts & Swatuk, 2012). Gone are the days when tourists insisted on eating the same food on vacation that they would eat at home.

Most urban people grow some amount of food, whether in a yard, on a balcony or rooftop, and as communities we highly value food production. There is keen interest, therefore, to learn from rural growers and a true appreciation for their labours. In 2115, most citizens understand the importance and aliveness of the soil (Jeffery *et al.*, 2010) and many want to spend some of their holiday time with their hands in the soil, working with professional growers. There is respectful dialogue as the guests strive to understand how the farmers are growing what they grow – their successes as well as challenges (Rilla, 2011).

Not that life in AgriTourism 2115 is all work and no rest. We fully value the importance of rest, even for farmers! The difference is that, historically, agritourism guests meant more work for already overworked farmers or ranchers, especially for the women. Now there are lots of people in the rural community ready to help with the guests. There are many people available to attend to AgriTourism 2115 guests because extended family members and non-related young people have chosen to live and work on the farm, and do not feel compelled to move to a city. Young people and families have access to many social opportunities and they joyfully participate in cultural activities within the local community as well as the surrounding villages and towns. Many people now choose to stay in their rural communities, or have moved from cities to a rural life on farms or villages, where they enjoy working in the fields or in small collaborative food production businesses such as cooperative cheese-making operations. In Latin and South America, many families work collaboratively to produce and sell high-end products such as organic chocolate directly to customers, and provide agritourist services such as cafés, while maintaining strong family and cultural relationships (Kallari, 2013).

Significant migration of people from cities to rural areas took place in the first half of the 21st century in many countries, including: Japan (Cheng, 2011), the United States (Winchester, 2012), Ireland (Connolly, 2013) and Africa (Potts, 2012). In Canada, there was a noticeable return to rural life, predominantly through organic and biodynamic farming on smaller farms, especially by women, many with advanced university degrees (COABC, 2013; Fisher et al., 2012). AgriTourism 2115 includes a great diversity of people in rural communities, which results in no shortage of interesting activities for the visitor.

Within AgriTourism 2115, our shared values are based on compassion and respect, therefore vacationers do not have a sense of entitlement to other peoples' labour.

We have addressed the problems of the past and no longer are women and rural poor made unhappier by tourism (Chok et al., 2007; Hashimoto & Telfer, 2011). In fact, women are now farm owners/operators in equal number to men as agriculture is fully organic, biodynamic or permaculture, and they have equal access to land ownership. Women are often the leaders in community tenure arrangements. In addition, transnational corporations no longer exist and their chemicals are long gone from agriculture; therefore, farms are profitable and farmers are healthy. Also, farmers and ranchers are now paid fairly for their goods, even by the large tourist hotels and resorts. No one expects food to be 'cheap' anymore; nor does anyone expect others to suffer for their food. So there isn't a group of rural 'poor', except the young people who are choosing to apprentice or hang around at farms while they figure out their futures, and they are happily housed and very well fed. We do not have the same dependency on money, as previous eras, so many people choose to live a subsistence lifestyle, focusing on trade and gift economies.

AgriTourism 2115 accommodations pride themselves on high standards, such as beautiful, comfortable beds with organic, fair-trade linens and delicious, locally sourced meals. In return, guests are respectful and grateful for the accommodations, the food and the staff.

Cooking classes in large, beautiful farm kitchens are often part of the offerings, sometimes in partnership with a local restaurant (Philo Apple Farm, 2013). And impromptu group cooking sessions often happen as guests become inspired by the local fruits and vegetables, wines, cheeses and productive landscapes. These are joyful events, where everyone participates in some aspect of the meal production – from harvesting to preparation and cooking to serving and cleanup. This conviviality is inspired by Slow Food (2013) who were early leaders in promoting sustainable agriculture and appreciation for joyful cooking and eating.

Birds and small animals have returned to the cities, but there is an even greater abundance of birds and other wildlife to observe and listen to on the farms. Organic, biodynamic growing has brought with it a return of flourishing bird and animal life – and bees! Many AgriTourism 2115 guests report a sense of awe at the diversity and abundance of wildlife that they observe and hear.

AgriTourism 2115 vacationers leave their agritourism experience feeling blessed by the beautiful, well-prepared meals, convivial conversation, and new knowledge in an aspect of growing food. They are physically and mentally restored by the quietness in the landscape, their healthy activities and by the healing time in nature and with farm animals.

Understanding how change happened to create AgriTourism 2115

Tourism research did an admirable job in the early 21st century by identifying tourism-related problems affecting humans and the environment. Joanna Macy's (2007) Great Turning, with its three aspects – *holding actions, alternative structures* and *new consciousness* – is a useful framework to understand how people created change that addressed the problems.

In the late 20th and early 21st centuries tourism caused much economic and cultural damage when rural communities were displaced to make room for tourist infrastructure in many countries, including: Botswana, Burma, Taiwan and Tanzania (Chok *et al.*, 2007). In AgriTourism 2115, rural communities are highly valued both as tourist destinations and as sources of local food to the broader tourist industry. History tells us how local activists used their bodies to stop the earth-moving machines and the hotel developers from taking their lands (*holding actions*); then they created new institutional *structures* to keep the land in agricultural production. Now, in 2115, rural economies are flourishing because farmers are paid a fair price for their goods, all production is organic or biodynamic and ethically raised (once *'alternative'* methods and now conventional) and many people choose to vacation at rural bed and breakfasts and cottages instead of posh resorts. Also, global *consciousness* has transformed to a point where compassion for others is fundamental to all actions, therefore, no one's home, community or agricultural land would ever be destroyed for another's benefit.

Historically, many resorts relied on imported cheap food, often at the expense of the local agricultural community (Rhiney, 2011). But this changed as resorts adopted farm-to-fork (*alternative*) strategies that connected local products to the resorts, at fair prices, and also vacationers were taken to the farms for visits and on-farm purchases (Berno, 2011). Also, many of the very large all-inclusive operations, most of which were dependent on under-waged workers as well as cheap food, closed because a *new consciousness* developed regarding right livelihood for all. In AgriTourism 2115 many of those closed resorts are schools, daycare centres, health care centres and libraries.

In the early days of agritourism, some women carried an unfair burden of the extra work of having guests on a farm or ranch because the accommodation, food preparation and management were considered 'women's work' (Rilla, 2011). For example, in Japan early in the 21st century, agritourism resulted in some women having to work in fields, cook and clean for their families as well as take care of the guests – at the expense of their personal sleep and health (Hashimoto & Telfer, 2011). Then there was a change in *structures* in society and on the farms. Roles became less gendered, in both the public and private spheres, and a shift in *consciousness* as men and boys understood that they were not more valued than women and girls and needed to do their fair share of the house work (Eisler, 2007). Women happily took up more active farming roles and farm ownership and men learned that they were responsible also for domestic duties and found themselves enjoying social interactions with visitors (Rilla, 2011). *Thank you for visiting future time.*

Concluding Remarks: The Implications for the Future of Food Tourism

The purpose of visions, as preferred futures, is to inspire and guide action towards positive and diverse futures. The vision of AgriTourism 2115 describes a preferred future where many of the issues identified by tourism researchers, in present time, have been addressed. The implications for the future of food tourism are: (1) seeing how agritourism can be a vibrant and flourishing component of tourism industry futures and, (2) that agritourism can be conducted in ways that honour farmers and the rural landscape. The preferred future of AgriTourism 2115 provides tourism scholars and practitioners with a vision of agritourism, within a just and sustainable world, as well as shining a light on what is not working in the present, and to guide action in support of the vision. In addition, Joanna Macy's (2007) theory of the Great Turning provides a framework to explore the nature of the changes that took place to reach the vision of AgriTourism 2115. This is useful to demonstrate how change towards sustainability will be multifaceted and will require many people making diverse contributions.

Preferred futures that include flourishing, peopled agricultural spaces are important to ensure that rural landscapes are valued and protected in the present. The hegemonic images of a solely urban future are not helpful in developing farm/farmer friendly land use and tourism-related policies and decisions. For example, much of the movement back to rural life or people staying in rural areas that is taking place today is resisted and ignored by many academics and governments who remain fixated on rural-to-urban migration and the 'collective impact of academic, urban advocates' and policy-makers' opinions is very hard to counter' (Potts, 2012: x). By including a description of people moving from cities to rural areas in the vision of AgriTourism 2115 I aim to lessen the power of the hegemonic view of the future as only urban, thereby, gaining support for policies and decisions that support rural well-being, including compassionate agritourism.

This chapter has also demonstrated that tourism scholars, and others who are writing about tourism and futures, have an opportunity, indeed a responsibility, to include visions of flourishing, healthy rural communities and farms in their diverse futures to guide action in the present. Tourism and futures studies scholars and practitioners can create an alliance that offers transformational ways forward, where respectful and compassionate tourism is part of ecologically sound and social just futures.

References

Agapito, D., Mendes, J. and Valle, P. (2012) The rural village as an open door to nature-based tourism in Portugal: The Aldeia da Pedralva case. *Tourism Review* 60 (3), 325–338.

Aikaterini, G., Loannis, S. and Thanasis, K. (2001) Is agrotourism 'agro' or 'tourism'? Evidence from agrotourist holdings in Lesvos, Greece. *Anatolia: An International Journal of Tourism and Hospitality Research* 12 (1), 6–22.

Ashford, M.-W. and Dauncey, G. (2006) *Enough Blood Shed: 101 Solutions to Violence, Terror and War*. Gabriola Island, BC: New Society Publishers.

Balkan, J. (2004) *The Corporation: The Pathological Pursuit of Profit and Power*. Toronto: Viking Canada.

Bell, Wm (2000) *Foundations of Futures Studies. Human Science for a New Era*. New Brunswick, NJ: Transaction Publishers.

Bergman, A.J., Karlsson, Ch and Axelsson, J. (2010) Truth claims and explanatory claims: An ontological typology of futures studies. *Futures* 42 (8), 857–865.

Berno, T. (2011) Sustainability on a plate: Linking agriculture and food in the Fiji Islands tourism industry. In R.M. Torres and J.H. Momsen (eds) *Tourism and Agriculture: New Geographies of Consumption, Production and Rural Restructuring* (pp. 87–103). Abingdon; New York: Routledge.

Boulding, E. (1988) *Building a Global Civic Culture: Education for an Interdependent World*. New York: Teachers College Press Teachers College Columbia University.

Brach, T. (2012) *True Refuge: Finding Peace and Freedom in Your Own Awakened Heart*. New York: Bantam Books.

Cannato, J. (2006) *Radical Amazement: Contemplative Lessons from Black Holes, Supernovas, and Other Wonders of the Universe*. Notre Dame, IN: Sorin Books.

Capra, F. (2000) *The Tao of Physics: An Exploration of the Parallels Between Modern Physics and Eastern Mysticism*. 4th ed. Boston, MA: Shambhala.

Cheng, C.L. (2011) Young people moving out from the City to the rural area. *Japan Sociology (blog)*. 19 December. See http://japansociology.com/2011/12/19/young-people-moving-out-from-the-city-to-the-rural-area/ (accessed 12 April 2013).

Chok, S., Macbeth, J. and Warren, C. (2007) Tourism as a tool for poverty alleviation: A critical analysis of 'pro-poor tourism' and implications for sustainability. *Current Issues in Tourism* 10 (2–3), 144–165.

COABC – Certified Organic Associations of BC (2013) What is organic farming? See www.certifiedorganic.bc.ca/aboutorganic/whatis.php (accessed 28 April 2013).

Connolly, J. (2013) Ireland Rural Resettlement Program. See www.ruralresettlement.com/index.html (accessed 12 April 2013).

De Graaf, J. and Batker, D.K. (2011) *What's the Economy For, Anyway? Why It's Time to Stop Chasing Growth and Start Pursuing Happiness*. New York: Bloomsbury Press.

Delio, I. (2013) *The Unbearable Wholeness of Being: God, Evolution and the Power of Love*. Maryknoll, NY: Orbis Books.

DeMotts, R. and Swatuk, L. (2012) Conflicts and conundrums: In southern Africa, there's no easy route to the ecotourist promise of stewardship and livelihood gains. *Alternatives Journal* 38 (4), 15–20.

Eckert, J. (2013) Agritour in 2013 to feature New Zealand. See www.eckertagrimarketing.com/articledir/eckert-agritourism-agritour-new-zealand.shtml (accessed 26 March 2013).

Eisler, R.T. (2007) *The Real Wealth of Nations: Creating a Caring Economics*. San Francisco, CA: Berrett-Koehler Publishers.

Ellyard, P. (2011) Designing 2050: Imagining and building a global sustainable society. *Journal of Futures Studies* 15 (3), 175–190.

Fisher, R., Stretch, H. and Tunnicliffe, R. (2012) *All the Dirt: Reflections on Organic Farming*. Victoria British Columbia, Canada: TouchWood Editions.

Gattinger, A., Muller, A., Haeni, M., Skinner, C., Fliessbach, A., Buchmann, N., Mader, P., Stoize, M., Smith, P., El-Hage Scialabba, N. and Niggili, U. (2012) Enhanced top soil carbon stocks under organic farming. *PNAS* 109 (44), 18226–18231.

Greer, J.M. (2009) *The Ecotechnic Future: Envisioning a Post-Peak World*. Gabriola Island, BC: New Society Publishers.

Greif, S., Rauscher, C. and Sontgerath, C. (2011) Agro-tourism. In A. Papathanassis (ed.) *The Long Tail of Tourism* (pp. 25–34). Wiesbaden: Gabler Verlag.

Hashimoto, A. and Telfer, D. (2011) Female empowerment through agritourism in rural Japan. In R.M. Torres and J.H. Momsen (eds) *Tourism and Agriculture: New Geographies of Consumption, Production and Rural Restructuring* (pp. 72–83). Abingdon; New York: Routledge.

Hurley, K. (2008a) Food in the future: Does futures studies have a role to play. *Futures* 40 (8), 698–710.

Hurley, K. (2008b) Is that a future we want?: An ecofeminist exploration of images of the future in contemporary film. *Futures* 40 (4), 346–359.

Jeffery, S., Harris, J.A., Rickson, R. and Ritz, K. (2010) Effects of soil-surface microbial community phenotype upon physical and hydrological properties of an arable soil: A microcosm study. *European Journal of Soil Science* 61, 493–503.

Kallari (2013) *The Kallari Café*. See http://kallari.com/cafe.html, and *The Family Life*. See http://kallari.com/family_life.html (accessed 15 March 2013).

Korten, D.C. (2006) *The Great Turning: From Empire to Earth Community*: San Francisco, CA: Berrett-Koehler/Kumarian Press

Lappé, A. (2010) *Diet for a Hot Planet: The Climate Crisis at the End of Your Fork and What You Can Do About It* (1st edn). New York: Bloomsbury USA.

Lappé, A. (2012) The hunger & food security myth: Do we really need industrial agriculture to feed the world? See http://foodmyths.org/myths/hunger-food-security/ (accessed 28 April 2013).

Lappé, F.M. (2011) *EcoMind: Changing The Way We Think, To Create The World We Want*. New York: Nation Books.

Lappé, F.M. and Lappé, A. (2002) *Hope's Edge: The Next Diet for a Small Planet*. New York: Jeremy P. Tarcher/Putnam.

Macy, J. (2007) *World As Lover, World As Self: Courage For Global Justice And Ecological Renewal*. Berkeley, CA: Parallax Press.

Macy, J. and Brown, M.Y. (1998) *Coming Back to Life: Practices to Reconnect Our Lives, Our World*. Gabriola Island, BC; Stony Creek, CT: New Society Publishers.

Meadows, D.H. (1996) Envisioning a sustainable world. In R. Costanza, O. Segura and J. Martinez-Alier (eds) *Getting Down to Earth. Practical Applications of Ecological Economics* (pp. 117–126). Washington, DC: Island Press.

Meadows, D.H. (1999) Chicken Little, Cassandra, so many ways to think about the future. *Whole Earth* Spring: 106–111.

Meadows, D.H., Meadows, D.L. and Randers, J. (1992) *Beyond the Limits: Confronting Global Collapse, Envisioning a Sustainable Future*. Post Mills, VT: Chelsea Green.

Milojevic, I. (2005) *Educational Futures: Dominant and Contesting Visions*. London: Routledge.

Ohe, Y. and Ciani, A. (2012) Accessing demand characteristics of agritourism in Italy. *Tourism and Hospitality Management* 18 (2), 281–296.

Oredegbe, A. and Fadeyibi, I. (2009) Diversification into farm tourism. Paper presented at the International Conference on Regional and Urban Modelling.

ORGANIG (2011) Why sustainable agri-tourism is a market opportunity for the organic sector, Organic Centre Wales. See www.organiccentrewales.org.uk/uploads/agritourisme_july11.pdf (accessed 30 April 2113).

Philo Apple Farm (2013) Stay and cook farm weekends. See www.philoapplefarm.com/cooking.php (accessed 7 May 2013).

Potts, D. (2012) What do we know about urbanisation in sub-Saharan Africa and does it matter? *International Development Planning Review* 34 (1), v–xxi.

Pritchard, A., Morgan, N. and Ateljevic, I. (2011) Hopeful tourism: A new transformative perspective. *Annals of Tourism Research* 38 (3), 941–963.

Rhiney, K. (2011) Agritourism linkages in Jamaica: Case study of the Negril all-inclusive hotel subsector. In R.M. Torres and J.H. Momsen (eds) *Tourism and Agriculture: New Geographies of Consumption, Production and Rural Restructuring* (pp. 117–138). Abingdon; New York: Routledge.

Rilla, E.L. (2011) Tourism and agricultural viability: Case studies from the United States and England. In R.M. Torres and J.H. Momsen (eds) *Tourism and Agriculture: New Geographies of Consumption, Production and Rural Restructuring* (pp. 173–191). Abingdon; New York: Routledge.

Rodale, M. (2010) *Organic Manifesto: How Organic Farming Can Heal our Planet, Feed the World and Keep us Safe*. New York: Rodale Books.

Scialabba, N. and Müller-Lindenlauf, M. (2010) Organic agriculture and climate change. *Renewable Agriculture and Food Systems* 25 (2), 158–169.

Shiva, V. (2004) The future of food: Countering globalisation and recolonisation of Indian agriculture. *Futures* 36 (6–7), 715–732.

Siegel, D.J. (2007) *The Mindful Brain: Reflection and Attunement in the Cultivation of Well-being*. New York: W.W. Norton.

Siegel, D.J. (2011) *Mindsight: The New Science of Personal Transformation*. New York: Bantam Books Trade Paperbacks.

SIPRI (2012) *SIPRI Yearbook 2012 Summary: Armaments, Disarmament and International Security*. See www.sipri.org/yearbook/2012/files/SIPRIYB12Summary.pdf (accessed 14 May 2013).

Swimme, B. and Berry, T. (1992) *The Universe Story: From the Primordial Flaring Forth to the Ecozoic Era – A Celebration of the Unfolding of the Cosmos*. San Francisco, CA: Harper.

Wheatley, M.J. (2006) *Leadership and the New Science: Discovering Order in a Chaotic World*. San Francisco, CA: Berrett-Koehler.

Winchester, B. (2012) Continuing the trend: The brain gain of the newcomers: A generational analysis of rural Minnesota migration 1990–2010. University of Minnesota Extension Center for Community Vitality. See www1.extension.umn.edu/community/brain%2Dgain/ (accessed 2 March 2013).

Yeoman, I. (2012) *2050 – Tomorrow's Tourism*. Bristol: Channel View Publications.

9 Making the Difference: The Experience Economy and the Future of Regional Food Tourism

Kevin Meethan

Highlights

- While exact future predictions cannot be made, certain scenarios and trends can be identified.
- Food tourism is part of the wider long-term trend that sees tourism become increasingly niched and specialised.
- Regionalisation can also be seen as a reaction against the homogeneity of global multinationals through the development of artisanal products and recognisably small-scale production.
- Part of this process involves the development of an experience economy which puts the consumer and the quality of what they consume at the centre of development.
- Such developments rely on the creation of regional clusters and modes of cooperation and collaboration within and across the food sector.

Introduction

Everyone has a tourism food story, whether that concerns the ubiquity of the full English breakfast (seemingly a global phenomenon) or the over-priced and/or barely edible, or the cheap and wonderful, the unidentifiable and the surprising, with the latter being either positive or negative. This pool of first-hand knowledge clearly underlines the indisputable fact that food is an essential part of one's individual and social identity: one way or another, food, the way we store it, prepare it, share it and consume it, helps define who we are and what our place in the world is.

We also have to consider the associations that relate particular food-stuffs to specific countries, regions or locales and in turn how this is manifested in patterns of tourism production and consumption. There is no doubt that for many tourists the essence of a place or region is derived from the uniqueness of the place itself as much as the goods and products that characterise it. Certain foodstuffs, cuisines and wines can also come to represent a specific place of origin, and by achieving iconic status can represent nations, people and ways of life (Everett, 2012; Everett & Aitchison, 2008; Henderson, 2009, Kittler et al., 2012; Lee & Arcodia, 2011; Mak et al., 2012; Manniche et al., 2009; Swislocki, 2009; United Nations World Tourism Organisation (UNWTO), 2012).

It is also necessary to make a distinction between what we may term gastronomic tourism, that is, tourism which has a special relationship with food as the primary motive for travel, and the role of food in other forms of tourism, given that nearly one-third of tourist expenditure overall is on food (UNWTO, 2012: 6). While cuisine may or may not be the motivation for certain types of tourism, it can still be a key element in holiday decision-making (Sanchez-Cañizares & López-Guzmán, 2012; Young et al., 2010). Some tourists are keen to seek out new food experiences, while others rely on, or demand, that which they are familiar with (Chang et al., 2010, 2011); but even with the most controlled and contrived forms of package holiday, a taste of the other is an essential part of the itinerary.

Food choices, regardless of tourism, result from a complex set of circumstances, including factors such as age, gender, socio-economic status, religion, cultural milieu, national differences and preferences and so on (see for example Chang et al., 2010, 2011; Henderson, 2009; Kittler et al., 2012; Young et al., 2010). What is important is how these are perceived and acted on, and how food producers create and sell products for the tourist market, and also how tourists (and others) perceive and consume the products. One useful way of approaching this is to see the producer–consumer relationship in terms of the experience economy.

The Experience Economy

The term experience economy was, to my knowledge, first coined by Pine and Gilmore (1999), who argue that over time the dominant mode of economics has undergone a number of changes, from agrarian to industrial, and then to a service and knowledge economy, and most recently to one in which experiences take centre stage. Despite its polemical and didactic approach which verges on the naïve at times, and leaving aside the easy criticisms that can be levelled against such periodisation, the term nonetheless has some utility in directing our attention to product marketing, and the fact that many businesses seek to provide products *as* experiences. Indeed the subtitle of their book, *Work Is Theatre & Every Business a Stage,* provides an overarching metaphor that attempts to put theatricality and performativity at the heart of consumption. All other things being equal, the differentiation of one product from another comes not in the inherent value of the goods or services per se, but the ways in which they are presented and consumed: the greater the experience on offer, the greater the added value that can be attached to it, and derived from it.

Pine and Gilmore's (1999) original formulation was primarily concerned with advocating an approach that would allow businesses to gain competitive advantage in a crowded marketplace, while at the same time driving up the value of their product. While this can be perceived as being rather cynical (customers are easily seduced by showiness) and somewhat overwrought in its claims for general applicability (everything must be fun, folks!), the notion of the experience economy accurately describes many aspects of tourism, and certainly more niched forms of tourism in particular, which rely entirely on the quality of experiences offered.

Even a cursory examination of tourism marketing shows this to be the case. What is offered is not merely a bundle of goods and services that includes say, accommodation, food and transport, but an experience, and adventure, something more than the sum of its parts that transports the tourist metaphorically as well as physically away from the routine of daily life. Now it is arguable whether or not tourist experiences can be bought in the simple way that Pine and Gilmore (1999) envisage. As Anderson (2007: 46) points out, it is the tourists themselves who actually assemble, so to speak, the different elements that together comprise a 'consumption set'. In other words tourists are active agents. The tourist experience implies active engagement and not simple passive consumption (Meethan, 2011, 2012). Bearing these points in mind, it could be argued that tourism per se can be seen as exhibiting many characteristics of an experience economy, and all the more so, I would argue, when we are dealing with gastronomic or food tourism which includes rarely and actively seeks out new tastes and new sensations: new experiences. I would argue therefore the basic premises of the experience economy are that what we consume has added value and is more than the sum of its parts, and that this process provides a useful starting point from which we can examine the production–consumption nexus that is involved in food tourism.

By examining selected case studies of regional cuisine in relation to tourism development, this chapter will identify a number of future trends that are likely to continue to influence the production and consumption of regionally branded food and drinks. More specifically, these include the development of localised and regional clusters, the development and protection of regional specialisms, often referred to as artisanal or heritage foodstuffs. In turn, these major themes are also underpinned by a drive to shift production into niche markets, and by how food and drink can contribute to a sense of regional identity and the development of an experience economy.

However before we can proceed, it is also necessary to establish some theoretical basis from which we can assess any claims to the future trajectories of culinary tourism. Making predictions of any kind is of course fraught with uncertainties. Commenting on what is known as future studies, Bergman *et al.* (2010) point out that a general trend is to focus on likely scenarios rather than more precise predictions. Clearly, the complicating factor for predicting events is the wide range of variables that have to be accounted for, as unlike the natural sciences, dealing with the social world does not always allow for the control of variables. 'The question is', they write, '. . . not whether a forecast is good or bad or wrong or right, but whether it is good enough' (Bergman *et al.*, 2010: 858). Such a pragmatic approach is to be welcomed, but more importantly perhaps is their typology, which offers us a choice between prediction and prognosis: the former concerned with the specificity of predictable outcomes, while the latter identifies general trends and likely future trajectories. What follows for the remainder of this chapter is, in the terms outlined above, an assessment and prognosis of some emerging trends that surround the issues of the experience economy and the development of regional cuisines.

Regions and Food

'A country's food', writes Henderson (2009: 320), 'can be a critical dimension of destination image and the theme has always been used in advertising'. In her useful overview of food tourism, she also notes the recent trend for regions to promote food as part of their tourism marketing. But before we pursue this further, there is a need to provide a wider perspective within which we can locate such changes, and that is the context of modern, globalised production and distribution networks and patterns of consumption. These not only fuel an increasing sense of individuation, but as a consequence also drive demand for product differentiation and more individualised niche markets (Meethan, 2012).

We are all familiar with both the spread of fast food chains such as McDonald's and the populist, knee-jerk criticisms directed against them, often as predictable and banal as the products they are criticising. However if we look beyond the familiar whipping boys, there is no doubt that the production of generically labelled foodstuffs and the global spread of ubiquitous international brands are at best a perceived threat to regional and local differences, and at worst, a direct challenge and threat to the distinctiveness of regional and national cuisines.

In part as a reaction against this homogenisation of food and drink production, we can see the emergence of regionally branded foodstuffs (this has long been the case with wine) that not only seek to develop new markets but also provide a sense of local and regional identity, acting as a means of re-establishing cultural differences and maintaining distinctions in a globalised world.

To argue this is to engage in a debate concerning the nature of globalisation that is associated with the work of Rugman (2000, 2005), who argues that claims for globalisation may in fact be over-exaggerated as many multinational enterprises (MNEs) are actually more rooted in their region of origin than was first imagined. Such claims have not gone unchallenged and have been subject to both negative and positive critiques (e.g. Fillippaios & Rama, 2008; Osegowitsch & Sammartino, 2008). It is enough to note here that there is sufficient evidence to suggest that, at the level of MNEs, the spread of globalisation is perhaps more assumed than actual. Now, in turn, this may well be a question of defining terms. Rugman's argument may well indicate that globalisation is uneven and patchy, and that some sectors may well be more globalised than others; tourism and travel, for example, are sectors which are in many ways paradigms of globalisation.

Yet there is more at stake here than simply economic phenomena or patterns of trade, for what is also evident is that whatever the overall trajectory of globalisation, we also have to account for the cultural and identity politics that are at both regional and local levels. For example, in the European Union (EU) we can also see statutory powers being used to label and protect certain regional foodstuffs in order to maintain their distinctiveness (see Fields, Chapter 10). It is such distinctions that form the basis of regionally-based gastro-tourism, a fact which has been increasingly recognised as both economically and culturally significant at both regional and national levels (Bottone & Maguire, 2011; Everett, 2012; Everett & Aitchison, 2008; Lee & Arcodia, 2011; Manniche *et al.*, 2009; Ohe & Kurihara, 2013; Sims, 2010; Spilková & Fiavolá, 2012; Swislocki, 2009). However before I proceed any further there are some terms that need closer definition, in particular the differences between region, regionalism and regionalisation

For the purposes of this chapter I will define regions as sub-units of sovereign nation states that exhibit distinct boundaries – cultural, religious or linguistic differences – and may include minority nationalisms. However, we also have to bear in mind that regions can also define larger entities that cross national boundaries, for example the Basque Country which straddles border of France and Spain on the Atlantic coast, or on a larger scale, can encompass a number of nation states that share some cultural attributes such as the Nordic region of Europe that is designed to encourage cooperation between its member states (Norden, 2013).

Just to add a further layer of complexity to the issue, in the case of the EU we also see an apparent paradox, in that the EU has always promoted the encouragement of regional identity through various policy initiatives that are on the one hand enacted at a supra-national level and on the other, delivered at a sub-national level (Keating, 2013).

In terms of regionalism and regionalisation, both of these terms are used extensively within the literature on globalisation and are most usually associated with transnational trading agreements and the development of supra-national organisations such as, for example, the EU and the North American Free Trade Association (NAFTA) (Dicken, 2003; Glenn, 2007; Keating, 2013). However, there is also an important difference between them, in that regionalism is a formal process of integration that may involve economic as much as political and cultural elements, whereas regionalisation refers to pure economic integration of the kind examined by Rugman (2000, 2005). Now in many respects such a distinction may be a matter of degree, as what they both have in common are forms of collaboration between sovereign nation states, but the role of the EU in actively promoting regionalism is of importance here (Borrás-Alomar et al., 1994; Keating, 2013). One way this is achieved in relation to cuisine is through the European Network of Culinary Heritage, whose goal is to '...develop our regions through regional food and culinary traditions [this] develops small scale business [and] concerns tourism, environment, employment and health' (European Network of Culinary Heritage, 2013).

The involvement of the EU shows the complexity (at least in that part of the world) of defining just what a region consists of, and arguably more so when we add the term culture. In our hyper-globalised mobile world, physical boundaries can no longer be assumed to simply coincide with significant cultural differences. However we also have to take into account that claims to authentic, regional cuisines are often founded on the assumption that such boundaries and differences continue to have salience in people's lives, and indeed, the use of culinary markers may be a way of both creating and maintaining such differences as much as satisfying any economic criteria. The question then is, how does it work in practice?

Clustering and Development

It has become accepted orthodoxy that localised and indeed regional economic growth can be encouraged and sustained through the development of clusters in many different economic fields (Beer & Meethan, 2007; Meethan & Beer, 2007) as much as gastro-tourism and the food sector in general (Hall, 2004; Manniche et al., 2009; Norrman & Pettersson, 2010; O'Hara, 2012; Steiner & Ali, 2011). A chapter of this length precludes a full discussion of clustering, however the basic characteristics are that the transfer and transmission of sector-specific knowledge that innovation requires is fostered by the close proximity of different producers and other related small and medium enterprises (SMEs), with a consequent shortening of supply chains.

Cooperation between such SMEs encourages the development of expertise within particular sectors and helps to drive up value of the goods and knowledge produced.

However, clustering per se does not require close spatial proximity and can be implemented to good effect if necessary by utilising large and spatially diffused networks across regions (Beer & Meethan, 2007). What is also clear from the literature is that SMEs lack the resources to develop new products and new markets, and that collaboration and networking are crucial elements for success. For clustering to develop and encourage local innovation, there is a clear need for strategic direction at a regional level which will allow smaller enterprises and food producers to work together towards defined goals. One example to hand is the case of Bornholm, a Danish Island in the Baltic with an economy once dominated by agriculture and fishing, and more recently by tourism and local craft production (Manniche et al., 2009). What this particular study shows is, first, the use of clustering as an organisational and developmental strategy, and second, the development and creation of regionally branded foodstuffs, both of which were designed to promote a culinary experience economy.

In common with many other regions, there is a need for Bornholm to further diversify the economic base of the island. Of particular significance was the formation of a regional association in the 1990s which encompassed both Bornholm and South Eastern Sweden (geographically their closest neighbour), and perhaps of greater long-term significance, the support of various EU regional programmes which directed funding to peripheral and rural areas. Such developments laid the basis for further action, and it was also apparent that such diversification required '...firms [to] define themselves not only as individual actors but also as part of a collective project' (Manniche et al., 2009: 11).

The role of the EU was also critical here in providing, among other things, the conceptual framework for the development of regional branding that extended beyond national boundaries, and built on the '...production and marketing systems for culinary heritage in other rural regions of Europe' (Manniche et al., 2009: 47) as mentioned above. Similarly Spilková and Fiavolá's (2012: 1) study of regional food branding in the Czech Republic argued for '...the need for a significantly more effective interconnecting body or agent at the regional level with the capability of creating fertile links between rural tourism and regional products in a specific entrepreneurial environment'. Such developments and the use of clustering are not however confined to the EU as other studies demonstrate (Hall, 2004; O'Hara, 2012; Steiner & Ali, 2011).

Such collaboration is a central element of regional food branding; as Manniche et al. (2009) note, there was no pre-existing sense of collective enterprise, nor of a Bornholm brand. This was created by the stimulation of small-scale artisanal food production and by adding 'experience elements' to the products in order to consciously build a Bornholm experience economy by creating the conditions where added value could be extracted from locally branded produce (Manniche *et al.*, 2009; Steiner & Ali, 2011). The point here is that the development of the experience economy cannot be achieved – or rather, was not achieved in this case – through the autonomous actions of individual producers, but by coordinated and collective strategy across an entire sector.

It has now become a widespread practice that strategic regional frameworks are required to encourage localised clustering and development, within which there will be national and regional differences in the implementation of strategic developments (Hall, 2004; O'Hara, 2012; Ohe & Kurihara, 2013; Steiner & Ali, 2011). In turn many of these may reflect cultural differences in attitudes towards political authority, and supra-national organisations such as the EU. Such considerations however are beyond the scope of this chapter. Organisational linkages are clearly of concern here, but while they may be a necessary condition, they are not in themselves a sufficient one, what is also required are sufficiently distinct products that collectively can define a place and a region, in this case heritage foodstuffs as markers of distinction that help define and maintain the differences between regions, and provide, as marketers would have it, the unique selling point.

Heritage and Artisanal Foods

As I noted above, one of the wider contextual issues in relation to food tourism is the increasing global trend towards niche production and consumption which in turn can also be seen as part of the shift towards a more individualised experience economy: the development of gastro-tourism requires both the creation and the promotion of products which are locally/ regionally specific, and one way that this can be achieved is to allow tourists to witness the process of food production, or at least some aspects of it.

This not only differentiates places, localities and regions but also supplies tourists with another form of experience other than that of simply consuming. At another level it is also a means of assuring potential consumers that at some level they are witnessing a form of counter-globalisation in which mass, anonymous factory production is replaced with something more local, individual and human in scale, which I would argue is a factor of crucial importance for the future development of gastro-tourism.

This latter point is the salient one, as Manniche *et al.* (2009: 14) point out, local food producers and local tourism are interdependent, as both rely on '...experience elements that cannot be separated from the production process'. Just as much as the production and commodification of tourist space involves the active participation of tourists (Meethan, 2011, 2012), allowing customers access to the production process also commodifies

'. . . the experience of personally seeing, hearing and smelling how products are produced' (Manniche *et al.*, 2009: 14). This sensory element is key and the actual engagement with production of foodstuffs as much as the consumption of them is what adds value, a factor that has also been recognised in other studies. For example, as Norrman and Pettersson (2010) argue, there is often an implicit as well as explicit assumption that haute cuisine restaurants will have access to local or regional suppliers that create high-quality artisanal products, a clear example of how clustering (access to and utilising local markets) drives up value, which in turn helps stimulate the local economy.

Similar findings have been noted in other studies. As an example, Sims (2010: 111), in her study of the south-west of England, found that one cider farm was a tourist attraction which

> . . . promoted local place, culture and tradition to its visitors. . . There was thus a temporal and cultural element to the understanding of local that was employed by the business.

The study by Everett and Aitchison (2008: 159), focusing on the same geographical area, also noted the importance of consumers recognising the point of origin of their food, recording that one of their interviewees remarked that tourists '. . . wanted to know it [fish] was caught in a small boat'. Venturing a bit wider afield we find similar concerns emerging in relation to gastrotourism in the Czech Republic (Spilková & Fiavolá, 2012), in Japan (Ohe & Kurihara, 2013) as well as Sweden (Norrman & Pettersson, 2010), Scotland and Ireland (Everret, 2012) and the USA (Bottone & Maguire, 2011). What is evident from these case studies and indeed others is the value that consumers attach to witnessing the actual processes involved in food production, and how the production of craft or artisanal or even heritage food has a number of parallels with other forms of craft production (e.g. Littrell *et al.*, 1993). It is tempting to surmise (but further study would be needed on this point) that the experience economy is also means by which cultural capital can be accrued; the extra value that is both attached to and taken from the consumption of certain commodities does not simply end at the point of consumption, rather the experience itself becomes an element of cultural capital than can then be utilised.

Another point to consider is the importance of food production being seen to be on a small and easily recognisable scale, I would argue that this also represents an older, widespread discourse and set of tropes that encompass not only the relationship between town and country, but also a critique of globalising modernity. We do not have (to my knowledge) tourists visiting industrial-sized burger factories, large bakeries or dairies that produce the bulk of mass marketed food, indeed to the culinary tourists such would be anathema. Witnessing food production is one way not only to be assured of the freshness and quality of ingredients but also a way to connect, at least vicariously, with something that is less removed from nature than that which can be purchased in a supermarket or at a fast food outlet, or is the product of a remote MNE. There is some evidence that a search for 'real food' (that is, locally or regionally produced and consumed) is not only another variation of heritage or craft production but also a reaction against the perceived totalitarian tendencies of globalisation (Mak *et al.*, 2012; Swislocki, 2009). The origins and preparation of food are clearly part of the culinary tourist experience, whether this is for the more committed epicurean who seeks out new tastes, or the tourists who wish to sample the local or regional, something that encapsulates the essence and experience of place, and by so doing, marks it as distinct.

Concluding Remarks: The Implications for the Future of Food Tourism

The implications for the future of food tourism, as outlined in this chapter, can be expressed as follows. First, it was argued that future developments need to be seen in the context of globalisation and the broad trend towards market niching that is evident within tourism as a whole. Within this broad trend we also see the development of both food tourism and cuisine as a marker of national and regional identity.

Second, that despite the hyperbole that surrounds the initial formulation, the concept of the experience economy has a lot to offer in terms of approaching the issue of gastro tourism and regional identity. In particular a focus on consumption as an active process that involves both producers and consumers creating experiences holds promise for future lines of research that focus on the micro and macro processes involved.

Third, that the current situation is apparently one of ambiguity and contradiction; globalisation has caused homogenisation and the eradication of difference in some sectors and sub-sectors, while at the same time, counter – globalisation encourages a celebration of the regional and the local. At the same time we also see a general shift into an economy in which individualised experiences assume a greater role in both motivation and consumption. Foodstuffs and cuisines then assume a greater cultural significance as both a marker of identity and a distinct product for growing, niched, tourist markets.

Fourth, such small scale development in turn relies on a number of institutional and regulatory frameworks that can assist the development of regionally-based foodstuffs. The use of policies which encourage the development of SMEs through clustering is a crucial factor, they not only stimulate development but also help add value and can create the conditions where a culinary experience economy can emerge. Small-scale production of high-value products is also at once economic and cultural, providing as it does the marker to cultural distinction that both creates and sustains difference in a globalised world.

Finally, the relationship between tourism branding and the production of foodstuffs is not a simple one of cause and effect, rather we need to see both in terms of a dynamic and even symbiotic relationship that may give rise to new forms of cuisine as much as preserve old ones. For example shortening supply chains in food production has a number of advantages that apply beyond tourism and help to push forward an agenda of environmental concern and sustainability. In turn, tourism that seeks to take advantage of such developments and emphasises the experiential, helps drive up demand for localised produce. In this broad sense we can see that the development of regional food tourism (and perhaps gastro-tourism as such) is indeed a form of experience economy that shows signs of a continued upper trajectory.

References

Anderson, T.D. (2007) The tourist in the experience economy. *Scandinavian Journal of Hospitality and Tourism* 7 (1), 46–58.

Beer, J. and Meethan, K. (2007) Marine and maritime sector skills shortages in the South West of England: Developing regional training provision. *Journal of Vocational Education and Training* 59 (4), 467–484.

Bergman, A., Karlsson, J.C. and Axelson, J. (2010) Truth claims and explanatory claims: An ontological typology of future studies. *Futures* 42 (8), 857–865.

Borrás-Alomar, S., Christiansen, T. and Rodriguez-Pose, A. (1994) Towards a 'Europe of the regions'? Visions and reality from a critical perspective. *Regional Policy and Politics* 4 (2), 1–27.

Bottone, E. and Maguire, D. (2011) Heritage foods: Born in Pennslyvania. In H. Hartwell, P. Lugosi and J. Edwards (eds) *International Conference on Culinary Arts and Sciences V11: Proceedings* (pp. 165–176). Bournemouth: International Centre for Tourism and Heritage Research.

Chang, R.C.Y., Kivela, J. and Mak, A.H.N. (2010) Food preferences of Chinese tourists. *Annals of Tourism Research* 37 (4), 989–1011.

Chang, R.C.Y., Kivela, J. and Mak, A.H.N. (2011) Attributes that influence the evaluation of travel dining experience. When bus matter West. *Tourism Management* 32 (?), 307–311.

Dicken, P. (ed.) (2003) *Global Shift: Reshaping the Global Economic Map in the 21st Century.* Oxford: Blackwell.

European Network of Culinary Heritage (2013) See www.culinary-heritage.com/ (accessed 15 June 2013).

Everett, J. (2012) Production places or consumption spaces? The place-making agency of food tourism in Ireland and Scotland. *Tourism Geographies* 14 (4), 535–554.

Everett, J. and Aitchison, C. (2008) The role of food tourism in sustaining regional identity: A case study of Cornwall, South West England. *Journal of Sustainable Tourism* 16 (2), 150–167.

Filippaios, F. and Rama, R. (2008) Globalisation or regionalisation? The strategies of the world's largest food and beverage MNEs. *European Management Journal* 26 (1), 59–72.

Glenn, J. (2007) *Globalization: North-South Perspectives.* London: Routledge.

Hall, C.M. (2004) Small firms and wine and food tourism in New Zealand: Issues of collaboration, clusters and lifestyles. In R. Thomas (ed.) *Small Firms in Tourism: International Perspectives* (pp. 167–181). Wallingford: CABI.

Henderson, J.C. (2009) Food tourism reviewed. *British Food Journal* 111 (4), 317–326.

Keating, M. (2013) Is there a regional level of government in Europe? In P. Le Gales and C. Lequesne (eds) *Regions in Europe: The Paradox of Power* (pp. 8–22). London: Routledge.

Kittler, P.G., Sucher, K.P. and Nahikian-Nelms, M. (2012) *Food and Culture* (6th edn). Belmont, CA: Wadsworth.

Lee, I. and Arcodia, C. (2011) The role of regional food festivals for destination branding. *International Journal of Tourism Research* 13, 355–367.

Littrell, M., Anderson, L. and Brown, P. (1993) What makes a craft souvenir authentic? *Annals of Tourism Research* 20 (2), 197–215.

Mak, A H N, Lumbers, M. and Eves, A. (2012) Globalisation and food production in tourism. *Annals of Tourism Research* 39 (1), 171–196.

Manniche, J., Topsø Larsen, K. and Petersen, T. (2009) Development and branding of 'regional food' of Bornholm. Bornholm: Centre for Regional and Tourism Research.

Meethan, K. (2011) Narrating and performing tourist space: Notes towards some conceptual and methodological issues. In C. Mansfield and S. Seligman (eds) *Narrative and the Built Heritage – Papers in Tourism Research* (pp. 129–140). Saarbrücken: VDM.

Meethan, K. (2012) Tourism, individuation and space. In J. Wilson (ed.) *New Perspectives in Tourism Geographies* (pp. 61–66). London: Routledge.

Meethan, K. and Beer, J. (2007) Economic clustering, tourism and the creative industries in Plymouth. In G. Richards and J. Wilson (eds) *Tourism, Creativity and Development* (pp. 217–229). London: Routledge.

Norden (2013) The Nordic Council. See www.norden.org/en/the-nordic-region (accessed 30 June 2013)

Norrman, M. and Pettersson, L. (2010) Gourmet restaurants and small scale food production: Swedish rural and urban regions. Paper given at the European Regional Science Association Congress, Jönköping, Sweden. See www-sre.wu.ac.at/ersa/ersaconfs/ersa10/ERSA2010finalpaper1664.pdf (accessed 30 June 2013).

O'Hara, J. (2012) Successful development of local and regional food systems: The New England story. *Communities and Banking* 23 (1), 11–13. Online at: http://www.boston fed.org/commdev/c&b/2012/winter/successful-development-of-local-and-regional-food-systems.htm

Ohe, Y. and Kurihara, S. (2013) Evaluating the complimentary relationship between local brand farm products and rural tourism. *Tourism Management* 35, 278–283.

Osegowitsch, T. and Sammartino, A. (2008) Re-assessing (home) – regionalisation. *Journal of Business Studies* 39, 184–196.

Pine, J. and Gilmore, J. (1999) *The Experience Economy: Work Is Theatre & Every Business a Stage*. Boston, MA: Harvard Business School Press.

Rugman, A. (2000) *The End of Globalisation*. London: Random House.

Rugman, A. (2005) *The Regional Multi-Nationals: MNEs and 'Global' Strategic Management*. Cambridge: Cambridge University Press.

Sanchez-Cañizares, S. and López-Guzmán, T. (2012) Gastronomy as a tourism resource: Profile of the culinary tourist. *Current Issues in Tourism* 15 (3), 229–245.

Sims, R. (2010) Putting place on the menu: The negotiation of locality in UK food tourism from production to consumption. *Journal of Rural Studies* 26 (2), 105–115.

Spilková, J. and Fiavolá, D. (2012) Culinary tourism packages and regional brands in Czechia. *Tourism Geographies* 5 (2), 1–21.

Steiner, B. and Ali, J. (2011) Government support for the development of regional food clusters: Evidence form Alberta, Canada. *International Journal of Innovation and Regional Development* 3 (2), 186–216.

Swislocki, M. (2009) *Culinary Nostalgia: Regional Food Culture and the Urban Experience of Shanghai*. Stanford, CA: Stanford University Press.

UNWTO (2012) *Global Report on Food Tourism*. Madrid: UNWTO.

Young, K.H., Goh, B.K. and Yoaun, J. (2010) Development of a multi-dimensional scale for measuring food tourist motivations. *Journal of Quality Assurance in Hospitality & Tourism* 11 (1), 56–71.

10 Food and Intellectual Property Rights

Kevin Fields

Highlights

- This chapter identifies and explains intellectual property rights (IPR) and considers why and how they are applied for.
- Problematic issues associated with IPR are identified, such as who the rights 'belong' to and the costs of applying for and policing the rights.
- IPR's relevance to food tourism is explored.
- It discusses potential future conflicts and challenges in relation to the ever-burgeoning list of foods awarded IPR status.

Introduction

Blakeney (2011: 8) has stated that IPR may be defined as, 'statutory monopolies conferred by the state for a prescribed term in relation to certain creations of the mind'. However, there is no all-embracing definition of IPRs to be found in any national laws or international treaties.

Much of the academic literature as applied to food and IPR focuses on issues of food security, not least because many in the world still do not have enough to eat on a daily basis. Food shortages affect many parts of the world. Africa, however, is a continent that suffers more than most in this respect. The United Nations Food and Agriculture Organization (2010) has noted that, '239 million people in sub-Saharan Africa were hungry/undernourished'. Boudreaux and Aft (2008) drew attention to the plight of Africans facing famine through the high cost of food, and identified part of the solution as making small-scale farmers more productive in growing and selling food. But Mushita and Thompson (2013) point out that global policies threaten the ability of the African smallholder to grow food through the controls being placed upon the seeds that would permit the farmer to grow useful crops. IPR, in relation to food, apply across science, technology, culture, heritage and sociology. In terms of science and technology, 'Intellectual property rights have effects on the incentives to create and diffuse innovations' (Trommetter, 2008: 7). In other words, companies investing in research can protect their innovations in order to recover research costs and generate profits. There is also the issue of food security and moral issues such as restricting the use of patented plants by causing second-generation seeds to be sterile (Wiber, 2010). So not only do African farmers have to buy seed, often at high prices, but they may also need to buy it again the following year if the seeds they bought were sterile and could only be used for one crop.

Adenle *et al.* (2012) identify how technology could play a part, via genetically modified food (GM), in helping to develop sustainable agriculture in developing countries. The difficulty lies in privatisation and increased intellectual property rights protection, meaning that those most in need of developing sustainable agriculture are essentially priced out of the market.

Within the developed world, IPR plays an altogether different role, though there are still cost implications for growers accessing seed and so on. There is a greater tendency to think of food in a much broader way than merely nutrition. Tansey and Worsley (1995: 49) have noted that it is also necessary to '... consider the basic psychological, social and cultural needs of individuals that food meets'. So the focus must go beyond issues of nourishment to understand the role that food plays within society. The importance of that role is now recognised to such an extent that destinations try to protect it. One of the ways of doing so is through intellectual property rights.

Many people in the developed world would be able to identify a country, and possibly a distinct region, merely from mention of a dish or food product. Paella, risotto, sauerkraut, foie gras, pizza, goulash, etc., have instantly recognisable national connections; the better informed would even be able to place their regional origins. This is despite the fact that these dishes are now available in many countries around the world. Their importance, locally, goes far beyond providing something tasty for tourists to consume. Wolinsky (2012: 189) notes that, '... it is important to remember that cuisine is inexorably intertwined with the history, economy, culture, climate, landscape, language, taste, and traditions of the country it belongs to'.

Tourism marketers have long recognised the value of creating tangible identities for destinations through images generated via products, specific geographic features, culture, heritage, attractions, and not least, food. Therefore, maintaining a strong link between the food and the locality is vital. Supporting this, Hall (2012: 7) states that, 'There is a growing recognition of the intellectual property dimensions of food, wine and tourism given that they are products that are often differentiated on the basis of regional identity.' Consequently, the stronger a food image or identity is connected to a region, the greater the value of protecting that identity. An increasingly prevalent way of doing this is via IPR.

IPR are the rights given to persons over the creations of their minds. They usually give the creator an exclusive right over the use of his/her creation for a certain period of time (World Trade Organisation, 2013). It can be seen in other chapters that global warming is redrawing the culinary map of the world. Together with IPR, this may be a significant problem for producers and consumers in the years to come.

For literary and artistic work, protection is granted through copyright. For creativity in the form of products or processes, patents can be applied for. For food and food products, the situation is more complex. For example, one needs to consider who 'owns' a dish or recipe? And who 'owns' a food product, cooking method or process?

The Micro Level

There have been cases reported in the press in recent years, in the UK and the US, where junior chefs have trained and worked under other chefs, then moved on and copied much of what they have learnt. An article published in the *LA Times* in October 2007 entitled, 'When chefs part ways, who gets custody of the recipes?' discussed the issue of recipe ownership and concluded that there was no easy answer to the conundrum. Similarly, chefs have moved restaurants and replicated dishes at their new place of employment, based upon dishes at their old place of employment. Even if producing exact replicas, should this be actionable in law? Who determines the first chef's right to 'ownership' of the dish? Haven't chefs always learnt from, and copied, each other? And if they've such an issue with it, why do celebrity chefs publish books of their own recipes? Perhaps the free publicity such cases attract for the restaurants and chefs concerned may be a factor?

There are literally no new dishes to be invented, except perhaps those involving molecular gastronomy, as practised by chefs such as Ferran Adria and Heston Blumenthal. But even those dishes have their origins in what has gone before. Blumenthal currently employs 300 staff, many involved in developing new dishes and concepts. No matter how 'creative' a chef is, he/she is drawing upon his/her existing knowledge and experience and experimenting to find new ways of applying that knowledge and experience. So the question remains, when a new dish is created, how much ownership belongs to the chef and how much to those who helped build their knowledge in the first place? In the Blumenthal case, what level of ownership should he have of the dishes his team develop?

Gastronomy is ever in a state of flux – it evolves and always has done. People learn from each other, begging, borrowing or stealing ideas. Sometimes they copy, sometimes they add value and take ideas forward into new dishes. Modern gastronomy is a migration of ideas, products and techniques. If IPR had been introduced years ago, would the gastronomic diversity which exists today have been available to the same degree?

All this remains a rather grey area, but what is certain is that ownership of the recipes behind dishes, by restaurants or chefs, can be an important commercial factor, promoting visits to those restaurants so customers can consume/experience a dish cooked and served by its 'creator'. This delivers the 'real' or 'authentic' experience much sought after by modern consumers (Scarpato & Daniele, 2003).

The Macro Level

This is the area which has the potential to have the biggest impact on food tourism in the future. It is becoming increasingly common for producers of food and drink to try and develop a strong geographic identity for their products. In some cases, they rely upon marketing campaigns with the use of key words: 'original', 'traditional', 'the home of', 'authentic'. Such campaigns are designed, therefore, to convince the consumer they are purchasing something special or unique. Sejal Sukhadwala in *The Guardian* (May 2012) questions this approach, pointing out that:

> One of the ideas underpinning Claudia Roden's cookery books is that food is an integral part of identity. At the launch of her most recent book, The Food of Spain, she spoke about members of an Egyptian chefs' organisation who didn't want to cook their mothers' food as they associated it with poverty. They have jettisoned authenticity in favour of aspiration; evolution at work.

Additionally, just how real or authentic does food have to be? Advances in knowledge of food hygiene and the advent of refrigeration have significantly improved the safety of food consumed, so in relation to authenticity, there needs to be a consideration that past food processes may not be welcomed by modern consumers. For example, Scarpato and Daniele (2003: 300) illustrate this by noting that, 'Ox carcasses slaughtered in a village two kilometres away from Paris, reached the French capital after 3 or 4 days and before selling them, the butcher had to cut away 3 or 4 inches of rotten meat infested by worms.' So in reality, it may be advisable to cherry-pick food and processes, when considering traditions and authenticity, before deciding what can be adopted from the past, and what is best discarded.

Legislation

In recent years, legislation, rather than just marketing strategies and campaigns, has been used to strengthen the link between geographic locations and food and drink production. For example, within Europe there is legislation surrounding the designation of food products. There are three designations: Protected Designation of Origin (PDO), Protected Geographical Indication (PGI) and Traditional Speciality Guaranteed (TSG). The key features of the designation process are as follows:

*   The application for designation is free (though gathering the relevant evidence may prove costly).
*   Provides protection for 10 years.
*   The process has the support of national governmental food agencies. For example, in the UK, the Department for Environment, Food and Rural Affairs (DEFRA), undertakes a preliminary examination of the application prior to submission to a designated European Union (EU) food agency.
*   The application is examined and the intention to protect is published (*European Food Journal*) inviting objectors who must provide a complete rational and justification for their objection.
*   The application is passed through a number of examining committees before receiving the designation.
*   It is a protracted procedure requiring resources, patience and forbearance.
*   The authentication process has to be paid for by producers (Gov.UK, 2013).

The three designations

Protection of Designation of Origin (PDO)
The product must be produced and processed and prepared in a specific geographical area. The quality or characteristics of the product must be essentially due to that area.

Protection of Geographical Indication (PGI)
The product must be produced and processed and prepared in a specific geographical area.

Specific quality, reputation or other characteristics must be attributable to that area.

Traditional Speciality Guaranteed (TSG)
The name must be specific in itself, or express the specific character of the food. It must be traditional, or established by custom. Distinguished features of the product must not be due to the geographic area. This product must be produced in or entirely based on technical advances in the method of production (Agriculture, Food and the Marine, 2013).

At this macro level, protection is not given to an individual or a restaurant, but granted to a defined geographic region associated with the food item or product. This obviously has major ramifications for food tourism as the

linkage between the food and a destination/region is transparent, clearly identifiable and likely to motivate visits to that region for food tourists, or tourists
with only a secondary interest in food.

Some of the protected food and drink items are high profile and knowledge of their protection is commonplace, for example Champagne and
Roquefort cheese. But coverage is far more extensive than the 'average' tourist will realise. As an example of the breadth of protection, the Table 10 lists
some of the UK and Irish food and drink currently protected:

As can be seen for the items listed in Table 10.1, the range of items is
varied and extensive, and it is constantly growing (European Commission,
2013a). A similar list for EU wines is also extensive and constantly growing
(European Commission, 2013b). In a global context, many countries or
regions have some form of protectionism for their food in relation to IPR.
There is also the global coverage offered by UNESCO (2013). Furthermore,
Fooladi (2011) notes that,

> The UNESCO World heritage list is probably well known to most, but
> there is also another list called the Intangible Cultural Heritage list
> intended to safeguard immaterial cultural heritage. In this list, at least
> four entries relate closely to food and food culture.

Table 10.1 Examples of UK and Irish protected food and drink products

Product	Examples
Meat	Traditional pasture reared beef, traditionally farmed Gloucestershire Old Spots pork, Melton Mowbray pork pie, Cornish pasty, traditional Cumberland sausage, Isle of Man Manx Loaghtan lamb, Northern Ireland beef, Northern Ireland lamb, South West of England lamb, South West of England beef, Welsh lamb, Welsh beef, Scotch lamb, Scotch beef, traditional grass-fed red poll beef, traditional farmfresh turkey, Shetland lamb, Orkney beef, Orkney lamb
Fish	Cornish sardines, Lough Neagh eels, traditional Grimsby smoked fish, Arbroath smokies, Whitstable oysters, Scottish farmed salmon
Fruit and vegetables	Yorkshire forced rhubarb, Armagh bramley apples, traditional bramley apple pie filling, Jersey royal potatoes
Dairy	Yorkshire Wensleydale cheese, Staffordshire cheese, Exmoor blue cheese, Dorset blue cheese, Cornish clotted cream, Teviotdale cheese, white stilton cheese, blue stilton cheese, West Country farmhouse cheddar cheese, Beacon Fell traditional Lancashire cheese, single Gloucester, Swaledale cheese, Swaledale ewes' cheese, Bonchester cheese Buxton blue, Dovedale cheese
Drink	Gloucestershire cider/perry, Worcestershire cider/perry, Herefordshire cider/perry, Kentish ale and Kentish strong ale, Rutland bitter

The UNESCO recognition is broad-based and in most cases does not apply just to one food item/product, though there are exceptions. Recent examples of recognition in 2010 are: The Gastronomic Meal of the French; Traditional Mexican Cuisine; The Mediterranean Diet; and Gingerbread Craft from Northern Croatia.

Problems to be Considered

Certain key issues have to be considered when attempting to protect food. These include the following.

- Identification of ownership, that is who actually 'owns' the product, if it can be owned at all?
- Established food producers may be banned from producing their product (e.g. Somerset Brie, French Brie). This could cause severe problems within local economies. Somerset Brie was developed to utilise excess milk production in the region, but French Brie predates Somerset Brie.
- Food miles will be increased if many products can only be sourced from their original area of production.
- The cost of establishing protected status. No actual charge but the time and effort required will have financial implications.
- Responsibility for determining the geographic limitations of production.
- The cost of policing protected status. A fee is payable for yearly inspections so there is an ongoing cost (The Scottish Government, 2013).

Relevance to Tourism

Once difficulties have been resolved and protected status achieved, the food identity of a destination or region can form part of a marketing strategy to attract tourists, '... not only because food is central to the tourist experience, but also because gastronomy has become a significant source of identity formation in postmodern societies' (Richards, 2002: 3). This is particularly important in what is an ever-increasing competitive marketplace. The process of globalisation has eroded national, regional and local identities to the extent that some mass tourism destinations in the Mediterranean region are differentiated only by the language spoken, with a certain amount of homogenisation having been applied to the food and drink offered to tourists. For example, Paella is seen by tourists as a national dish, when its origins are actually regional. However, a locally or regionally defined gastronomy will re-introduce the differentiation that once existed across holiday destinations (though for dedicated food tourists that differentiation has always been there if sought out).

The issue of cost should also be considered. Sourcing food from outside a region can sometimes be cheaper as economies of scale mean that major producers can deliver products more cheaply than local suppliers, but this needs to be countered to avoid economic leakage of tourism income. As noted by Paarlberg (2010: 149), 'Survey evidence reveals that the average food buyer is now willing to pay a premium to purchase locally produced foods.'

Though surveys such as these reflect the views of domestic consumers, rather than those of tourists, it would not be unreasonable to assume that tourists may also develop similar spending habits.

To some extent, the feeding of tourists has gone full circle. The earliest tourists to a destination would have been faced with the local cuisine and little else. As tourism grew, many hotels and restaurants attempted to improve their market share by offering food styles similar to the tourists' home regions. As tourists gained experience and became more knowledgeable, their interest in local cuisines grew and demand changed, away from the foods they were familiar with at home, and towards what was traditional for the locality. However, 'tradition' is a moving target. As cuisines evolve, what is traditional for a current generation is not necessarily traditional for their parents or grandparents. As Gillespie (2001: 86) stated, 'A good deal of what are now acknowledged as essential elements of the various national cuisines of Europe are imports.' For example, peppers, tomatoes and potatoes, three staples of many European cuisines, originated in the 'New World' and were introduced to Europe by Portuguese and Spanish explorers in the 15th and 16th centuries. Clearly, tradition has a date stamp.

Consumption of local food is not just an issue connected to culture and heritage, but also an economic one. Income from tourists purchasing food will stay longer in the local economy if food is sourced from within, rather than outside, the region. Technological advances in transport and refrigeration have cancelled out issues of seasonality and lack of availability. It is always summer somewhere in the world and produce can be chilled or frozen and moved quickly to a destination anywhere in the world – but at a cost. As noted by Andress and Harrison (2002),

Freezing is expensive when you add up the cost of packaging, of energy use and of the freezer itself. More energy is used in cooking, freezing and reheating than in cooking from scratch and serving immediately.

This means that not only does the cost of food need to be inflated to cover these costs, but also that a large percentage of money spent on food will be an economic leakage, not staying in the destination where the food was actually purchased and consumed. Not only will local food often be cheaper, but the economic benefit will be more direct and accrue to local producers and processors. In addition the local area will benefit from increased employment opportunities for local farms and food producers.

So regardless of tradition, culture, heritage, fashion, style and IPR (which may all be used to create a food identity for a destination), the key issue in relation to tourism is the economic value of food and its ability to attract tourists, and provide a focus for their spending once they arrive. Destinations are increasingly aware of the value of food and drink as a tourism resource, hence the increasing interest in IPR.

Where to Next?

Using a suitable food-related metaphor, the advice to tourism destinations is, 'Don't put all of your eggs in one basket.' Once the market is saturated with regions extolling the virtues of their local food and drink, the impact of food and drink as a determinant of demand is likely to wane, if only through over-familiarity. However, a bigger danger is if anything happens to change a region's ability to produce the food and drink for which they have become famous. Changing what may have become a strong identity, via regional food and/or drink, would not be easy. The following scenario is useful in illustrating this situation.

Potential Scenario: Champagne

Sparkling wine can only legally be called Champagne if produced within a very carefully designated region, centred on the city of Reims, France. That region has a soil structure and climate which particularly suits the type of grapes used for the production of Champagne, as a lack of sun means the grapes struggle to ripen and have high levels of acidity and low levels of sugar. Champagne evolved as grapes grown in the region were not suitable for more robust styles of wine. Early Champagne was pink and still and often made from Pinot Noir grapes. Today, the prosperity of the Champagne region is almost solely due to the sparkling wine they produce and the level of tourists drawn to the area because of it. The impact if they could no longer make wine of the type currently recognised as Champagne would be substantial. A reduction in the level of rainfall in the area, and a corresponding rise in the average ambient temperature, could both be caused by global warming. If the grapes then had a reduction in acidity levels and an increase in sugar levels, it would become impossible to produce Champagne in the current style. As IPR in this instance are conferred by geographic boundaries, whatever the wine growers produced could still be called Champagne, providing the *méthode champenoise* was still employed, but would the market accept it? Champagne has evolved over time but modern consumers have a very distinct appreciation of what the product should be.

If global warming then creates the conditions for a sparkling wine which is the equal of Champagne in a region, or even a country, not previously associated with Champagne, what would they call it? What would be the way forward for the Champagne region? Accept that the nature of the product has changed and carry on regardless? Or, change the product to one conducive to the new climatic conditions? To some extent, that situation already exists with the Spanish sparkling wine, Cava.

This conundrum could be faced by every region whose products are determined by the prevailing climate. The greater the connection between place identity and product, especially through IPR, the greater will be the conundrum faced.

Global Warming and Potential Problems

To date there does not seem to have been a major problem caused for IPR-protected food and drink by global warming, but possible issues cannot be too far away. Certain food staples are already affected. Agriculture, as Santilli (2012) has commentated, is one of the activities most affected by climate change, as it depends directly on temperature and rainfall conditions. Within the UK, one of the wettest winters and coldest springs on record (2012–2013) meant that crops of many vegetables are in short supply, and imports are replacing a lot of products normally home grown. Potatoes, very much a staple of the UK diet, have been a particular problem as the ground was too wet for farmers to plant seed potatoes at the usual time. In this instance, the impact will be purely economic. The cost of living will go up due to the higher prices of imported vegetables. However, a bigger long-term worry is that farmers may struggle to survive with a reduced amount of produce to sell, making the UK even more dependent on imports in the future. In a similar vein, Lobell et al. (2008, cited in Santilli, 2012) has estimated that that southern Africa may lose 30% of its main agricultural product (corn) in the next two decades, and southern Asia over 10% of its corn and rice harvests. In these regions the issue may go beyond economic impact, and result in hardship and famine. At that point IPR may become an irrelevance. However, some multinationals are attempting to get ahead of the game by developing climate-ready crops which allow for the impacts of global warming (Abergel, 2011).

Looking from the Present to the Future

Accurately predicting the future in terms of food is largely dependent upon looking back at how food and food products have developed and considering what future developments there will be. It is a given that climate change will affect food supply, but how much will the climate change and over what period? Experts are offering many different scenarios. Initially, small increases in average temperatures will benefit some regions but harm others. The Intergovernmental Panel on Climate Change (IPCC) produced an assessment in 2007 which claimed that a 1–3°C increase in average temperatures would increase crop productivity at mid to high latitudes, but at lower latitudes just a rise of 1–2°C would decrease crop productivity. They also claim that any rises above 3°C would decrease crop production globally. So not very significant temperature rises could have catastrophic impacts on food production. With these scenarios it could be argued that IPR again becomes irrelevant.

Concluding Remarks: The Implications for the Future of Food Tourism

This chapter has discussed IPR in relation to food, and identified the issues which are most relevant to food tourism, while acknowledging there is also a much wider agenda beyond the scope of this chapter. In terms of developing a tangible image for a destination or region, IPR can help build tourists' perception of a locality. Food can be both a primary and secondary motivator for visits as all tourists need to eat, and some will travel primarily to eat. Regardless of the level of interest in food across the full spectrum of tourist types, spending on food and drink in a destination delivers significant economic benefits, providing the majority of that food and drink is produced in or near the destination.

But are IPR a necessary part of the image-building process? At the current time it is easy to argue 'yes', as the process of applying for IPR gets a certain level of media coverage and the details can be included in promotional literature. But as the process reaches saturation level (witness the 50+ products already protected across the UK and Ireland) the impact is likely to be increasingly less effective over time. That is not to say that IPR does not have its benefits, but that in the long term those benefits may apply more directly outside tourism.

History, tradition, heritage, authenticity, culture, education, society, economy, and not to forget pleasure, are all linked to food and drink. Achieving IPR status will deliver benefits across all of these factors. In turn, all of these factors can be motivators for tourism. So, IPR has a value for tourism but it should not be a direct one, rather it should be connected to associated strategies to develop the overall resources that can maintain a destination in relation to tourism. Focusing too much on IPR as a tourism resource is building on a foundation of sand, as the long-term impacts of global warming may mean the destination or region will not be able to continue producing the food and drink it becomes famous for in the long term.

References

Abergel, E.A. (2011) Climate-ready crops and bio-capitalism: Towards a new food regime. *International Journal of Sociology of Agriculture & Food* 18 (3), 260–274.

Adenle, A.A., Sowe, K.S., Parayil, G. and Aginam, O. (2012) Analysis of open source biotechnology in developing countries: An emerging framework for sustainable agriculture. *Technology in Society* 34 (3), 256–269.

Agriculture, Food and the Marine (2013) See www.agriculture.gov.ie/gi/pdopgitsg-protectedfoodnames/ (accessed 15 December 2013).

Andress, E.L. and Harrison, J.A. (eds) (2002) Preserving food: Freezing prepared foods. The University of Georgia College of Agricultural and Environmental Sciences. See http://nchfp.uga.edu/publications/uga/FreezingPreparedFoods.pdf (accessed 15 December 2013).

Blakeney, M. (2011) *Trends in Intellectual Property Rights Relating to Genetic Resources For Food And Agriculture*. Report for the Commission on Genetic Resources for Food and Agriculture, United Nations. See www.fao.org/docrep/meeting/022/mb684e.pdf (accessed 17 June 2013).

Boudreaux, K.C. and Aft, A. (2008) Fighting the food crisis: Feeding Africa one family at a time. *Environs: Environmental Law & Policy Journal* 32 (1), 131–181.

European Commission (2013a) See http://ec.europa.eu/agriculture/quality/door/list.html;jsessionid=pL0hLqqLXhNmFQyFl1b24mY3t9dJQPflg3xbL2YphGT4k6zdWn34!-370879141 (accessed 15 December 2013).

European Commission (2013b) http://ec.europa.eu/agriculture/markets/wine/e-bcchus/index.cfm?event=pwelcome&language=EN (accessed 15 December 2013).

Fooladi, E. (2011) Food accepted as cultural heritage – Food is surely culture. See www.fooducation.org/2011/01/food-accepted-as-cultural-heritage-food.html (accessed 21 May 2013).

Gillespie, C. (2001) *European Gastronomy into the 21st Century*. Oxford: Butterworth Heinemann.

Gov.UK (2013) Protected food names: Guidance for producers. See www.gov.uk/protected-food-names-guidance-for-producers#how-to-apply (accessed 15 December 201).

Hall, C.M. (2012) Culinary tourism: Why the interest in the cuisine, food and tourism relationship. In M. Mair and D. Wagner (eds) *Culinary Tourism: Products, Regions, Tourists, Philosophy* (pp. 3–12). Vienna: Springer.

IPCC (2007) Global crop yield is at risk of decline at a temperature increase of 1°C. WG 2 Technical Report 07. See www.climatechange-foodsecurity.org/edited_copy_of_ipcc.html (accessed 4 June 2013).

Los Angeles Times (2007) When chefs part ways, who gets custody of the recipes? See www.latimes.com/local/la-fo-journal3oct03,1,1161214.story#axzz2wPbqbnBT (accessed 22 May 2013).

Mushita, A. and Thompson, C. (2013) More ominous than climate change? Global policy threats to African food production. *African Studies Quarterly* 13 (4), 1–25.

Paarlberg, R. (2010) *Food Politics*. New York: Oxford University Press.

Richards, G. (2002) Gastronomy: An essential ingredient in tourism production and consumption. In A.-M. Hjalager and G. Richards (eds) *Tourism and Gastronomy* (pp. 3–21). London: Routledge.

Santilli, J. (2012) *Agrobiodiversity and the Law*. Oxford: Earthscan.

Scarpato, R. and Daniele, R. (2003) New global cuisine: Tourism, authenticity and sense of place in postmodern gastronomy. In C.M. Hall, L. Sharples, R. Mitchell, M. Macionis and B. Cambourne (eds) *Food Tourism around the World* (pp. 296-313). Oxford: Butterworth Heinemann.

Sukhadwala, S. (2012) The bogus quest for authentic food. *The Guardian*, 28 May. See www.theguardian.com/lifeandstyle/wordofmouth/2012/may/28/bogus-quest-for-authentic-food (accessed 4 June 2013).

Tansey, G. and Worsley, T. (1995) *The Food System*. London: Earthscan.

The Scottish Government (2013) Protected food names. See www.scotland.gov.uk/Topics/Business-Industry/Food-Industry/national-strategy/rep/PFNs/faqs (accessed 15 December 2013).

Trommetter, M. (2008) *Intellectual Property Rights in Agriculture and Agro-Food Biotechnologies to 2030*. Report for OECD International Futures. See www.oecd.org/sti/futures/long-termtechnologicalsocietalchallenges/40926131.pdf (accessed 10 June 2013).

UNESCO (2013) Lists of intangible cultural heritage and Register of best safeguarding practices. See www.unesco.org/culture/ich/en/lists (accessed 15 December 2013).

UN Food and Agriculture Organization (2010) Africa hunger and poverty facts. See www.worldhunger.org/articles/Learn/africa_hunger_facts.htm (accessed 12 December 2013).

Wiber, M. (2010) Intellectual property rights and food security: The international legal battle over patenting staple crops. In O. Hospes and I. Hadiprayitno (eds) *Governing Food Security* (pp. 272–291). Wageningen: Wageningen Academic Publishers.

Wolinsky, C. (2012) Travel, eat, learn. Discovering the world through food. In M. Mair and D. Wagner (eds) *Culinary Tourism: Products, Regions, Tourists, Philosophy* (pp. 189–195). Vienna: Springer.

World Trade Organisation (2013) What are international property rights. See www.wto.org/english/tratop_e/trips_e/intel1_e.htm (accessed 15 December 2013).

Part 3

Food Tourism and the Future Tourist

11 Back to the Future: The Affective Power of Food in Reconstructing a Tourist Imaginary

David Scott and Tara Duncan

Highlights

- The chapter focuses on future food experiences through the tourist imaginary.
- The future food tourist becomes reflexive, engaging with multiple 'scapes' as they travel.
- Future food tourists make use of food as an agent to reconstruct global imaginaries.
- Future food tourism moves from a focus on leisure to a focus on the embodied search for belonging.

Introduction

In order for the body to become corporeally mobile in travel, one must first construct an imaginary to sustain that mobility; this includes, for example, not only motivations but also performances of everyday life, a kind of performative baggage that allows an individual to be-in-the-world. Increasingly however food can be seen as a significant motivation to travel: as a key constituent of the tourist imaginary as well as an essential part of humans' biological and social existence.

In thinking about and discussing the future – it is already *in-becoming* (if it has not already become) a 'reality' in the mind. In a world of liquid modernity (Bauman, 2000) one of the only resources one has to anchor oneself is an interpretation of the spaces and places which are individually constructed. Thus, how sense is made of the world is an inherently imaginative process. In this chapter the focus is on future food experiences through the tourist imaginary.

In much of the toured world (and indeed much of the 'emergent' touring world) food is vaunted as an attraction, yet often remains an impediment to travel (Cohen & Avieli, 2004). Consequently, in order to maximise the potential value to be extracted from tourism (i.e. to get as many people travelling as possible), food has been, and generally remains, operationalised and marketed in a way that seeks to minimise any possible risk to the individual which in turn might negatively impact on destination selection. The focus of much marketing attention is not on food itself but rather on its symbolic relations with an individual's ontological security (Giddens, 1991). Food therefore appears emblematic of the tension within tourism. It is a supposed escape from the everyday (in that one can 'try' new and exotic foodstuffs) as it simultaneously challenges the very thing one seeks to escape – the mundane performance of everyday life (or rather, what is cooked at home). Becoming corporeally mobile brings into sharp relief the differences between daily life and those places and people who are 'toured'. Thus, to all intents and purposes, much of the tourism literature posits the tourist existing within de Certeau's (1984) rationalised bubble.

There has been (in the West) an increase in demand for opportunities to perform and consume food in different ways and different places. Not only in the places and spaces that might be called home, but also in those that are visited as tourists. In the toured world this is made evident through new and innovative experiences that cater to the so-called gastronomic/culinary/food tourist. Accordingly, these food-situated experiences have moved from being a support activity to becoming primary attractions themselves, where food (and its concomitant experiences) becomes a motivation for corporeal mobility and subsequent destination choice.

This chapter sets out to give priority to the imaginary of the contemporary food tourist in order to 'think' of and about the future. The chapter follows Bergman et al. (2010: 050) in that the futures suggested here are 'a loose coupling between mechanisms and outcome' where critical social science is utilised to explain the possibilities for the future. Through a blurring of prediction and prognosis (after Bergman et al., 2010) the chapter recognises the role of the present as a mechanism for future imaginaries. Through this lens, the chapter looks to what might influence the future imagination of the individual rather than the future of the tourist. It moves past thinking about food in the context of future trends to consideration of future influences on the imagination and performance of the consumption of food and the construction of the identity of the food tourist.

As such, the chapter illustrates the role of the imaginary in becoming (virtually) mobile and finishes by exploring how the meeting of east and west might necessitate re-imaginings of the experience of the tourist interested in food. The chapter thus concurs with Aradau and Munster (2011: 2) who suggest, 'imagination and sensorial experience play an increasing role, alongside more traditional forms of knowledge, [in] our attempts to inhabit unknown futures'.

'We Are What We Imagine We Eat' – The Food Tourist in Late Modernity

Food is, of course, an essential part of any travel experience. However, whilst it is integral to travelling experiences, it is necessary to consider the role food currently plays in the tourist imaginary and how the food and drink imaginary might be deconstructed to offer fertile ground for 'future' tourism researchers. It is the imagination of the tourist and the consequences of those imaginings that result in the tourist-in-becoming. Moreover, whilst the imagination is about the future, it is also integral to the present. Therefore, for those tourists who are motivated by food, past experiences can mediate the imagined future.

At this point, it is necessary to take issue with and problematise the motivations of food tourists that have resulted in a conflation of tourist typologies. Whilst the idea of the food tourist might well encompass multiple motivations, by not thinking of these motivations separately there is a risk of apoliticising food tourism. In doing so the food tourist might be seen as occupying a space of consumerist characteristics where other aspects concerning the construction of individual identity and consumptive experience become overlooked, for example, those of food and health (Foxall, 2010), hedonism, and the 'body'. Moreover, limiting the study of food and tourism to *one* 'identity' – that of the food tourist – suggests the (imaginary of the) food tourist is constructed primarily around the notion of (consumer) consumption. There is, of course, production involved. However the means of production (the interaction or 'experience' in the case of tourism and hospitality) are commoditised in order to attract and be attractive to the consumer thus claiming the focus of the research agenda and neglecting other, possibly more constructive but less or even non-economic – forms of consumption (Goodheart, 2012).

Understanding motivation is important in thinking about the future; there is the suggestion, for example, that the idea of futurist cooking was not only politically motivated but potentially fascist in its alignment (Poole, 2012). Likewise, the unproblematic appropriation of the notion of the 'gastronomic' individual as a cover-all for anyone with an interest in food also needs addressing. Gastronomy is inherently about class distinctions. As Powell and Prasad (2010: 114) suggest, it can act as 'disseminator of certain lifestyle preferences and critic of others'. Here for example one is reminded by Bourdieu (1984/2010: 33) that 'it must never be forgotten that the working-class "aesthetic" is a dominated "aesthetic" which is constantly obliged to define itself in terms of the dominant aesthetic'. The performance of gastronomy is *not* available to all – it is a function of capital – economic, cultural and social. To neglect this is to essentialise the study of food and tourism.

While Hall and Mitchell (2001: 308) define food tourism as 'visitation to primary and secondary food producers, food festivals, restaurants and specific locations for which food tastings and/or experiencing the attributes of specialist food production regions are the primary motivating factor for travel', it is necessary to highlight characteristics that go towards constructing the food tourist 'imaginary' (rather than those characteristics individuals respond to when questioned). As such, and taking inspiration from Hall and (2006), it is worth moving away from seeing the food tourist as based on economic impacts towards developing an understanding of social identity, framed in the case of this chapter within symbolic interactionism. In using 'food tourist' rather than any other term, there is not an assumption of subsuming other definitions or understandings of tourists' relationships with food. Here, the 'food tourist' encompasses the reflective (reflexive), experiential, local and global nature of much food-related tourism.

What is the Imaginary?

It is generally understood that imagination is used to articulate a sense of self and at the same time a sense of who one wants to be(come). As such, it is these processes that lead to imagined communities and, indeed, societies of the future; for example the belief in a sustainable future (Powell, 2012). It is therefore important to understand the complexities of imaginaries. After all, as Althusser (2008) would suggest of neoliberalism, the relationship (and power) between an ideology – in this case (neoliberal) consumerism – and the individual is through the imaginary. Here one is led to believe they can have it all through the power of economic capital and a free market economy. How the imaginary is understood can range from the construction of cultural beliefs and subsequent negotiation of identity (Hall, 1990) to Lacan's fantasy (see Jameson, 1977) to a way of being (Lévi-Strauss, 1966). In this chapter, the key concepts put forward by Lee, Taylor, Warner, Gaonkar are made use of as a way of conceiving the social imaginary (in Gaonkar, 2002). For the purposes of this chapter:

> social imaginaries are ways of understanding the social that become social entities themselves, mediating collective life … They are first person subjectivities that build upon implicit understandings that underlie and make possible common practices. They are embedded in the habitus of a population or are carried in modes of address, stories, symbols, and the like.

The imaginary in a double sense: they exist by virtue of representation or implicit understandings, even when they acquire immense institutional force; and they are the means by which individuals understand their identities and their place in the world. (Gaonkar, 2002: 4)

The emergence of food as a leisure activity as well as motivation to travel results in a rationalisation of the individual-as-consumer. Thus the food tourist, at least to date, remains primarily a discursive construction. Moreover this can result in a valorisation of the role of food and drink in authentic and meaningful tourist experiences. Hence current or contemporary images that surround food result in a lack of imagination, or at least, a 'thoughtless' imagination which Poole (2012: 20), borrowing from Adorno, argues results in 'the rage of the belly without any consequent sublimation into mind'.

One does not only imagine 'food' but makes use of food as an agent to construct global imaginaries (Phillips, 2006). In the tourism context this is enacted through the (co)development of explicit tourist (mobile) foodways that may or may not go on to become part of emplaced as well as non-placed foodways. One example is the rise of McDonald's as both a globalised and globalising space (Ritzer & Liska, 1997). McDonald's, itself built around notions of mobility (the drive-thru), has, in part, mobilised on a global scale for at-risk-bodies (the tourist) and in turn becomes a locus of globalisation in and of itself. Thus, in understanding food as a base biological need, McDonald's and the like have facilitated the development of mass tourism on a global scale – where the individual is able to become (imaginatively) the global subject.

As such there is, as Phillips (2006: 43) argues, a deterritorialisation of particular foodways enabled through the phenomenon of tourism which, however, is 'at the same time re-embedded in some [distant] place, as changing ideas about food and the world are reinscribed by people'. In turn, both consumer and consumed become 'embedded in the social institution of globalisation' (Jerome, 2007: 72). Given the mobilities of food (and food culture), along with tourists consuming in-situ, food, both in the present and into the future, remains central to the production of a global imaginary – positively in remembered food experiences (see Kauppinen-Räisänen et al., 2013) and negatively such as through food scares, droughts, etc. It can be suggested that many in the West, whilst attempting to distance themselves from the images (and imaginings) of mass-produced and globalised foodways, remain embedded in such globalising imaginaries. Here one engages with a somewhat postmodern desire to decrease 'speed' as evidenced by a rise in 'slow' movements, for example slow food (see Andrews, 2008), but simultaneously want imported ('authentic') foods, and the ability to travel to gastronomic sites/sights at distant locations in record times (and in record numbers). It is to representations of the mobility/mobilising of the imagination that the chapter now turns.

The glossy magazine, television show, food blog and tourist brochure are spatial practices. They are representations but also exist as representational spaces; where there is a mediation of particular ideological positions (i.e. neoliberalism, capitalism and so on). Thus the social construction of such 'space' is important to note in order to understand what it is that is being offered, or not, in constructing the imaginary. By thinking of food as a (very real) challenge to the economic benefits to be derived from tourism there is an institutional imperative to mediate and regulate the imagination of the individual. It is through such mediatised images and representations that the tension between neophilia (enthusiasm for the new or novel) and neophobia (fear of the new or of new experiences) arises. The desire to consume food-as-culture is pitted against the need to mitigate the risk of food to the 'body'. Consequently, imaginings of future (touristic) food experiences comprise this friction between desire and risk. Thus in the context of food one can recognise a positioning of the social actor as lacking agency. Rather, one is positioned as the rationalised individual-as-consumer where practicalities (such as risk) dominate the 'offering', in this case food.

In saying this, understanding tourism as an institutional (economic) force is to acknowledge how the system makes use of individuals' need to construct images of the world around them, to give sense to their daily lives and their imagined futures, and thus to not challenge their sensibilities. This again supports the suggestion that the 'imagination is absent' or is at least encouraged to be absent. This is increasingly challenged by the proliferation of food-as-lifestyle magazines and food television shows. Along with the position within (Western) society of those involved in the production of these representations, many aspire to emulate the people and foods within these media. Yet, it is more than the food they seek to emulate. One could suggest that this is a democratisation of 'taste' through food and culture, perhaps however it is about the massification or industrialisation of 'taste' (and so back to Bourdieu, 1984/2010; Mitchell & Scott, 2013).

In much of the current 'food' media two defining characteristics can be noted: food as a support activity and food as performed. In the first, food represents the experience of tourism or leisure, even luxury, yet is often hidden behind the façade of service. In the second, individuals are encouraged to imagine themselves consuming both food and also 'culture'. The latter can be seen as the valorisation of authentic and meaningful tourist experiences, where one is encouraged to valorise or perform culture through food, imaginings of food and knowledge (or lack thereof) of food practices.

Understanding the media as representational space can then lead to thoughts of how such representations might drive consumer consumption, act to hide otherness (for example what type of food is portrayed, how is culture displayed or not displayed?) and highlight mechanisms being used to romanticise our current and future encounters with food. Thus, discursively and performatively, food media constructs and mediates imaginings of everyday food practices, urging the individual to 'do' travel. Such experiences constructed and consumed within everyday lives are therefore central to constructing a tourist imaginary. TV food shows, the glossy food-travel magazines and the increasing proliferation of 'foodie' blogs, lead to a consumptive performance that is 'experiential, vicarious and at times voyeuristic' (Stevens & MacLaran, 2005: 290). However mediatised representations of food also attend to '[t]he frustrations that attend embodied reality' (Nast & Pile, 1998: 49). While squirming and gagging in sympathy – there is the opportunity to live vicariously through Anthony Bourdain's consumption of snake blood, bile and liver in a voyeuristic orgy of virtual 'eatertainment' in the television show 'No Reservations Required' (see Bourdain, 2006). Here the paradox of relative corporeal stillness within a form of virtual mobility can be recognised. While more often than not bodies are 'still' when imagined travelling with Bourdain, food is consumed virtually through such armchair, and kitchen table, travel.

Media sources thus act as a confluence of 'dream-worlds' which can be made real by a visit to the restaurant, and where further imaginaries are then constructed through design and performance. Through aesthetic labour – the reconfiguration of space through encounters with staff and media (posters on the wall, soundscapes from other places) – the 'ethnic' restaurant becomes a place which an individual can step into and out of as they wish. It allows the individual to be both nostalgic and to imagine future travels; the real and virtual consumption of food thus enabling imaginative outcomes.

Molz (2004), for example, talks of the individual as the culinary tourist – visiting the (local) Thai restaurant, often in search of knowingly (staged) authentic experiences. Here the imaginary is pre-constructed through both (potentially) past travel experiences and TV shows, food magazines and, so, 'understandings' of what Thai food and culture is. Or week by week the individual is a voyeur like in Luke Nguyen's TV show, 'Greater Mekong'. Over a period of 10 weeks, minds and taste buds are 'mobilised', moving from Vientiane to Vietnam, as those same bodies physically move from his restaurants in Sydney's Surrey Hills to Kings Cross. In seeking to authenticate these experiences one makes future destination choices based on these experiences. Thus, the imaginary is used to 'book' the reality. The ethnic restaurant allows one to 'play' with their imagination, to negotiate the space between the virtual and the possibility of a future embodied reality.

However, whilst imaginations can and do travel – without the body one cannot become a corporeally mobile tourist and thus there is a need to pull the 'imagination back to the place of the human body and the physical world that can never become entirely virtual' (Hillis, 1998: 51). These imaginings lead to what might be considered trans-global knowledge experiences where shared 'images' act to construct communities of practice, or perhaps, in the case of food, market cultures. The individual thus attempts to construct both a virtual and real camaraderie by constructing and performing 'relations of mutual interdependence, including engagement in shared projects of imagining a better future' (Calhoun, 2002: 171). However in constructing the imaginary of the food tourist, vestiges of Anderson's (1991) imagined community can clearly be seen, where the food tourist seeks to define themselves as part of a community 'based not on physical proximity and relations with close intimates but on an imagined proximity to distant others' (Bajde, 2012: 360). Therefore, it is not only those upon whom the food tourists gaze and (culturally) graze, but also with those whose wider food values are shared through collective consumption of both mediated and tourist experiences that are implicit in the imaginary.

The Future: Reflexivity in Action

Thus, to understand the food tourist of the future one must not neglect how and to what extent alternative world views and knowledge(s) have and are impacting on the construction of the imaginary. However one must also acknowledge that tourism can be considered a shared community of practice produced and reproduced through the individual's imaginative engagement of affect and desire.

TV shows, magazines, blogs and such like cannot be considered a neutral space as they offer representations of both the 'real' and the 'imagined'. Thus, it is a space that captures the imagination and therefore 'cannot remain indifferent space...It has been lived in...with all the partiality of the imagination' (Bachelard, 1994: xxxvi). The social actor, through constructing the imaginary, is able to appropriate and challenge the representational space of the mediated images of food (Lefebvre, 1991). There is a move by an increasing number of individuals (for example, Feifer (1985) post-tourist) to engage in the search for what might be considered existential authenticity through food (Wang, 2000). Simultaneously, the rise in post-consumerism (or even anti-consumerism) shows an increasing awareness of and attempt to perform of an ethics-of-consumption.

In becoming the reflexive self, the food tourist has begun and will continue to question the orthodoxy of current relationships between, for example, food and health. There will be a move away from the food tourist (as foodie) performing orthoexia (having a preoccupation with food) built around the search for the perfect identity and a supposed reconnection with spirituality (Janas-Kozik et al., 2012). Rather there will be a move towards a more embodied and performative engagement with the multiple 'scapes' through which the food tourist travels. Here, for example, the mainstream food tourist will engage in experiences such as wwoofing (worldwide opportunities on organic farms), as well as seeking the possibility for other existential encounters with the lived everyday food practices of the 'toured-other'. As such, the imagined self will seek to challenge a capitalist identity and (re)move the everyday self to other-selves in the search for (meaningful) inter-subjective encounters. While the food tourist – in any iteration – will remain a small part of the overall tourist market, increasing numbers of tourists will show interest in this type of tourism. Driven not by an imaginary recon-structed through cooking shows and food magazines, their motivation will be derived from (re)engagement with media images derived from more gen-eral, local, national and world events. This will come from an array of con-tested media spaces, for example education, images of famine, food shortages and security as well as new modes of nationalism driven by food security and thus resulting in the construction of new imaginaries (at least in the 'West').

The previous discussion has presented a privileged viewpoint which has been dominated by a Western, middle-class discourse. However, global food-scapes are rapidly changing. No longer is the (mass) production of food des-tined for Western tables, nor the type of foodstuff, production methods or places of production dominated by Western ownership. Here the imaginary becomes about constructing a fantasy (and internally) performed in order to deal with the psychological issues (real or imagined) of contested landscapes (ownership, use, representations of, as representational spaces). Domestic political, cultural and social landscapes become increasingly understood by the reflexive self as representational spaces of contested performance. Local takes on a new (and renewed) significance. Tying in with restrictions on corporeal mobility brought about by the reflexive selves' engagement with climate change and increasing value placed on 'not travelling', travelling locally or domestically (or not at all) becomes the new way to perform dis-tinction. However, this imaginary is illusionary – after all, the farmer, espe-cially in food-producing nations such as New Zealand and Australia, needs to sell outside the area, businesses need inbound consumers and tourists, and locals do not necessarily want to be limited to 'local' food.

West Meets East?

Whilst much tourism research to date has privileged the developed world, there is a need to also attend to the future as it relates to the individual in and from the (economic) developing world. As with changing markets within tourism more broadly, a change in the demographics of those motivated by 'food' – from an ageing Western tourist to a younger Eastern (Asian) tourist – will also be seen. However, whilst many of these younger Asian tourists may have been born in, for example, China, an increasing number will have lived and/or been educated in the West.

Subsequently, both shared imaginaries and parallel imaginaries will be evident where the toured-other and touring-other renegotiates the con-struction of touristic space. Chinese and Australian tourists configure the same (mutual) touristic space through conflicting (but parallel) images. For example, imaginings of 'local' where the Chinese individual tours the source of their food and wealth whilst the Australian tourist visits the same destinations for a glimpse of their 'own' heritage through the very same foodscapes.

Thus there will be increasing demand for inbound tourists from parts of Asia to view or 'gaze' and interact with sites of food production. As such there will, for example, be an increase in demand for visits to sites (and sights) of food production like dairy farms in New Zealand or wheat farms in Australia that are owned by companies based within particular tourist-generating markets, where images of food and production mediate the future tourist imaginary – much like current Western tourists' visits to tea plantations (Cheng et al., 2010). From this, initially at least, there may be increasing tensions between two contested imaginaries – one constructed as the capitalist-focused production of food for its subsequent consumption as a leisure activity placing the individual as a consumer performing the myth of consumer sovereignty (Korczynski & Ott, 2004), the other driven by a reflexive engagement with a politics of food.

This will not only occur in spaces of production, but also consumption, often in negative ways. As there are increases in visitation by food tourists from emergent markets, so too is there a market response to these tourists. Businesses will develop food offerings based on Western notions of consumer markets with tensions being caused when the 'local' imaginary is challenged by cultural discourses centred on, for example, the use of halal production methods. Whilst this is widespread at the industrial level (for example, in New Zealand most meat production is carried out to meet halal certification) there is little mediation of this in the space of local consumption – the restaurant and supermarket. Such images, including prominent certification in marketing collateral of food-related businesses will act to problematise notions of 'local'. Contrastingly, as suggested in the discussion of the culinary tourist above, this may result in further authentication of the 'ethnic' imaginary linked to the local ethnic restaurant. The question then becomes: is all this leading to an increasingly alienated imagination where the Western individual is feeling increasingly threatened by a future mediated imaginary and if so, to what extent is tourism implicated? On the other hand, does this 'authentication' allow 'other' tourist markets to mitigate their 'fears' about the food they consume on their travels?

In attempting to answer this question, this chapter sees the future as being about an emergent, hopeful food tourist. Here there is a blurring of cultural boundaries – where the shared production and consumption of food, at multiple scales and spaces, results in food tourism as a truly cosmopolitical endeavour (Rorty, 1998). For this to happen there is the requirement for a reflexive and thoughtful consumption of images (and experiences) which in turn will result in an embodied (re)imagining of the food tourist. The images and texts of the future will be mediated through technologies that encourage the individual to construct their imaginary through not just what is currently thought of as the consumer imagination, but increasingly via embodied performances and encounters with and through virtual spaces. New and imaginative mobilities along with emergent technologies encourage the performance of the reflexive individual resulting in a sharing of what might historically have been regarded as divergent imaginaries. Thus rather than tourism being about discordant performances and understood through binary distinctions, there is blurring if not crossing of such (imagined) borders (not only national or political borders but also social and furthermore, borders of the body).

As such the use of affective technologies will begin to engage all the senses, realigning the tourist-as-consumer to the tourist-as-citizen which enables the individual to construct an imaginary embedded within what they perceive as an ethics of consumption. This will result in a subsequent re-invention of the food 'tourist' (e.g. Carrier & Luetchford, 2012; Grasseni, 2012). The mediation of food narratives by new technologies illustrates that the imagination is not disembodied; rather it is embodied, affective and performative – it can and does 'do things'.

Concluding Remarks: Implications for the Future of Food Tourism

The implications for the future of food tourism include multiple challenges to the current commodified, economic model of food experiences performed by the tourist. The impact of wider social change, for example the massification of eating out in the Western context, will challenge previously understood hedonistic imaginaries constructed historically through the practice of gastronomy as a form of social distinction.

This will result in new cultural modes of production and consumption that will appear as a result of such social change but will also be attributed to resistance to, and a confrontation with, globalisation as the absolute horizon of the future (McSweeney, 2011). This will offer an opening up of, and awareness to, the possibilities afforded by the action and praxis of food and eating to a wider global audience. However this change in the emergence of a reflexive consumer will result in the destabilising of space and place. A result of this will be a movement of the periphery to the centre and the centre to the periphery enabled through new technologies and networks of mobility(ies).

As such there are two aspects of the future that stand out. Modes of consumption: here the performance of food tourism becomes an increasingly contested space as the ideology of conspicuous consumption and marketplace consumerism become ever more challenged. Overt displays of (destructive) consumption become, to many people, socially unacceptable. The result is that new forms of production and consumption will emerge in the imaginary. For example, food security and associated issues will come to dominate the tourist discourse. Similarly there will be a reimagining of landscapes. As has happened in the UK, what was once agricultural land will be taken out of production and made use of as simulacra in order to spectacularise agriculture, food production, culture and society. Here the future food imaginary will be built around the space of nostalgia with increasing use made of technologically mediated signifiers that engage the rural idyll as an ethical consumerscape comprising landscape, taskscape and experiencescape. Second, the future will also see a rise in demand from individuals coming from emergent economies who wish to engage with the spaces and places of food production and consumption. As such there will be a blurring of national boundaries whereby international ownership of both touring and land leads to the blurring of what is understood to be 'home' and 'citizenship'.

Hence the mediation of tour(ing) experiences becomes more complex. Undoubtedly food remains a source used in the search for cultural identity both individually and collectively. However this will move from the use of food tourism experiences as primarily leisure to a focus upon the embodied search for belonging. Thus, rather than an emphasis upon the food tourist-in-being there will be a refocusing upon the importance of understanding the food tourist-in-becoming, where food will allow the individual a sense of belonging in multiple locations as well as subject positions. The demand for existential experiences (mindful, meaningful, affective) will encourage the development and communication of images that result in the reimagining of the future food tourist. Consequently, the concerns of this (newly) reflexive 'consumer' will result in an imaginary embedded within a praxis of ethics.

References

Althusser, L. (2008) *On Ideology*. London: Verso Books.
Anderson, B.R.O.G. (1991) *Imagined Communities: Reflections on the Origin and Spread of Nationalism*. London: Verso Books.
Andrieu, G. (2000) *The Slow Food Story: Politics and Pleasure*. Montreal: McGill-Queen's University Press.
Aradau, C. and Munster, R.V. (2011) *Politics of Catastrophe: Genealogies of the Unknown*. London: Routledge.
Bachelard, G. (1994) *The Poetics of Space*. Boston, MA: Beacon Press.
Bajde, D. (2012) Mapping the imaginary of charitable giving. *Consumption Markets & Culture* 15, 358–373.
Bauman, Z. (2000) *Liquid Modernity*. Cambridge: Polity Press.
Bergman, A., Karlsson, J.C. and Axelsson, J. (2010) Truth claims and explanatory claims – An ontology typology of future studies. *Futures* 42, 857–865.
Bourdain, A. (2006) *The Nasty Bits Collected Cuts, Useable Trim, Scaps and Bones*. London: Bloomsbury.
Bourdieu, P. (1984/2010) *Distinction: A Social Critique of the Judgement of Taste*. London: Routledge.

Calhoun, C.J. (2002) Imagining solidarity: Cosmopolitanism, constitutional patriotism, and the public sphere. *Public Culture* 14, 147.

Carrier, J.G. and Luetchford, P. (2012) *Ethical Consumption: Social Value and Economic Practice*. Oxford: Berghahn.

Cheng, S.-W., Xu, F.-F., Zhang, J. and Zhang, Y.-T. (2010) Tourists' attitudes toward tea tourism: A case study in Xinyang, China. *Journal of Travel & Tourism Marketing* 27, 211–220.

Cohen, E. and Avieli, N. (2004) Food in tourism. Attraction and impediment. *Annals of Tourism Research* 31, 755–778.

de Certeau, M. (1984) *The Practice of Everyday Life*. Berkeley: University of California Press.

Feifer, M. (1985) *Going Places: The Ways of the Tourist from Imperial Rome to the Present Day*. London: Macmillan.

Foxall, G.R. (2010) Invitation to consumer behavior analysis. *Journal of Organizational Behavior Management* 30, 92–109.

Gaonkar, D.P. (2002) Toward new imaginaries: An introduction. *Public Culture* 14 (1), 1–19.

Giddens, A. (1991) *Modernity and Self-Identity: Self and Society in the Late Modern Age*. Cambridge: Polity.

Goodheart, E. (2012) Our consuming problem. *Society* 49, 212–215.

Grasseni, C. (2012) Re-inventing food: The ethics of developing local food. In J.G. Carrier and P. Luetchford (eds) *Ethical Consumption: Social Value and Economic Practice* (pp. 198–216). Oxford: Berghahn.

Hall, C.M. (2006) Culinary tourism and regional development: From slow food to slow tourism? *Tourism Review International* 9 (4), 303–305.

Hall, C.M. and Mitchell, R.D. (2001) Wine and food tourism. In N. Douglas, N. Douglas and R. Derrett (eds) *Special Interest Tourism: Context and Cases*. Brisbane: John Wiley & Sons Australia.

Hall, S. (1990) Cultural identity and diaspora. *Identity: Community, Culture, Difference* 2, 222–237.

Hillis, K. (1998) The human language machine. In H.J. Nast and S. Pile (eds) *Places Through the Body* (pp. 39–53). London: Routledge.

Jameson, F. (1977) Imaginary and symbolic in Lacan: Marxism, psychoanalytic criticism, and the problem of the subject. *Yale French Studies*, 338–395.

Janas-Kozik, M., Zejda, J., Stochel, M., Brozek, G., Janas, A. and Jelonek, I. (2012) Orthorexia – A new diagnosis? *Psychiatria Polska* 46, 441–450.

Jerome, K.P. (2007) A case of McDonald's restaurant, the built environment and the perpetuation of the phenomenon of globalisation. In C. McCarthy and G. Matthewson (eds) *Proceedings of the Third Conference of the Interior Design/Interior Architecture Educators Association: Inhabiting Risk* (pp. 71–79). Wellington: New Zealand.

Kauppinen-Räisänen, H., Gummerus, J. and Lehtola, K. (2013) Remembered eating experiences described by the self, place, food, context and time. *British Food Journal* 115, 666–685.

Korczynski, M. and Ott, U. (2004) When production and consumption meet: Cultural contradictions and the enchanting myth of customer sovereignty. *Journal of Management Studies* 41, 575–599.

Lefebvre, H. (1991) *The Production of Space*. Oxford: Blackwell.

Lévi-Strauss, C. (1966) *The Savage Mind*. Chicago: University of Chicago Press.

McSweeney, J. (2011) Finitude and violence: Žižek versus Derrida on politics. *Kritike* 5, 41–58.

Mitchell, R.M. and Scott. D.G. (2013) A critical turn in hospitality and tourism research. In A. Murcott, W. Belasco and P. Jackson (eds) *The Handbook of Food Research* (pp. 229–252). London: Bloomsbury Academic.

Molz, J.G. (2004) Authenticity and culinary tourism in Thai restaurants. In L.M. Long (ed.) *Culinary Tourism* (pp. 53–75). Lexington: University Press of Kentucky.

Nast, H.J. and Pile, S. (1998) *Places Through the Body*. London: Routledge.

Phillips, L. (2006) Food and globalization. *Annual Review of Anthropology* 35, 37–57.

Poole, S. (2012) *You Aren't What You Eat: Fed Up With Gastroculture*. London: Union Books.

Powell, F. (2012) 'Think globally, act locally': Sustainable communities, modernity and development. *GeoJournal* 77, 141–152.

Powell, H. and Prasad, S. (2010) 'As seen on TV' the celebrity expert: How taste is shaped by lifestyle media. *Cultural Politics* 6, 111–124.

Ritzer, G. and Liska, A. (1997) 'McDisneyization' and 'post-tourism': Complementary perspectives on contemporary tourism. In C. Rojek and J. Urry (eds) *Touring Cultures: Transformations of Travel and Theory* (pp. 96–109). London: Routledge.

Rorty, R. (1998) Justice as a larger loyalty. In P. Cheah and B. Robbins (eds) *Cosmopolitics: Thinking and Feeling Beyond the Nation* (pp. 45–58). Minneapolis: University of Minnesota Press.

Stevens, L. and Maclaran, P. (2005) Exploring the 'shopping imaginary': The dreamworld of women's magazines. *Journal of Consumer Behaviour* 4, 282–292.

Wang, N. (2000) *Tourism and Modernity: Sociological Analysis*. Oxford: Pergamon.

12 The Changing Demographics of Male Foodies: Why Men Cook But Don't Wash Up![1]

Ian Yeoman and Una McMahon-Beattie

Highlights

- Men see food as a leisure activity rather than a chore.
- *The Man Foodie* is British, male, aged between 25 and 44 years old, is upwardly mobile, from the socio-economic categories ABC1,[2] loves to cook for sexual desire and holidays abroad.
- From a future tourism perspective, a conceptual framework is presented that represents the trend as authenticity, place, foodies and craftsmanship.

Introduction

Food is a hot topic, constantly on our television screens and part of popular culture. Consumers want to know about the food they are eating and are genuinely interested in cooking food. Indeed food tourism is classed as a mainstream experience (Sharples, 2003). This interest in food means men do a greater share of cooking at home than at any point in time since records exist; furthermore, it seems likely that this represents a greater contribution to what has become an essential part of our lives in modern history. Younger men, both singletons and those living with their partner, are playing a greater role in the kitchen, far more than their fathers did. Furthermore, they are enjoying this greater involvement. In fact it is viewed as both a passion and a leisure activity by this new generation of men in the kitchen (FSR, 2013).

Men are claiming a stake in the kitchen in a particular way. These are young, upwardly mobile and unabashedly masculine men who love to cook and love to be seen to cook. This trend has been created by a wide range of forces from multiculturalism, travel and the single lifestyle and is one which will continue to grow in the future. *The Man Foodie* is about pleasure, praise and potential seduction. He is British, aged between 25 and 44 years old and from the socio-economic categories ABC1. This chapter explores how *The Man Foodie* has evolved and what it means in British society. It examines the relationship between food and culture and concludes with a discussion on the future implications for the food tourism industry.

Gastronomy is the New Rock 'N' Roll

Richards (2013: 12) has written in the magazine of the *Sunday Star Times*:

Today's gastronomy provides the thrills that rock'n'roll used to. New restaurants appeal to sense of discovery. Our diets can reflect our identities, our politics. For fans of thrash metal and/or live octopus sashimi, food is a way to sate cravings for the maximal, visceral and extreme. Cuisine exists in a cultural realm where people can engage in status displays.

So food is the new rock 'n' roll by which men express their masculine identity. It is Jamie Oliver in the TV series *The Naked Chef* who cooks with passion, fun and as a lifestyle activity rather than a domestic chore (Hollows, 2003). Jamie Oliver is a man who negotiates the tension between 'The Man Foodie' and 'new lad' with references to football, music, booze and babes but avoids any reference to seriousness as 'you gotta laugh' (Jackson *et al.*, 2001: 27). Heston Blumenthal's aspirational wizardry aligns the preparation of food with history, folklore, nostalgia and science and Hugh Fearnley-Whittingstall's presents production-conscious, thinking man's real food. Gordon Ramsay's represents the macho man stance, turning cooking into a heroic task equal to the labours of Hercules. These celebrity chefs play an important role in society, by both mediating how consumers understand food and the role of cooking within society.

By 2030, the British man will be swapping football for culinary skills as chefs such as Gordon Ramsay become the new male icon. Why is this? Upwardly mobile men, aged between 25 and 44 are becoming passionate about food and the rewards it brings, such as pleasure, praise and love. No longer will conversations in the bar be about the Premier League or Manchester United but tips and recipes about the best food and wine. Across the world societies are changing. By 2040, there will be 10% more men in China than women (Yeoman, 2008) so men will have to work harder to impress those ladies – all in the hope of love. Society is observing a micro trend of men taking cookery courses, learning to appreciate wine, taking charge in the kitchen and food is becoming 'the' new hobby (Yeoman, 2012).

Simply put, *The Man Foodie* is on the increase especially in the ABC1 socio-economic category. This upwardly mobile singleton has had his overseas experience – travelled to Europe, Vietnam and Patagonia and beyond – and tasted a variety of foods, whether it is an authentic curry in India or steak from Argentina. These travels and experiences ensure they acquire cultural capital about food which means once they return to Britain they will shop in local ethnic supermarkets for authentic ingredients or search out the finest cheeses in specialist food shops (Yeoman, 2008).

Men like being in the kitchen, as modern kitchens are full of gadgets whether it is an ice-cream maker, electric food steamer or a chef's oven range. A modern kitchen also means less washing up as the built-in dishwasher takes care of that. Contemporary society and culture are also witnessing other changes such as a significant increase in the number of women entering the workforce, which can result in creating new pressures in the home. In these circumstances it might be expected that men would do their fair share of household duties, whether it is childcare, cleaning or shopping. However men have chosen to make their greatest contribution by involving themselves in the most creative area of housework – the kitchen. The male does not see this as a chore, but rather a hobby and a leisure experience. The kitchen for the male has become the 'new battle ground of the sexes' – somewhere to be better and to outdo their partner. It is also a place to escape, away from the drudgery of everyday life and the pressure of work. To men, the kitchen is the equivalent of a spa treatment or somewhere to create a masterpiece. From the love angle, men have an opportunity to seduce women, as according to Gravity (2012), one in six of British women struggle to cook basic dishes and 79% of women find cooking as a hobby attractive in men. So, what does this all mean?

Please Don't Ask *The Man Foodie* to Wash Up as Gender Does Matter

From a historical perspective men have generally had little involvement with the preparation of food; the growing importance of men in the nation's kitchens is a recent development. Indeed, until the development of the stove in the 18th century, kitchens did not form part of the typical home. Instead food was largely bought out of home and warmed in front of an open fire. Technological developments play an increasingly important role in kitchens and the amount of time spent on cooking and washing up has declined significantly in recent years. While there is a temptation to attribute this change to declining standards in kitchens, it is linked rather to the existence of a greater number of dishwashers, microwaves and other labour-saving devices. Consumers are eating out more as affluence rises and a greater proportion of time is being spent on leisure activities out of the home. The simultaneous growth of interest in food and cooking with the continued growth in the purchase of convenience foods has often been seen as a contradiction of sorts. It is proposed here, however, that these developments are in fact complimentary. According to the Office of National Statistics (ONS) British men in 1961 spent on average five minutes per day cooking and washing up, in 2005 this had risen to 27 minutes per day which is a five-fold increase.

However, this does not mean men are domestic goddesses. According to research by the Future Foundation (2012) there is a clear gender disparity across a range of domestic responsibilities and chores. While men are more likely to undertake a handful of responsibilities, such as putting out the bins, it is women who play a much greater role in areas such as cooking and cleaning. In many instances, men are also more likely than women to think that various domestic tasks are a shared family responsibility. Certainly men are cooking more frequently than in the past, motivated by many different reasons. A crucial development is that cooking for this new generation of males is not simply a matter of refuelling but rather cooking is seen as an enjoyable experience which to be relished. According to Szabo (2012), men are able to enjoy cooking because of gender inequalities. For example, home cooking is primarily done by women as they are the prime homemaker, whereas men have more flexibility as far as how they cook and when they cook. Having less identity invested in feeding and caring for others on a day-to-day basis, men tend to cook on a weekend, over a barbecue or on a special occasion. Szabo (2012) concludes that men may see cooking as leisure because when they do it, they are positioned as culinary artists or creative hobbyists. So, why do men, especially those aged between 25 and 44 years old have a passion for food and cooking?

I Want to be Jamie Oliver: Passion, Love and Food

Food is important to *The Man Foodie*. It is not simply for refuelling or the basic provision of sustenance. Food is a passion and a leisure activity as well as a necessity. However, this passion for food is in itself not the group's defining characteristic; it is their motivations that really distinguish them. The sensuality of food is key. This involves the richness of the experience, through the ability to control that richness by enhancing one flavour with another and the effect this has on other people. The display of this skill brings about other benefits such as the gaining of praise and the ability to impress others. The term, *The Man Foodie*, also expresses the growing acceptance that for men, cooking and masculinity are not mutually exclusive; rather they can be part of an attractive form of male identity. *The Man Foodie*

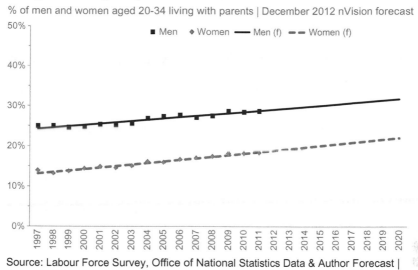

Young adults living with parents - forecast

% of men and women aged 20-34 living with parents | December 2012 nVision forecast

Source: Labour Force Survey, Office of National Statistics Data & Author Forecast | Base : Individuals aged 20-34, UK

Figure 12.1 Young adults living with parents
Source: ONS.

includes people from a wide variety of backgrounds but has some salient qualities. As noted earlier, they are especially heavily concentrated in men aged between 25 and 44. Indeed younger men still largely live in their parents' homes with 28.8% of 20 to 24-year-old men (see Figure 12.1) living at home in 2012. This is forecasted to rise to 31.7% by 2020.

The Man Foodie is upwardly mobile. This is not to say they are a lofty social elite. It is simply the case that they are often paid somewhat more than the average and therefore as a consequence are disproportionately in the ABC1 social grades. After all, this makes sense; cooking ability carries more status in these higher grades. Put simply, the wealthy cook more, and are in turn more impressed by skill shown in the kitchen. The rising affluence of these groups also means they can more readily afford the ingredients and are people who enjoy foreign cuisine. This ties into a wider trend in which foreign travel has become an almost necessary part of the lives of British people.

British Society and Cooking

Within just a few generations British society has been transformed. Many important aspects of British lives have changed fundamentally. The role of women in society is now very different. On the whole people marry later and also choose to have children later in life (Yeoman, 2008). The paths of people's lives and the expectations they have for themselves are, therefore, very different. These tectonic shifts in Britain's social make up have changed the way people eat and prepare food and the new male 'cook' has been propelled forward by these changes. He has risen to the challenges and opportunities of this new society and will continue to do so as these trends become ever more prominent. In this section the trends that are shaping British society from a food and cooking perspective will be explored.

Singleton society

It is well documented that the number of single person households is on the rise (Yeoman, 2008). Back in 1961 nearly half (48%) of all English homes consisted of a couple living with their children. However, by 2011 this had fallen sharply to 21.4% and at the same time some 3 million 20 to 34 year olds were living at home with their parents (a figure 20% higher than in 1997). Some have taken this as a worrying sign of family breakdown but the evidence shows a different picture. Yeoman (2008) notes that singletons are becoming more important as the pre-family life stage is lasting longer. Single-person households represent about 30% of all households. The problem for men is that single women in their 30s and 40s have well-developed social networks and confidence that men lack. Men define themselves more by their work, and relax with too much unhealthy food and drink, a recipe for isolation and loneliness. Single women, by contrast, are more likely to see friends, explore their spiritual side and relax with yoga. Consequently, single men need to find a strategic lever, hence one of the reasons for the emergence of *The Man Foodie*.

For the single man, cooking can also offer other benefits. Forty-eight percent of people say that being able to cook makes a person more attractive to them, and this is a message clearly not lost on young, single men in particular. Research has shown that 23% of 18 to 34-year-old men say that they cook to impress or potentially seduce a partner as opposed to just 11% of women in the same age range (Future Foundation, 2013b). In choosing to live as a single man a growing proportion of men are thereby taking on the responsibility for all aspects of running a home. However, this is not always an unwelcome responsibility and it is clear that many young men are aware that cooking can be considered to be an attractive skill for a single man to have.

Women at work

However, men are not the only people to influence the rise of *The Man Foodie*. In part, the growth of the man who cooks is a reaction to the increasing independence of women and the desire and need for men to play their part in running the British home. Yet even with the rapid growth of the singleton generation, the majority of men are either married or live with their partner. Clearly men living with their partners face a different sort of necessity than the singleton male, as expectations have changed. Women have played a key role in changing men's attitude to cooking, as they are more independent than ever before and consequently men have had to share in some of what was once considered the female domain.

Historically, cooking, cleaning and the general running of the home has been part of the woman of the house's domain. The domestic home, the private sphere, was also the female sphere. This strict division has changed substantially. A large part of this change in division of labour has been caused by the movement of women into the workforce. In addition, with every year that passes, the social capital of women (Future Foundation, 2013a), defined here as the acquisition of market-relevant skills, swells in their favour and, theoretically at least, balances the see-saw between men and women as they each search for jobs, careers, incomes and general success in life.

But this is a Britain where women are marrying much later than before, having fewer children and building – certainly on the basis of their presence in tertiary education – stronger careers. Thus, the politics of gender difference just do not seem as intense as they once did (Yeoman, 2008).

Battle of the sexes

The famous dual burden of domestic work and paid employment has been alleviated somewhat by the arrival of men in the kitchen. Many women, especially younger women, are very positive about the cooking ability of men. Approximately 20% of women agree that their partner is a better cook than them; this percentage is at its highest with women who are less than 34 years of age, where 25% agree their partners are better cooks (FSR, 2013). Men are very positive about their new responsibilities in the kitchen. For many cooking is a form of leisure rather than a household chore. This is a crucial point, as men have taken up the spatulas and started to cook more frequently and spend much more time in the kitchen than their fathers ever did. However, men have not embraced the other traditionally female tasks of home upkeep with same gusto. Women still do four-times as much cleaning and laundry as men.

Cooking for leisure

The Man Foodie cooks more than just to satisfy his hunger – his cooking says a lot about him. It is leisure more than work and his ability to cook (and cook well) shows his friends, his partner and the outside world just how accomplished and sophisticated a man he is. Simply put, *The Man Foodie* is what he cooks; cooking is an important part of his identity and his social life. It is often suggested that men are better able to enjoy cooking as a hobby because they have only occasional involvement with this most necessary of activities. The frequently cited idea is that men only cook for dinner parties and at barbecues – where they can show off and do 'fun' cooking (FSR, 2013). The argument goes that as men only do the fun and interesting cooking they naturally find cooking more engaging, whereas women are saddled with the responsibility of providing food on a daily basis and so are not given the same opportunities to enjoy the act of making a meal.

Desire for new experiences

Consumerism is fuelled by society's desire to accumulate more goods and services (Pine & Gilmore, 2011). However, rising access to items once seen as luxuries has encouraged many to place a greater focus on the pursuit of experiences, whether this is in addition to, or in place of, more material-based forms of consumption. The consumer of the 2010s thus differentiates him or herself not only through the goods and services they buy, but also by the experiences they enjoy, such as holidays abroad, cultural events, fine dining and cutting-edge leisure activities. This trend is known as the *Experience Economy* (Pine & Gilmore, 1998), which encapsulates the desire for people to enrich their daily lives by experiencing new things and undertaking activities which deliver a sense of improvement, enjoyment and refreshment (Pine & Gilmore, 2011). Thus the aspirational and experiential types of consumption are underpinned by the attitude that, in sampling new and unique things, consumers gain the opportunity to develop new skills, acquire new knowledge and thus boost their share of social and cultural capital. As Yeoman (2008) notes, food and cooking in the experience economy is about new tastes, knowledge and concepts, thus food creates a new experience in which consumers capitalise on its formation and creation. As consumers have travelled further afield, visited new countries and tasted new cuisine, food has become a symbol of the experience economy.

The Leisure Society and Everyday Exceptional

As society grows wealthier, the need for organised fun, the search for reasons to interact informally with others and the pursuit of endorsed cultural identity increases. From a food perspective, the virtually organised community group, *Diner en Blanc* (http://dinerenblanc.info/) works on a simple premise, in selected cities around the world. A secret location is revealed to Diner en Blanc followers who then descend upon the special public location to have a mass, chic, picnic, dressed all in white. According to the organisers, diners can enhance their night by taking full advantage of the city's public space and participating in the unexpected. Beyond the spectacle, guests are brought together from diverse backgrounds by a love of beauty and good taste. Without doubt food is a lifestyle issue and plays an important role in a leisure society.

The social capital of cooking

Leisure has established itself to be of importance in British society and as a consequence work has become of less importance. British consumers define themselves not by their work but by their leisure activities, that is, by books they read, the places they visit and their hobbies. Consumers are constructing their own identities using leisure and other signifiers in a post-traditional modernity where they are no longer given an established pattern to follow (Giddens, 1991). The essence of social capital is that as consumers grow wealthier and better educated they place their 21st century sophistications on display, talking about where they have been or what they have done (Bourdieu, 1976). This is the knowledge, skills, personal accomplishments and fulfilling experiences which they want to share with others. Having the knowledge to explain a rare ingredient's origins coupled with gourmet cookery skills can carry as much cultural credit as dining in a Michelin-starred restaurant.

So, food is an important element of social capital. For *The Man Foodie* cooking is a passion which requires a rich knowledge and skill base. Being a good cook carries with it social status and also helps the chef to get a sense of 'themselves', where the food actually helps to form part of their identity. Men do not see cooking as a chore, but rather as an extension of masculine lifestyle (Szabo, 2012). Cooking to men is an expression of creativity and the importance of creativity is an aspiration for the consumer. Regardless of gender and age, Britons in general seem keen to fulfil themselves as individuals through creative expression. People want to learn new things and enjoy a sense of success when they do. Currently four in five men agree that they are confident in their culinary skills, with one in five claiming to feel very confident. This growth in confidence further reinforces the desire for self-actualisation. Ultimately cooking has evolved as a specific symbol of creativity

As Hollows (2003) observes, Jamie Oliver represents the cool, masculine lifestyle. Oliver re-affirms domestic cookery as a leisure practice but also affirms the dispositions associated with the new petit-bourgeoisie in which there is a 'morality of pleasure as duty' (Bourdieu, 1984: 367). It is Moseley who argues that Jamie sells 'a discourse of accessibility and achievability' (2001: 39). He suggests that this is only achieved by obfuscating the extent to which cooking is seen as both domestic labour and lifestyle.

Linked to social capital is *glory*. In a world where identity is created by the individual rather than handed out by the accident of fate and social circumstance, *The Man Foodie* approaches the preparation of food in a very male way. He makes it a competition and a way of gaining social capital through showing skill and taste.

Praise can come to the accomplished *Man Foodie*. The vivid examples of household names, such as Jamie Oliver, Gordon Ramsay, and Heston

Blumenthal are continually fuelling the efforts of the nation's budding chefs. Food has become big business, an entertainment product, a lifestyle and even a philosophy. The amateur Jamies and aspiring Hestons are clear examples of the close association between gastronomic skill, high motivation and public success.

Dinner party cult

One way to express creativity and gain social capital through sharing is the concept of dinner parties. Dinner parties represent people's relationship with their home and food. The desire to own, furnish and enjoy one's home is a force which shapes consumer behaviour (Yeoman, 2008). For so many people home ownership can exert a potent influence over purchasing decisions, lifestyles and leisure portfolios and even contribute to their sense of security or self-worth. Consumers have a cultural relationship with their home through strong emotional attachments and the creation of living spaces. As such, the home and home-making skills intertwine so that homes become spaces to entertain friends and kitchens become showcases for creative expression. The home is the place where Britons accrue social and cultural capital (Hollows, 2013). This process of socialisation is symbolised by dinner parties. Moreover, it is the younger age groups who cook most often for guests. Dinner parties are, it seems, the new house parties or at least house parties represent a time to display one's skill in the kitchen with 16% of the 25–34 age group most likely to host one (Future Foundation, 2012).

An age of affluence

The exploits of male chefs have been greatly facilitated by the steady and profound rise of mass affluence in the United Kingdom. *The Man Foodie* has been given new opportunities to express their tastes and skills. Growing disposable income has opened up new foods, products and experiences which were uncommon only a short time ago. Affluence has changed the way in which we eat and the way in which we cook. A range of products previously unavailable have flooded the supermarket shelves and kitchen cupboards across the whole of the United Kingdom. Cooking has long been an area where social status and economic clout are important discriminating factors. Whilst *The Man Foodie* comes from all backgrounds and walks of life, they are more concentrated at the middle and wealthier end of society. Research by the Future Foundation (2013a) highlights that the socio-economic categories ABC1 and the 25–34 age group are the groups that like to experiment with new dishes and are the most likely to prepare meals with separate ingredients. This is in part because cooking carries greater social status in middle-class society than it does elsewhere. Rising affluence continues to underpin the growth of the new male cook. More money has primarily meant greater opportunity, but it has also broadened horizons and changed values and attitudes towards the preparation of food.

Authenticity and local produce

Although people live in a society of convenience and fast food, authenticity is an important aspect. As Yeoman (2008) notes, authenticity is the individual who enjoys finding experiences that have clear links to a place, time or culture. Consumers searching for authenticity have a desire to reject anything artificial, generic or mass-produced. The desire for food authenticity is central to *The Man Foodie*, with men, aged between 16 and 34 more likely to choose local ingredients compared to other demographic cohorts or women. In addition, this trend has grown significantly since 2010 (Future Foundation, 2014). The importance of authenticity is underpinned by research by Gravity (2012) who commented:

> Whether local, traditional, regional, seasonal, artisan, organic or home-made, food conveys a message of quality. And it is always happy. The meat comes from happy cows grown by kind smiling farmers cared for in beautiful sunny nature resorts. Regardless of where you are, the food stories are identical and keep repeating as marketers and producers are stuck in a loop. Basically, it feels like selling food to people who care more about the story than taste or nutrition. This creates successful rupture between the food and its origin, which we chose to buy into, as most of us do not want to know the truth about our food any more. Our food is full of self-deception.

Therefore, without doubt authenticity and local preference are of core importance. Consumers have an association with the attributes of 'local' and 'quality', culminating in a desire to support local producers. For many, authenticity offers and products can be a route to social capital (Oliver, 2001), with mobile technology and online services making it ever easier to access them in convenient ways. For example, www.gothambox.com delivers boxes of location-inspired foods on a monthly basis, allowing people to enjoy cuisine from a specific city. Another location-based food application, www.fiddme.com, allows people to post pictures of their cooking achievements and share local recipes with others. May 2012 saw the opening of a new Whole Foods supermarket in London's Piccadilly Circus. This store places an emphasis on local produce, customer comfort and difficult-to-obtain items (www.wholefoods-market.com/stores/piccadilly). Inside the branch, shoppers can find a range of London-based brands (including St John Bakery, Neal's Yard Dairy and Monmouth Coffee) as well as purchase a specially created 'Piccadilly Piccalilli' wrap or freshly baked in-house pizza, breads, cupcakes and other items from the patisserie counter.

Health and hedonism

Hedonist activity is defined as pleasure seeking. However, obesity in Britain is on the rise and so from a food perspective *The Man Foodie* must balance pleasure with health considerations to impress the female gender. Celebrity chef Myra Kornfeld (as cited in Grumdahl, 2008) has said:

> People do think that something healthy is just going to be sort of sad and not flavorful or fun or luscious. But I don't think there's any conflict between luscious eating and healthy eating. That's why my cookbooks have words like 'hedonist' and 'voluptuous' in them – people need to know that good food doesn't have to be monastic.

The health and hedonism trend will strengthen in coming years due to the size of our waistlines (Yeoman, 2012). Consumers are beginning to focus on foods which have a health-focused proposition and will seek ever more detailed and transparent information about product ingredients. Therefore, it is very important for *The Man Foodie* to have health awareness as part of his seduction process.

Food and Culture

Food practices in the 1950s have been seen as essentially feminine and the domestic kitchen in particular was seen as a female domain. Popular culture reproduced the idea that cookery was a female pursuit, that competent cooking was central to a woman's role and that it was a woman's responsibility to be knowledgeable about food (Hollow, 2013). But the commercial kitchen has always been a male domain. As the experience economy matures, the social and cultural capital of food, along with demographic changes, have seen food emerge as central to modern society and masculinity. Food is a distinguishing factor and a central symbol of identity. So how does food and culture manifest itself from *The Man Foodie* perspective?

Cooking, celebrity, craft and male identity

Man's relationship with cooking has traditionally been defined as a hobby (Coxon, 1983), a means of 'helping out' for special occasions (DeVault, 1991), or as the domain of the professional chef who is a 'talented and competent craftsman' (Fine, 1995: 248). Studies analysing the gendering of foods have examined entrenched associations between masculinity and meat and how 'hard' masculinities are constructed in opposition to supposedly feminine discourses of gourmet food and dieting for weight loss. The FSR (2013) identified a consistent level of social acceptance for the man who cooks. Gone, it seems, are the days where to cook was somehow seen as being less than macho. Men have moved into cooking with much more enthusiasm than they have moved into other areas of the previously female domestic sphere, for example, cleaning, tidying and laundry. Male identity has been reconciled with the art of preparing food, although not, it seems, with cleaning. Crucial to this development has been the prominence of men who cook.

Celebrities were once remote and mysterious idols to be admired reverentially at a distance. Nowadays their cultural visibility has reached such a pitch that the public has continual and unlimited access to their private lives. Celebrities are often seen as public property and, for some, access to their personal information feels more of a right than privilege. This can be seen clearly in the rise of the celebrity chef in society.

Celebrity chefs can be very visibly laddish, macho or just plain angry when cooking. If there had been any doubt that real men could cook, it has been dispelled by a decade of unabashedly male chefs. Jamie Oliver remains one of Britain's most popular food heroes. His popularity started with his book and TV series *The Naked Chef* (Oliver, 2001). Hollows (2003: 231) describes why *The Naked Chef* was so successful:

> The power of Jamie as a brand stems from his show's negotiation of the television cookery format to emphasize the importance of lifestyle The Naked Chef is distinguished by the way it incorporates cooking sequences in Jamie's apartment within a wider display of the 'Jamie lifestyle', in which he is shown riding his trademark Vespa around London, shopping, eating with friends and engaging in a range of leisure pursuits. The Naked Chef doesn't simply educate the viewer about 'how to cook', but how to use food as one element 'in an expressive display of lifestyle'. This is accentuated by the show's visual style which draws on pop videos and employs 'a grainy realist aesthetic' to create the sense of The Naked Chef as a 'docu-soap' about Jamie's life.

Hot on the heels of Jamie Oliver is Gordon Ramsay, Britain's second most popular celebrity chef, who is a no-nonsense ex-footballer turned chef, restaurateur and television star. Dreams of a promising football career were cut short while he was still in his teens. By comparison to Jamie Oliver, Gordon Ramsay makes it clear that he is a chef, not a cook. As Scholes states (2011: 52):

> Ramsay obsesses about the inadequacy of the men who surround him, taking every opportunity to contest their virility, as if penis size equates to cooking skill; 'this is nothing to do with your bollocks or the size of your cock is it?' he asks one Briton – whose dream of running a restaurant in Spain has turned into a nightmare of unsatisfied

customers and huge expenses – when he refuses to take Ramsay's word as law. Ramsay later drags his victim down to the local bull-ring and forces him to man-up Spanish style (though Ramsay doesn't play matador himself).

Cooking can be stylish, fiercely passionate and, indeed, in the case of the successful *MasterChef* format, directly competitive. Ironically, therefore, by disassociating cooking from the traditionally female worlds of home and family, celebrity chefs have encouraged men into domestic kitchens often to cook for their girlfriends, wives and children. *The Man Foodie* need not be embarrassed about his passion for cooking. It no longer seems un-male but can be seen as heated, exciting and competitive.

Multicultural men: Cooking in modern Britain

British food remains popular but the influence of foreign cuisines, especially those from Asia, is strong. Indeed, many believe Britain's favourite dish, the Indian curry, is a symbol of Britain's identity (Leung, 2010). According to the ONS Integrated Household Survey (2011), 11.6% of the British population identifies itself as an ethnic minority (or non-white), with 25.5% of all babies born in the United Kingdom being to foreign-born mothers. Both the inflow of new immigrants and outflow of those choosing to leave Britain have increased as global mobility continues to rise. The experience of migration has itself changed through political and social developments. This has seen migrants settling in areas of Britain where they would not have previously done so.

According to Leung (2010), ethnic foods are found to be most popular amongst young male adults from a higher socio-economic grouping who fit *The Man Foodie* profile. It is most likely that members of this group have travelled more widely and have greater levels of disposable income, with four out of 10 consuming ethnic food at least twice a week. This *Man Foodie* has a stronger preference for emerging cuisines, for example Japanese food, than lower socio-economic groupings and is more adventurous with his food habits. *The Man Foodie* is likely to buy ethnic food from specialist shops, such as Chinese supermarkets or Italian delicatessens, hence the importance of authenticity. The growth of emerging cuisines like Japanese or Thai is attributed to concerns about healthy eating as these cuisines are considered lighter and healthier, particularly by females.

The restaurant industry has been an area which has facilitated the entry of many immigrants into the national culture and society. Chinese and Indian restaurants are regular features on high streets nationwide. Indeed, as Melanie Howard (cited in FSR, 2013) points out, food was one of the first areas where migrants from non-English-speaking countries were able to enter the national consciousness in a positive way.

Future Thoughts: A Food Tourism Perspective

What does this all mean? Figure 12.2 represents a conceptual framework of the *Man Foodie*. From a tourism perspective the importance of place and authenticity, master craftsman and the food and food tourist present implications for the future. This section explores these concepts.

The importance of place and authenticity

The language and style of Jamie Oliver and his programme *The Naked Chef* exudes Cockney authenticity and Britishness (Hollows, 2003). The TV programme is set against a backdrop of metropolitanism and cosmopolitanism in which cooking sequences in domestic space are intercut with sequences tracking Jamie's movements around several London locations such as Soho, Notting Hill and Islington, with lots of red buses and barrow boys. The locations embody the language of Londoners with an emphasis on the 'bacon sarnie' and English breakfast. 'Comfort Grub' is also linked

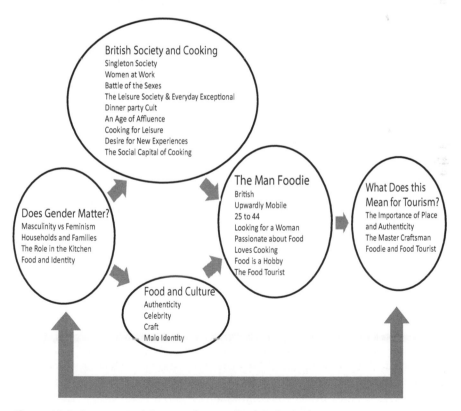

Figure 12.2 A conceptual framework: men, food and travel

to a nostalgia for 'British' dishes associated with 'memories of childhood …
coming home shivering and wet after playing footie with the boys' (Oliver,
2001: 20). Throughout the programme, references are continuality made to
Brit Pop and The Beatles and Jamie appears to be an ideal advert for Visit
Britain (Hollows, 2003). This association with place is not lost on destinations as the contemporary tourist is more cultured than visitors of 20 years
ago; they are well travelled, searching for new experiences, concerned about
the environment, interested in taking part in a health/well-being lifestyle
and want to experience the local culture when they go on holiday (Yeoman,
2008). When on holiday, the cooking and eating of food becomes the social
occasion where busy people create a 'time oasis', but is also as a means to
connect with family members and friends who may in general be less time-
impoverished. Food becomes a human-space within, frequently, much-
harried lives; the notion of the meal as a 'time oasis' seems to be a very
powerful theme. As the consumer desire for new experiences increases, the
'authentic' restaurant or food experience becomes more important.
Authenticity is about food that is simple, rooted in the region, natural,
ethical, beautiful and human.

The Man Foodie

The visibility of the male celebrity chef along with books, magazines and
blogs about men cooking seem to indicate, according to Szabo (2012), a
growing enthusiasm for cooking. Cultural discourses about cooking have an
influence on this growing enthusiasm, with research by Swenson (2009),
Hollows (2013) and Parasecoli (2008) observing that men cooking on TV and
film can be framed as a display of professional skill or leisurely entertainment. Fundamentally, men see cooking as leisure because they are positioned
as culinary artists or *The Man Foodie*. As Gravity (2012) observes:

> As most of us have lost the skills to build a boat or skin a sheep, the
> kitchen represents the last refuge for craftsmanship. Anyone is welcome
> to try the tricks of the old trade and look good by wearing that trendy
> apron. Cooking and baking are the last crafts we can master. They offer
> control and social gratification – something that might lack in other
> areas of our stressed everyday. Connecting to traditional values, the jour-
> ney is the reward. Having time for DIY today is a romanticized luxury.
> That's what makes baking sexy (again).

The Man Foodie metaphorical interpretation is directly linked to the changing
meaning of luxury (Yeoman, 2008), in which luxury is shifting from materialism to enrichment, where sources of pleasure and gratification are sought.
Here *The Man Foodie* prepares romantic meals and is confident to experiment
with new cuisines. Hence, the man in the kitchen represents food as a craft

which allows man to make and construct something. Cooking and baking are the new metalwork and woodwork of the modern era, offering control and social gratification: they are a sort of romanticised kitchen DIY. Therefore cooking and being a chef are about getting back to basics, hence the interest in heritage, tradition and craft.

From a tourism perspective, *The Man Foodie* can be associated with urban tribes and cookery schools. Watters (2004) coined the term *Urban Tribes* in the 1990s where friends are your new family. From the 1990s the TV show *Friends* is a representation of this, where friends get together to talk in the local coffee shop. These friends are highly educated, and want to learn and acquire new skills. These people are also single, urban and, like Bridget Jones, need a social network. As Sharples (2003) points out, the cookery school is about the desire for new experiences drawing on the dimensions of culture, as tourists learn about new foods immersed in the destination. In addition, tourists are learning a new skill and will probably have an interest in food.

The foodie and food tourist

Foodies are people with a longstanding passion for eating and learning about food but they are not food professionals. Cairns *et al.* (2010: 592) note that:

> Foodie is portrayed in culture as referencing a new, omnivorous cultural interest in a wide range of foods ranging from high-brow classics (e.g. duck à l'orange) to low-brow culinary treasures (e.g. handmade tacos). Our analysis demonstrates that while foodie culture is by no means gender-neutral, foodies are enacting gender in new ways that warrant closer inspection. Alongside evidence that foodies are contesting particular gendered relations within the food world, we explore how broader gender inequities persist.

An important trend for the foodie is cultural capital (Yeoman, 2012). The importance of cultural capital defines identity and status; it becomes the critical currency of conversation, notably in phrases like, 'have you been to France and dined at the Hotel George V' or 'made authentic Thai Green Curry at the Elephant Cookery School in Krabi'? It is the knowledge and experiences of the food, hobbies and craft that help define who foodies are rather than their socio-economic grouping. Sociologists (Sharples, 2003) argue that consumers are moving from an era of industrial to cultural capitalism, where cultural production is increasingly becoming the dominant form of economic activity and securing access to the many cultural resources and experiences that nurture human psychological existence becomes an important aspect in shaping identity. The well-travelled *Man Foodie* can be viewed as a foodie and food tourist.

Concluding Remarks: The Implications for the Future of Food Tourism

Food helps men to form part of their identity like work, politics and sport. Men and food are also related to the importance of owning a home – an aspiration the majority of the British strive for. Homeownership is connected to the importance of dinner parties, which in recent times have become the new party scene for the upwardly mobile set. Dinner parties represent a chance for men to show off their skills. Some would say, the 'new going out' is the 'new staying in' – a chance to socialise in an environment of plasma screens, fine wines and food.

Mass affluence in society has meant men have been able to try out new experiences, broadened their horizons and raised their expectations. Affluence has changed the way in which society eats and the way that people cook. Cupboards in our kitchens are laden with important delicacies from far afield. Do not think for one moment that tomorrow's male will be metrosexual or someone that has found his feminine side. The new wave of celebrity chefs is visibly laddish, macho or just plain angry when cooking. They assert their aggression in the kitchen, just like footballers on their field of play.

As pollster Mark Penn (2007: 222) observes, 'micro trends are based upon the idea that the most powerful forces in society are the emerging, counter-intuitive trends that are shaping tomorrow before us'. Therefore, moving into the future, tomorrow's food tourist will be the upwardly mobile male, aged 25 to 44 years old who will seek cultural capital and social cachet in the United Kingdom's food experiences. In general, men are becoming more interested in food. This means more connectivity between food and wine, whether it is as an incentive product for those involved in business tourism or just more men taking food tours. Deluxe kitchen manufacturers will probably offer cookery lessons with the celebrity chefs in a wonderful location so consumers can learn how to use all those gadgets. Cookery schools will probably offer 'Man Food' courses for those who want to know how to 'cook a decent curry'. Restaurants will be taken over by budding Gordon Ramsays, who will fight it out just like in *Hell's Kitchen*. These budding celebrity chefs will pay for the privilege of doing so and they will invite their friends and relatives to consume that food (which they will charge for) and they will then sell them a DVD of the experience.

Notes

(1) The authors would like to acknowledge the support of the Future Foundation in the writing of this chapter who provided access to their omnibus survey of global household consumption and behaviour patterns via http://nvision.futurefoundation.net/.
(2) ABC1 is a demographic classification used in the United Kingdom to equate to middle-class society. The grades were first developed by the National Readership Survey but are now widely used in market research.

References

Bourdieu, P. (1976) *La Distinction: Critique Sociale du Judgement*. Paris: Les Editions de Minuit.

Bourdieu, P. (1984) *Distinction: A Social Critique of the Judgement of Taste*. London: Routledge.

Cairns, K., Johnston, J. and Baumann, S. (2010) Caring about food: Doing gender in the foodie kitchen. *Gender & Society* 24 (5), 591–615.

Coxon, T. (1983) Men in the kitchen. In A. Murcott (ed.) *The Sociology of Food and Eating* (pp. 172–177). Aldershot: Gower.

DeVault, M. (1991) *Feeding the Family: The Social Organisation of Caring as Gendered Work*. Chicago: University of Chicago Press.

Diner en Blanc. See http://dinerenblanc.info/ (accessed 12 June 2013).

Fine, G. (1995) Wittgenstein kitchen: Sharing meaning in restaurant work. *Theory and Society* 24 (3), 245–269.

FSR (2013) Future foundation studies show trend of 'Gastrosexuals' in the kitchen. See http://www.fsrmagazine.com/content/future-foundation-studies-show-trend-gastrosexuals-kitchen (accessed 10 September 2014).

Future Foundation (2012) Food trends. See http://nvision.futurefoundation.net (accessed 10 January 2013).

Future Foundation (2013a) Gender matters. See http://nvision.futurefoundation.net (accessed 10 January 2013).

Future Foundation (2013b) Home cooking and social capital. See http://nvision.future foundation.net (accessed 24 May 2013).

Future Foundation (2014) Authent-seeking. See http://nvision.futurefoundation.net (accessed 24 May).

Giddens, A. (1991) *Modernity and Self-Identity: Self and Society in the Late Modern Age*. Stanford, CA: Stanford University Press.

Gravity. (2012) Food thinking. See www.food-thinking.com/insights/ (accessed 30 May 2013).

Grumdahl, D.M. (2008) Healthy hedonism. See http://experiencelife.com/article/healthy-hedonism/ (accessed 1 June 2013).

Hollows, J. (2003) Oliver's twist: Leisure, labour and domestic masculinity in *The Naked Chef*. *International Journal of Cultural Studies* 6 (2), 229–248.

Hollows, J. (2013) The bachelor dinner: Masculinity, domesticity and food practises in playboy 1953–63. See http://oregonstate.edu/instruct/nutr216/ref/symposium_hollows.html (accessed 30 May 2013).

Jackson, P., Stevenson, N. and Brooks, K. (2001) *Making Sense of Men's Magazines*. Cambridge: Polity.

Leung, G. (2010) Ethic foods in the UK. *Nutrition Bulletin* 35, 226–234.

Moseley, R. (2001) Real lads do cook … but some things are still hard to talk about: The gendering of 8–9. *European Journal of Cultural Studies* 4 (1), 32–39.

Office of National Statistics (2011) See www.ons.gov.uk/ons/index.html (accessed 10 April 2013).

Oliver, J. (2001) *Happy Days and the Naked Chef*. London: Michael Joseph.

Parasecoli, F. (2008) *Bite Me: Food in Popular Culture*. London: Berg.

Penn, M. (2007) *Microtrends: The Small Forces Behind Tomorrow's Big Changes*. New York: Twelve.

Pine, J. and Gilmore, J. (1998) Welcome to the experience economy. *Harvard Business Review* 76 (4). See http://go.galegroup.com/ps/downloadDocument.do?actionCmd=DO_DOWNLOAD_DOCUMENT&bucketId=&inPS=true&prodId=ITOF&userGroupName=vuw&tabID=T002&documentTitle=Welcome%2Bto%2Bthe%2Bexperience%2Becon&docId=GALE%7CA20916746&currentPosition=&tagId=&dynamicEtoc Avail=&pubDate=&workId=&callistoContentSet=&useNewPubSvc=&download Format=HTML (accessed 10 June 2013).

Pine, J. and Gilmore, J. (2011) *The Experience Economy.* 9th ed. Boston, MA: Harvard Business Review.

Richards, C. (2013) Gastronomy killed the rock n' roll star. *Sunday: Magazine of the Sunday Star Times,* 26 May.

Scholes, L. (2011) A slave to the stove? *Critical Quarterly* 53 (3), 44–59.

Sharples, L. (2003) The world of cookery school holidays. In M. Hall and L. Sharples (eds) *Food Tourism Around the World: Development, Management and Markets* (pp. 112–120). London: Routledge.

Swenson, R. (2009) Domestic divo? Televised treatments of masculinity, femininity and food. *Critical Studies in Media Communications* 26 (1), 36–53.

Szabo, M. (2012) Foodwork or foodplay? Men's domestic cooking, privilege and leisure. *Sociology.* See http://soc.sagepub.com/content/early/2012/08/30/0038038512448562 (accessed 12 January 2013).

Watters, E. (2004) *Urban Tribes: Are Friends the New Family.* London: Bloomsbury.

Yeoman, I. (2008) *Tomorrow's Tourist.* London: Routledge.

Yeoman, I. (2012) *2050 – Tomorrow's Tourism.* Bristol: Channel View Publications.

13 The New Food Explorer: Beyond the Experience Economy

Jennifer Laing and Warwick Frost

Highlights

- The food explorer is emerging as an important future niche market in tourism.
- These tourists do not fit within the experience economy model.
- Food explorers are concerned with authenticity, sustainability and prestige.
- The experience economy model needs to be revisited in light of this development.

Introduction

The *food explorer* is an example of a growing tourism niche that is likely to be increasingly important in the future to destinations. These individuals are keen to experience food or wine that is authentic to a region or destination; and enjoy learning about different styles, traditions and heritage. They are often independent travellers, and eschew packaged experiences in favour of discovering things for themselves. This travel bestows a form of status or prestige, distinguishing them from the mass tourist. They also seek out sustainable experiences, conscious of their ecological footprint, and are strongly desirous of keeping cultural heritage alive.

This goes beyond the Pine and Gilmore's experience economy model (1998, 1999), which extols the importance of staging and uses the term *performance* to describe what is being delivered to a tourist – something scripted, slick and stylised, where 'products are "props" and staff are "actors"' (Frost & Laing, 2011: 135). The experience economy model emerged at a time when it was understood that the future of business growth lies not in providing products or services, but in delivering *experiences*. These are conceptualised across two dimensions – (1) the level of participation involved in the experience and (2) the connection or relationship between the customer and the performance, resulting in four *realms* of an experience – entertainment, educational, escapist and esthetic (sic). This chapter argues that this model needs to be extended to cover a fifth realm – *exploration* – and will use the example of the food explorer to discuss this proposed extension of the Pine and Gilmore model, as well as the implications of these trends for the future of food tourism.

This chapter adopts a *science fiction* paradigm to examine the food tourist of the future. According to Bergman *et al.* (2010), there are four paradigms of futures thinking – predictions, prognoses, utopias/dystopias and science fiction, which differ based on whether truth claims and/or explanatory claims are made. The forecasts contained in this chapter make explanatory claims, but not claims about 'the truth'. This approach is appropriate when considering the future of tourism, given the likely rate and uncertainty of change (Yeoman, 2012).

The Food Explorer

Food is often regarded as a *supporting* experience in tourism – akin to accommodation or transport – a mere foil to the peak tourist experience, which is normally conceptualised as an attraction, and the main reason for visiting a destination. If the supporting experience is professionally executed, there's no problem; if it isn't, it affects overall satisfaction with the tourist experience (Quan & Wang, 2004).

There are however tourists for whom food – and beverages such as wine – is the prime focus of and motivation for their travel and forms peak tourist experiences (Quan & Wang, 2004). Hill (2013: 19) labels this behaviour 'the 21st century equivalent of the Grand Tour…today the questing class seeks enlightenment not in galleries and museums but in eating houses' Some travel *solely* to visit a particular restaurant (Hill, 2013). As a dedicated food tourist from Melbourne observes, 'I have not made travel plans for many, many years that do not first involve thinking about where to eat' (quoted in Hill, 2013: 19). These tourists can be conceptualised as examples of *food explorers*.

Three main hallmarks of the food explorer can be identified. First, they want surprises, rather than certainty (Albrecht, 2011). They eschew tourist menus and tours, preferring to eat like the locals and discover for themselves what the destination has to offer. There is an educational element to this travel, but it goes beyond that. Their learning needs to be emergent, rather than pre-packaged, uncovering things that are novel and distinctive in their eyes (Image 13.1). They seek out hidden treasures in back streets, wineries

Image 13.1 Chocolate Easter eggs in patisserie, Dijon, France
Source: W. Frost.

with cellar doors only 'open by appointment' and culinary haunts that their friends have recommended via social media or that they have read about in food or wine-related magazines. There is social cachet to be earned in finding these hidden gems, but also in telling others about them.

This extends to destinations. Albrecht discusses the propensity of some tourists to avoid 'non-places', which he defines as places with 'no ostensible history that affirms their identity or uniqueness', exemplified by the Olive Garden chain of restaurants in the United States. The food explorer conversely looks for 'the "real places" that distinguish one place from another' (Albrecht, 2011: 102). What these real places *are*, however, remains open to conjecture, much like the multiple interpretations of authenticity discussed below.

Second, food explorers display a strong interest in experiencing food and wine that is *authentic* to a destination, particularly involving local produce and regional specialities. They flock to markets to see what is in season and pertains to the region, and prefer to frequent restaurants and cafés run and staffed by locals (Image 13.2). The food explorer's concern with authenticity is akin to Florida's (2002, 2005) creative classes, who enjoy lives 'packed full of intense, high quality, multidimensional experiences' (2002. 166) and prefer grunginess to sterility. The postmodern view of authenticity is relevant here, which argues that this concept is to be judged from the perspective of the individual concerned, whether or not there is any relevant objective standard (Bruner, 1994; Cohen, 1988). These tourists may perceive something as authentic, and that is all that matters.

Image 13.2 The main square outside the cathedral in Antwerp is lined with cafés – The perfect image of European outdoor café culture
Source: W. Frost.

Third, food explorers are concerned with *sustainability* issues such as minimising food miles and thus privileging locally produced and grown food over costly imports; patronising establishments with philanthropic or green goals or values that are in synchronicity with their own; and embracing organic and slow food offerings. Restaurants which employ locals and provide them with a sustainable livelihood, and aim to keep the local food heritage alive as a way of building identity, appeal to the food explorer.

The backdrop to the emergence of the food explorer is complex. Higher levels of disposable income give these consumers a greater ability to travel than in the past, and they are more likely to have a tertiary qualification and to have been educated overseas than previous generations. Societal trends focused on the search for meaning are manifested in a growing desire for the opportunity to be one's true or authentic self (Wang, 2000), and a search for self-actualisation and personal growth.

Trends Associated with the Food Explorer

Slow food

There is a burgeoning interest in slow food (Frost & Laing, 2013b; Hall, 2006), described as a movement promoting 'locally sourced ingredients, traditional recipes and taking time to source, prepare and enjoy food' (Dickinson & Lumsden, 2010: 80). It forms part of a philosophy of slowing down life in general. Slow food means making things from scratch, with loving care, and not taking short cuts – the very opposite to the McDonald's culture of convenience food (Miele & Murdoch, 2002). The food explorer will not expect (or want) an eat-and-run style meal, beloved of tour groups. Food – or the ritual of a meal – will be a major part of their day, not an add-on or inconvenience. Restaurants that are a member of the slow food movement display their credentials by posting a sticker on their door, featuring the snail symbol (Image 13.3). Others may present their philosophy on their menus, as a statement of their commitment to the slow food ethos.

Image 13.3 Slow food symbol on the door of a restaurant in Pistoia, Italy
Source: J. Laing.

Artisan and organic food and produce

Interest in artisan food and produce and organic food and wine is similarly a growing trend. Places like Milawa or the King Valley in Victoria's north-east (Image 13.4) pride themselves on the quality of the region's produce, its wines – mainly Italian varietals of growing reputation – and its hand-made food products (Laing & Frost, 2013). They develop food and wine trails for tourists to explore, with maps and often on a bicycle (e.g. the South Canterbury Food and Wine Trail in New Zealand). Milawa has become a magnet for clusters of artisanal local businesses like Milawa Organic Beef, Milawa Mustards, Milawa Cheese Company, the Olive Shop and Blue Ox Berries. Organic wineries such as Mount Edward in the Central Otago region of New Zealand promote their 'small batch, estate grown, single vineyard wines'. Other wineries, like Two Paddocks, owned by actor Sam Neill, grow organic produce adjacent to the vines (Image 13.5).

Even supermarkets have picked up on this trend. Eataly in Italy relies on small producers, and consults with representatives of Slow Food Italy to bring these wares to consumers, keeping this food heritage, in many instances, alive. It 'has brought fast food to slow food, injecting standardization and mass marketing into the artisanal-food industry' (Faris, 2013: 38). There is a market for hand-crafted cheeses, cured hams, and home-made sauces, but many consumers are not able to access these things without the help of a retailer (Faris, 2013).

Allied to this is a fascination with the history of food and recreating the past, albeit with a modern interpretation for current tastes (Backhouse,

Image 13.4 La Dolce Vita Festival, King Valley, Victoria, Australia
Source: J. Laing.

Image 13.5 Organic produce grown at Two Paddocks Winery, Central Otago, New Zealand
Source: W. Frost.

2012). Television shows like *The Super Sizers Go…* give us hosts who live off food from a particular historic epoch for a week (Frost & Laing, 2013a), while *Heston's Feasts* features leading chef Heston Blumenthal who creates banquets for his guests based on English culinary heritage. The Melbourne Food and Wine Festival in 2012 was partly themed around traditions of food and drink. There was a Grecian Banquet in the Hellenic Museum, a recreation of Queen Victoria's 1887 Golden Jubilee dinner at the Hotel Windsor, Drinks of the Gold Rush Era and Cocktails of the Highest Order, featuring drinks from the early 20th century (Backhouse, 2012). The kitchen gardens of many restaurants, such as l'Arpège in France, grow heirloom vegetables and experiment with reviving past varieties (Gopnik, 2011).

Hands-on experience

One exception to the food explorer's aversion to tours is the gourmet food tour or cooking school experience. These are most popular where they are 'hands-on' and vary with the season and what is available. Tourists can learn to make pasta in Italy, rice paper rolls in Vietnam and laksas in Thailand. It is a modern twist on the tradition of sending girls to Paris to learn the art of *cordon-bleu*, like Audrey Hepburn in *Sabrina* (1954), but taken much more seriously – this is not for the dilettantes but the serious epicure. To emphasise this, Unique Group Travel (2013) labels one of their gourmet tours a 'food pilgrimage' and 'foodie heaven'. An Australian company offers 'gourmet safaris', using the metaphor to connect to the idea of food as the object of discovery. The owner, high-profile TV chef and author Maeve O'Meara, instructs prospective tourists to 'join us to experience new and delicious worlds' (Gourmet Safaris, 2013).

Even tours not themed around food are keen to highlight the 'adventures' that participants can take part in – less about group dining and more about discovering the local market. Intrepid (2013) now promote the culinary opportunities available on their tours, using language aimed at the food explorer:

> Let's be honest, travelling goes hand in hand with eating. And sustainable travelling goes hand in hand with sustainable eating. That's why Intrepid has partnered with The Perennial Plate – the filmmaking, travelling, sustainably-eating, chef and documentary-maker duo, Daniel Klein and Mirra Fine…They'll help you discover the stories behind global cuisine, and have you wanting to eat your way around the planet in no time.

Chef Julian Bond takes small groups through the Granville Island Public Market in Vancouver, and covers everything from 'hydroponics to pod fishing' (Richardson, 2013: 6). He emphasises the choices people can make with regard to food, and how 'small choices' count (2013: 7), which appeals to the food explorer's desire for autonomy.

Sustainability

Disquiet about the long-term sustainability of food products manifests itself in various trends. Concerns over declining levels of seafood have led Vancouver to develop the Ocean Wise programme. Local restaurants and suppliers who take part in this initiative pledge to colour-grade seafood based on the health of the population. Seafood which is endangered or with low stocks will not be served, while diners can be reassured about some forms of seafood which they might otherwise have assumed were scarce or threatened. This level of information has become commonplace, such that 'savvy diners all but expect it in their choices' (Richardson, 2013: 6). The mania for knowledge extends to the provenance of the produce on one's plate. A programme started in Vancouver, ThisFish, allows people to trace their meal or purchase back to a particular time or location of catch, down to the boat that was used (Richardson, 2013).

Apprehension over extinction is not limited to animal species. There is also a realisation that food heritage is often fragile and prone to be overlooked, substituted by standard fare or the victim of the McDonaldisation of cuisine (Albrecht, 2011), where food is labelled *international* and pertains to no single country. Food explorers increasingly search for traditional but scarce delicacies (Leung, 2012) or resurrect ingredients such as quinces or heirloom tomatoes. This is not limited to older demographic segments. Hong Kong chef Daniel Chui has observed many younger tourists 'hunting down forgotten dishes' (Leung, 2012: 196).

There is a growth in restaurants with a philanthropic goal. Jamie Oliver's *Fifteen* restaurants were a means of giving employment to young people who had otherwise little future ahead of them, but also appealed to patrons who watched Jamie's television programmes and liked the thought of doing something altruistic, while enjoying a good meal. They demonstrate the use of food as a political tool (Smith, 2012). The Friends International restaurants in Cambodia provide local youth with valuable skills in a country still traumatised by war, and help them to reclaim their cultural (food) heritage and sense of identity as a result (Friends International, 2013). These restaurants appeal to the altruistic side of the food explorer, who wants to do good things for others, while not compromising on eating well.

Niche spaces

The small-is-chic craze can be seen in the increasingly tiny spaces that have been turned into cafés, bars and restaurants and the popularity of small gourmet coffee sellers (Frost *et al.*, 2010). Hole-in-the-wall spaces provide atmosphere and exclusivity, rather than the barn-like settings of the past, and may dispense their speciality, be it coffee, pastries or burgers, to those 'in the know', who find out about these places via word-of-mouth. Melbourne has become known for its diminutive and groovy bars down laneways or on rooftops, with hidden doorways and low-key signage (Tan, 2013). The trend in food trucks or vans, which started in Los Angeles, was partly due to the frisson of their random location and being hard to catch, rather like the ice-cream trucks of childhood. Social media then stepped in with apps advising their whereabouts, re-emphasising the desirability of 'being in the know'. They became the hipster form of fast food, using great local ingredients and a dash of cool (Dubecki, 2011; Gill, 2012). Melbourne has its Taco Truck, with Mexican street food, and Gumbo Kitchen, with its Cajun fare.

The exclusivity of the extreme

Cashed-up foodies, who might otherwise want the prestige of climbing Mount Everest or swimming with sharks, are making room in their diaries for a new adventure – visiting the world's top restaurants in what has been termed 'extreme dining':

> The combined force of global restaurant rankings, the mass media's infatuation with all things edible and the relative ease of air travel have spurred a race of globetrotting gourmets with an unprecedented obsession with eating. (Hill, 2013)

Restaurants like Heston Blumenthal's The Fat Duck in Berkshire and René Redzepi's Noma in Copenhagen are culinary shrines that aficionados have to experience. It becomes an obsession for some; a frenzy of eating at the right places and marking off the Michelin-starred restaurants that one has visited (Hill, 2013). The difficulty in getting reservations (Noma receives an average of 1.2 million reservation requests each year) makes them more prestigious and sought after (Hill, 2013). Some secure highly coveted invitations to dine in small groups, such as the private rooms of famous restaurants like Noma – for astronomical sums. One group paid €1500 a head for the privilege (Hill, 2013). New food destinations such as Cuba (Bell, 2013) are also being discovered by food explorers, with a race to be amongst the first to try them out.

Independent and experimental ordering

Some restaurants eschew tourist menus with translations and fixed-price specials, in favour of offering the opportunity to eat what the locals eat. There is a swing towards experimenting with food, exemplified by the *tasting plate*, with its multiple small offerings, or *degustation menus*, involving five, six or seven small courses, often with matched wines, allowing the tourist to sample unusual dishes and the chef to experiment with textures, tastes and ingredients. Harden (2012: 65) notes that we are in an era of 'swotted-up diners hungry for the untried and untasted'. Certain cuisines lend themselves to this sampling approach, such as the Spanish *tapas*, often consumed as bar snacks, and the Italian *antipasto*, as an appetiser.

George Calombaris, a chef of Greek origins living in Melbourne, encourages this sharing of food on platters as convivial and true to his ethnic roots. He aims to serve 'home food', respectful of his heritage and reminiscent of what his mother would cook for him, and looks for restaurants when he travels that have 'soul' (Calombaris, 2009: 213). The occasional off-note is not a problem for the food explorer when they feel the chef's heart is in the right place. This is part of the charm of discovery. As Albrecht (2011: 108) notes:

> One of the promises that discourses of travel hold is that the process of authentically visiting and engaging with other cultures holds a degree of danger that cannot be achieved without leaving the culture zone of contemporary modernized Western culture. The same desire for a bit of danger is present in consuming ethnic cuisines; there is a danger in consuming raw fish, seemingly alien fruits and vegetables, and animal parts that are not usually a part of Western cuisine.

The ultimate in moving away from a mass menu can be seen at Christopher Kostow's Restaurant at Meadowbank in California's Napa Valley. Kostow's staff quiz prospective diners when they make a booking on what they like to eat, why they are visiting the valley and where else they have eaten in the vicinity of the restaurant. This helps the staff tailor the perfect menu for their guests' dining pleasure. As Kostow puts it: 'If they ate at the [French] Laundry for lunch, I'll lighten it up...And I'll serve them different stuff than what's going out to tables nearby, to create a sense of...lively excitement' (Arnold-Ratliff, 2013: 41).

Local is best

The growing popularity of eating local produce and seeking out regional specialities can be seen in the rise of farmers' markets and *enotecas* (shops that sell produce as well as meals). Some restaurants advertise the *food miles* of their dishes and emphasise the fact that mostly local produce has been used to produce their menu. A number of chefs have their own kitchen garden and use their produce on their menus – the ultimate in low food miles. Annie Smithers, chef at Du Fermier in Trentham, Victoria, features photos and a diary about her one-acre garden in her new book *From Garden to Table* (2012): 'The garden supplies both the restaurant and the café with up to 90% of their produce at specific times of the year along with many of Annie's beautiful seasonal jams and preserves' (Smithers, 2013). Christopher Kostow has his own on-site restaurant in the Napa Valley but also created a garden and greenhouse at the nearby St Helena Montessori school (Image 13.6), which will help to inspire the next generation to appreciate good, local produce

Image 13.6 Students of St Helena Montessori School serve customers at the St Helena Farmers' Market, Napa Valley, USA
Source: J. Laing.

(Arnold-Ratliff, 2013). Alain Passard, chef at L'Arpège, takes visitors through his organic garden with small-crop rotation in the Sarthe, and transports his vegetables 200 km by the morning TGV train to Paris, where they appear on the tables of his restaurant by lunchtime (Gopnik, 2011).

Foraging

Being presented with a plate of regional specialities is not enough for many food explorers. They enjoy the thrill of the chase – collecting or *foraging* for the ingredients of their meals, just like the chefs on television, such as the 'always game Hugh Fearnley-Whittingstall – who'll whip up a meal using little more than a handful of weeds and a brace of calves' (McCabe, 2012). Glazebrook Lodge in New Zealand's Marlborough region offers diners the chance to gather the ingredients (e.g. saffron, salmon, crayfish and plums) that chef Simon Gault will use to create their dinner (McCabe, 2012). In a sense this trend is nothing new. TV chef Antonio Carluccio 'was out in the woods gathering mushrooms and herbs before today's enthusiasts were even conceived' (Schofield, 2013: 76). Truffle hunting has always been a national pastime in France and parts of Italy, and there are now foraging courses in the United Kingdom to train people to find everything from elderflowers to nettles.

Moving Towards the Explorer Economy

The emergence of the food explorer has led to a need for a new dimension or realm of the experience economy, covering *exploration*. This refers to the intense and memorable pleasure which some tourists get from discovery – seeking things out for themselves rather than gaining access to them too easily, and unearthing or encountering things that the mass of tourists might miss or overlook. This exploration realm arguably comprises elements of all four experiential realms identified by Pine and Gilmore (1998, 1999). There is an educational element, where the tourist learns about a new cuisine or food heritage. These experiences are enjoyable and often fun, so entertainment may be involved. The tourist can escape the everyday world, and the aesthetics inherent in food tourism are manifest, including the tastes, smells, sights and sounds of markets, retail stores, bars, cellar doors and restaurants and their ambience and atmosphere. One could regard them as sacred experiences in some instances, with references to pilgrimages and the intense devotion to finding new experiences and tracking down the unknown and the untried.

Pine and Gilmore (1999) argue that experiences that encompass all four realms represent the optimum experience: highly memorable and highly authentic (Frost & Laing, 2011). Yet the exploration realm, exemplified by the food explorer, goes *beyond* merely combining those four realms identified by Pine and Gilmore. There are several distinct elements to this realm. First, there is a touch of *ego* about this behaviour – these tourists see a prestige bestowed in being different to the masses. In this way they are akin to the frontier traveller (Laing & Crouch, 2011), who visits risky and faraway places like the poles, Mount Everest and outer space, beyond the wallets and comprehension of the average person.

Second, these travellers seek out a high degree of *authenticity* in what and who they interact with in a tourist setting. As Cohen (2004: 321) notes with respect to the frontier traveller, they are challenging a 'world of increasing sameness in which travel tends to be reduced to "mere" leisure, enjoyment and fun'. Many of these individuals would not regard themselves as tourists. In their minds, they are *travellers*, given they largely journey independently and do not expect infrastructure developed just for them. They prefer to use the facilities and activities that locals engage in to a large extent, seeking out home stays, trying regional cuisines and trying to live as the locals do. Whether this goal is ever possible is beyond the scope of this chapter, although it is notable that even home stays are often regulated and run along business lines, with the owners not even present in some cases, and the interest in local cultural specialties might not be shared by the resident community and thus be particularly authentic.

Third, these tourists have strong social values and seek experiences that are *sustainable* in a broad sense – economically, environmentally and socioculturally. They concern themselves with the ramifications or impacts of their tourist activities and seek to minimise their footprint where possible. They attend events that link with this ethos (Laing & Frost, 2010) and seek out tourist experiences that are a strong fit with their green principles and way of life.

This chapter does not merely advocate a change to the Pine and Gilmore model to include an exploration realm. The existence of the explorer tourist more broadly suggests that the *model itself* needs to be rethought. Rather than assuming that all tourists want a staged, scripted and pre-packaged experience, which underpins Pine and Gilmore's thinking with respect to the experience economy, it is time to think of tourist experiences as more *organic and dynamic* phenomena, which may occur serendipitously, based on a suite of elements or ingredients which tourists select based on their individual preferences and interests (Frost & Laing, 2011). They are thus within the control of the tourist, or at the very least a *co-creation*, rather than being created or developed for them by the tourism industry. The tourist experience will therefore be different for each individual (Chronis, 2005; Frost & Laing, 2011; Ooi, 2005). Pine and Gilmore (2011: xx) themselves recognise this, with their comment in the introduction to a revised edition of their 1999 work: 'to a degree all experiences are co-created'.

Pine and Gilmore's emphasis on charging for experiences is often anachronistic in a food explorer context. The experiences they seek out might be expensive (the participatory cooking school experience, the meal at the Fat Duck in Berkshire or Noma in Copenhagen), yet it costs nothing to stroll through a produce market in Florence and next to nothing to pick up a taco from a food truck in New York. It may lead them to pay handsomely for their meal that lunchtime or in the evening, or it may not. That is the serendipity inherent in the tourist experience, which the Pine and Gilmore model, as it currently stands, fails to acknowledge.

Concluding Remarks: The Implications for the Future of Food Tourism

Trends discussed in this chapter have various implications for the future of food tourism. While the food explorer is currently a niche market – and proud to be so – it is likely that their numbers and influence will continue to grow. There will therefore be a movement away from homogeneity and an increasing desire to be different and *seen to be different*. According to Vernon (2013: 37), this drive for novelty is based on 'the urge to be interesting', and in an era of Facebook, Twitter and 'selfies': 'We now competitively showboat our eccentricities, penchants, tendencies, proclivities, and outlandish pastimes'. Tourists will seek out experiences that allow active engagement and learning, providing them with cultural capital and social status. This will lead to burgeoning dissatisfaction with standardised food tourism offerings aimed at the mass tourist.

Image 13.7 Fish on display in the streets of Bologna, Italy
Source: W. Frost.

An emphasis on commodification of experiences, particularly for a premium, risks downgrading the value of immersion in the atmosphere of a destination. Simply being a *flâneur* on the streets of a gourmet hub like Bologna (Image 13.7) or Paris, admiring the street stalls and window displays of greengrocers, butchers, delicatessens and bakeries, may be priceless in the food explorer's eyes, even if followed by a meal in the priciest of restaurants.

Destinations and the tourism industry will have to focus less on scripting and staging, and more on providing the elements that the food explorer can use to create their own personalised experience. It will be important for them to create the right environment for these elements to be present in a destination, such as regulations that encourage window and street displays of food or facilitate the presence of small bars and cafés, giving the tourist something surprising to discover. The creation of more slow cities (Frost & Laing, 2013b) might lead to more destinations that value food as a centrepiece of a lifestyle that is both sustainable and authentic.

References

Albrecht, M.M. (2011) 'When you're Here, you're family': Culinary tourism and the Olive Garden Restaurant. *Tourist Studies* 11 (2), 99–113.

Arnold-Ratliff, K. (2013) Regional champion. *Time*, 21 January, 40–42.

Backhouse, M. (2012) Savouring the favour of history. *The Saturday Age*, Lifestyle, 3 March, 14–15.

Bell, L. (2013) Viva a food revolution. *The Saturday Age*, Travel, 16 March. See www.theage.com.au/travel/activity/food-and-wine/viva-a-food-revolution-20130314-2g2js.html (accessed 22 March 2012).

Bergman, A., Karlsson, J.C. and Axelsson, J. (2010) Truth claims and explanatory claims: An ontological typology of futures studies. *Futures* 42 (8), 857–865.

Bruner, E.M. (1994) Abraham Lincoln as authentic reproduction: A critique of postmodernism. *American Anthropologist* 96 (2), 397–415.

Calombaris, G. (2009) *Greek Cookery from the Hellenic Heart*. Chatswood, NSW: New Holland.

Chronis, A. (2005) Coconstructing heritage at the Gettysburg storyscape. *Annals of Tourism Research* 32 (2), 386–406.

Cohen, E. (1988) Authenticity and commoditization in tourism. *Annals of Tourism Research* 15, 371–386.

Cohen, E. (2004) *Contemporary Tourism: Diversity and Change*. Kidlington: Elsevier.

Dickinson, J. and Lumsden, L. (2010) *Slow Travel and Tourism*. London: Earthscan.

Dubecki, L. (2011) Would you cross Melbourne for a taco? *The Age*, The Melbourne Magazine, 25 November, 92.

Faris, S. (2013) Italy, fast & slow. *Time*, 21 January, 36–38.

Florida, R. (2002) *The Rise of the Creative Class: And How it's Transforming Work, Leisure, Community and Everyday Life*. Cambridge, MA: Basic Books.

Florida, R. (2005) *Cities and the Creative Classes*. London; New York: Routledge.

Friends International (2013) Friends the restaurant. See www.friends-international.org/shop/friendstherestaurant.asp?mm=sh&sm=fr (accessed 15 March 2013).

Frost, W. and Laing, J. (2011) Up close and personal: Rethinking zoos and the experience economy. In W. Frost (ed.) *Zoos and Tourism: Conservation, Education and Entertainment?* (pp. 133–142). Bristol: Channel View Publications.

Frost, W. and Laing, J. (2013a) *Commemorative Events: Memory, Identities, Conflict*. London: Routledge.

Frost, W. and Laing, J. (2013b) Communicating persuasive messages through slow food festivals. *Journal of Vacation Marketing* 19 (1), 67–74.

Frost, W., Laing, J., Wheeler, F. and Reeves, K. (2010) Coffee, culture, heritage and destination image: Australia and the Italian model. In L. Jolliffe (ed.) *Coffee Culture, Destinations and Tourism* (pp. 99–110). Bristol: Channel View Publications.

Gill, R. (2012) Right on. *The Saturday Age*, Lifestyle, 25 February, 15.

Gopnik, A. (2011) Treasures of the soil. *The Weekend Australian*, 19–20 November, Indulgence, 8.

Gourmet Safaris. (2013) See www.gourmetsafaris.com.au/ (accessed 20 February 2013).

Hall, C.M. (2006) Introduction: Culinary tourism and regional development: From slow food to slow tourism? *Tourism Review International* 9 (4), 303–305.

Harden, M. (2012) Stellar surprise. *Gourmet Traveller*, July, 65–67.

Hill, K. (2013) The Gourmet Club. *Good Weekend*, 26 January, 18–20.

Intrepid (2013) Real food world tour. See www.intrepidtravel.com/real-food-world-tour (accessed 20 February 2013).

Laing, J.H. and Crouch, G.I. (2011) Frontier tourism: Retracing mythic journeys. *Annals of Tourism Research* 38 (4), 1516–1534.

Laing, J. and Frost, W. (2010) 'How green was my festival': Exploring challenges and opportunities associated with staging green events. *International Journal of Hospitality Management* 29 (2), 261–267.

Laing, J. and Frost, W. (2013) Food, wine ... heritage, identity? Two case studies of Italian diaspora festivals in regional Victoria. *Tourism Analysis* 18 (3), 323–334.

Leung, J. (2012) The disappearing dishes of Hong Kong. *Gourmet Traveller*, December, 194–200.

McCabe, C. (2012) Full forage ahead in New Zealand. *The Australian*, Travel, 5 May. See www.theaustralian.com.au/travel/full-forage-ahead/story-e6frg8rf-1226344061077 (accessed 12 March 2013).

Miele, M. and Murdoch J. (2002) The practical aesthetics of traditional cuisines: Slow food in Tuscany. *Sociologia Ruralis* 42 (4): 312–328.

Ooi, C.-S. (2005) A theory of tourist experiences: The management of attention. In T. O'Dell and P. Billing (eds) *Experiencescapes: Tourism, Culture and Economy* (pp. 51–68). Copenhagen: Copenhagen Business School Press.

Pine, J.B. II and Gilmore, J.H. (1998) Welcome to the experience economy. *Harvard Business Review* (July–August), 97–105.

Pine, J.B. II and Gilmore, J.H. (1999) *The Experience Economy: Work is Theatre and Every Business A Stage*. Boston, MA: Harvard Business School Press.

Pine, J.B. II and Gilmore, J.H. (2011) *The Experience Economy*. Boston, MA: Harvard Business School Press.

Quan, S. and Wang, N. (2004) Towards a structural model of the tourist experience: An illustration from food experiences in tourism. *Tourism Management* 25, 297–305.

Richardson, L. (2013) Guilt free gourmet. *Sydney Morning Herald Weekend Edition*, Traveller, 12–13 January, 6–7.

Sabrina (1954) Movie. United States: Paramount Pictures.

Schofield, L. (2013) Il Maestro. *Gourmet Traveller*, March, 76.

Smith, G. (2012) Barthes on Jamie: Myth and the TV revolutionary. *Journal of Media Practice* 13 (1), 3–17.

Smithers, A. (2012) *From Garden to Table*. Melbourne: Penguin.

Smithers, A. (2013) From garden to table. See www.anniesmithers.com.au/garden-to-table (accessed 4 March 2013).

Tan, M. (2013) Melbourne's hidden bars. *Travel*. See http://travel.ninemsn.com.au/holi daytype/winedine/8222571/melbournes-hidden-bars (accessed 1 March 2013).

Unique Group Travel (2013) Eat your way around Vietnam. See www.uniquegrouptravel. com.au/default.asp?action=article&ID=21627 (accessed 20 February 2013).

Vernon, P. (2013) A life more ordinary. *The Age Good Weekend*, 23 November, 37.

Wang, N. (2000) *Tourism and Modernity: A Sociological Approach*. Oxford: Pergamon.

Yeoman, I. (2012) *2050 – Tomorrow's Tourism*. Bristol: Channel View Publications.

14 The Future of Dining Alone: 700 Friends and I Dine Alone!

Brian Hay

Highlights

- The construct of the family is forever changing and the future of the single diner will be determined by both the long-term changes in the structure of the population and the future growth of single-person households.
- The traditional model of three square meals/day at set times was driven by the regularity needs of the industrial society, in the future this will change as both work and lifestyle patterns continue to adapt to the demands of the 365/24/7 society.
- To meet the future needs of these changing work and lifestyles choices, including the single diner, restaurants will need to develop different dining options, designs and eating layouts.
- With the continuing development of technology and the adoption of increasingly informal communications structures, there will be a meshing and merger of functional and leisure activities, and in the future dining alone will become part of a multi-functional leisure activity.
- In the future, dining alone will no longer be associated with the lonely nor seen as an unacceptable social activity, but as a positive lifestyle choice.
- Irrespective of distance or location, it will be possible in the future, through the projection of full-size holographic images, for the single diner to have the option of sharing their meal experiences in real time with their friends and family.
- The future of food tourism is dependent on meeting the needs of the single diner, and failure to meet these needs may have a detrimental impact on the quality of all our lives.

Introduction

This chapter explores the key drivers of change that may influence the growth of the single diner market and provides foresights into possible future trends and developments of this market segment. Eating as a social activity is often perceived as family and friends appreciating good quality food and enjoying each other's company, but almost half of the meals eaten at home are taken alone (Poulter, 2003). Dining alone in a restaurant is often considered an unacceptable social practice, with the single diner almost perceived as a social outcast, and as suggested by Skidelsky (2005: 56), the best the single diner can expect is 'dingy-looking eating exotic eateries (and) ramshackle stalls adjacent to bus and railway stations'. However, the hospitality sector has always found space, if not exactly an open welcome, for the single diner. The historic suggested social isolation and loneliness of the single diner is reflected in images such as Edward Hopper's iconic 1942 painting of the diner in *Nighthawks*, in the 1958 movie of life in a Bournemouth (UK) residential hotel *Separate Tables*, and in the design of the 1960s classic American diner with its rows of single seating. Even today this social isolation is reflected in the design of airport restaurants, with their single-person dining booths, television screens and ipad docking stations.

While business tourists often represent the iconic image of the single diner, population and social changes are afoot, which will have a major impact on the future of food tourism. People from single households have long been perceived as being both alone and lonely, and this trend has been highlighted in a number of influential books and reports by social commentators, such as: Riesman (1950) in *The Lonely Crowd*, Galbraith (1969) in *The Affluent Society* and Putnam (2000) in *Bowling Alone*. However, more recently, being single is seen as a positive lifestyle choice, as embraced by Feldon (2003), supported by data from the United Kingdom (UK) government (Office of National Statistics (ONS), 2011) and the traditional negative connotations have been challenged by Klinenberg (2013). These authors have questioned whether the decline in social capital and an increase in loneliness and isolation in the West can be attributed solely to the growth in single-person households.

Although the focus of this chapter is about the future of single diner eating out, not all dining takes place outwith the home environment. As a study by the Future Foundation (2011) suggests, for about one-third of the UK population, the singleton supper is now the most common way to eat dinner, this rises to 60% for single males. What is interesting is that the singleton supper is now a multi-purpose activity, and is as much an entertainment event as a dining event, with the meal taken in conjunction with other functions, such as watching the TV, tweeting or Facebooking friends. Neither is dining alone restricted to the home, hotel or restaurant, as the BBC (2013) has suggested, over half of UK office workers regularly have lunch alone at their desks.

In addition, there has been rapid development in new technology and social media, which have led to changing work and leisure behaviours, and one result of these trends is the growth in the number of our online 'friends'. There has also been a growth in what has been termed 'individualism', accompanied by a breakdown and disconnection of the individual from the wider society. This trend is illustrated, for example, by the provision of dogs for hire to single diners in a Korean restaurant so they do not feel alone (Vittachi, 2002); by Jones (2011), who questions why he is eating alone when he has so many (online) friends; and in a recent study for the Future Foundation (2011) on the future dining styles of people who eat alone.

In the last decade, there have been three fundamental trends in society that are relevant for this chapter, and although they are country-specific, they nevertheless reflect these wider trends:

- Trend 1. In the USA in 2010, the number of prepared meals overtook the number of home-cooked meals (Lucchesi, 2011).
- Trend 2. Almost half of all meals eaten in the UK at home are taken alone (Poulter, 2003), and when we do share meals with others at home, more than a third of us do not speak to our dining companions (Red Tractor, 2013).
- Trend 3. In 2006, according to the Future Foundation (2008), society experienced a profound shift, when for the first time the nuclear family was no longer the predominant household form.

An Exploration of Issues Affecting the Future of the Single Diner

Before we go much further there is a need to be clear as to the meaning of 'dining alone'. While the emotional term 'alone' is normally associated with being single, this does not suggest that dining alone means dining by yourself. For example, going on holiday by yourself does not mean that your meals are lonely experiences, single backpackers often enjoy meals with their fellow travellers. The term 'dining alone' for the purpose of this chapter is taken to mean 'through necessity or choice eating a meal (either cooked, prepared or as a take-away) by oneself in your home, or eating and paying only for your own meal in a restaurant outside your home environment'. It does not preclude meeting strangers at restaurants, sharing the enjoyment of preparing meals in communal facilities and does not make any assumption as to household status/lifestyles.

Dining alone is not an activity confined to a specific segment of society, namely the young and single. For example, the importance of social contact for the single elderly is just as important as the nutritional value of eating, as reported by Lewis (2010) in a study about lunch clubs. With our increasingly busy lives, even members of the traditional nuclear family may develop different eating patterns, including dining alone, as parents may work different hours and children are involved in a diverse range of school activities or have part-time jobs. This trend is reflected in many families not even owning a dining table (Poulter, 2003), and some local authorities in the UK questioning the need for a dining room at all (Woolf, 2013).

As suggested by Bennett and Dixon (2006), the growth of single-person households in the future will be driven by four key trends:

(1) Increasing life expectancy, especially among elderly women.
(2) Increased growth in their absolute numbers (relative to other age groups) of both genders in the 25–44 age group.
(3) An increase in single living as a lifestyle choice by young males.
(4) Single living becoming a more permanent lifestyle choice for all age groups.

In conjunction with these general trends, there are four major specific trends that will influence directly the future growth of the single diner.

Changing household structures

There is no doubt that the population structure is changing as it ages – marriage is postponed or even rejected, family size is reducing and more people are actively choosing to remain single as a positive lifestyle choice. Living with other people, whether in marriage or not, along with the concept of the nuclear family, has long been embedded into human development (Murdock, 1949). However, as Klinenberg (2013) has noted (albeit within a United States (US) context) we now spend more of our life unmarried, rather than married, and for most of this time people who are unmarried now live alone. In 2006 in England, single-person households accounted for 6.82 million of the 21.52 million households, some 32% of all households (Table 14.1). However, in the future there will be a significant increase in single-person households, and they are forecasted to be the largest segment, accounting for 39% of all households, in England by 2031.

This growth is not unique to England, as global population projections from Euromonitor International (2012) show; the number of single-person households may grow from 277 million in 2011 to 331 million by 2020, accounting for almost 15% of all the world's households. Of course, this trend is not uniform across all countries; by 2020 over 36% of all households in the US will be single-person households, 32% in China, 31% in Western Europe, but only 18% in Japan, 17% in India and 15% in Germany. The reasons for this growth are numerous: the breakdown of family structures,

Table 14.1 Number of households by household type in England (millions)

Household type/year	2006	2016	2026	2031	As a percentage of all households in 2031
Married	9.40	9.12	9.13	9.18	33
Cohabiting	2.19	3.03	3.57	3.80	14
Lone parent	1.66	1.85	1.97	2.02	7
Other multi-person	1.45	1.65	1.82	1.91	7
Single person	6.82	8.46	10.18	10.90	39
All households	21.52	24.10	36.67	27.82	
% of single-person households	32	35	38	39	

Source: Communities and Local Government (2009).

delays in marriages due to people focusing on their education and careers, rise in female employment with delays in marriage and subsequent lower birth rates, increases in divorces and the number of single parents. As well as an aging population, there is also an increasing global old-age dependency ratio (% of person 65+ to persons aged 15–64) from 21% in 2001, 24% in 2011 and 30% by 2020 (Euromonitor International, 2012). There are also another two important impacts resulting from this growth in single-person households: they tend to concentrate in city centres and metropolitan areas (Summerfield & Babb, 2004) and due to their employment status and income they are likely to be both poorer and more richer than average (Department for Work and Pensions (DWP), 2005).

Growth of the single tourist

Although single-person households are not necessarily an indication of the number of single tourists, some destination marketing organisations (DMOs) are now recognising their presence. For example, VisitWales defines the single tourists as 'my good self' (VisitWales, 2012), with some 13% of the respondents to one of their 2012 marketing campaigns describing themselves as such. There are limited data on the number of tourists who travel by themselves; nevertheless, Table 14.2 provides at least an indication of the size of the market, in terms of overseas tourists to the UK who travel alone (38%), and, not surprising, some 68% of business tourists and 44% of visiting friends and relatives (VFR) tourists also travel alone. However, travelling alone does not necessarily mean that they dine alone, especially in case of VFR tourists.

As well as overnight tourists, there is a growing awareness of the day visitor market, where in 2011, in the UK alone, some 235 million day trippers travelled by themselves, spending some £4,600 million (Table 14.3). Although

Table 14.2 Overseas visitors to Britain by type of group

Type of group	Percentage
Traditional family of spouse/partner & children	8
Spouse/partner, but no children in travel group	21
Children in group, but no spouse/partner	9
Not alone, but no children or partner in group	24
Travelling alone	38

Source: VisitBritain (2010).

Table 14.3 Day trips in Great Britain by type of group

Type of group	Number of trips (millions)	Spending (£millions)
Spouse/partner	694	29,726
With my children	238	10,156
With other members of my family	288	10,944
With friend(s)	394	12,282
With an organised group	47	1,359
With someone else	17	548
No one, I was on my own	235	4,601
Total	1,545	52,040

Source: VisitEngland (2012).

some of them will prepare their own meals when on a day trip, most will choose to eat meals away from home.

Changing technology and communications trends

There is no doubt that both businesses and personal communications have changed dramatically in the last few decades: from letters, faxes and emails to Facebook, Twitter and YouTube. However, what is not clear is whether these new communication methods have led to an increase in our ability to understand the messages. There is an assumption that with greater face-to-face communications, individuals are less likely to be lonely, while with more online communications they may become lonelier (Gillespie, 2012). The degree to which social media reflects loneliness or drives loneliness is open to debate, and some argue it is not possible to dine alone if at the same time you are accessing social media (Horwitz, 2009) or are engaging with your own social world (Jones, 2011). It can be argued that social media in itself does not make people lonely, but its use is a reflection of the increasing number of single-person households who are trying to connect with their friends. However, Ryan and Xenos (2011: 1663) argue that there is a 'tendency for neurotic and lonely individuals to spend greater amounts of time on Facebook per day than non-lonely individuals', but some people like to be alone, and for them using social media is a positive choice.

Social media is also influencing the way we learn about life in general and food in particular. According to the Hartman Group (2012), about half the population learns about food from social networking sites, and what they call 'digital food' is replacing the sensory experience with the visual experience. This is especially so for the single diner, where they use social media to share their dining experiences with their online friends. It is rare even today for the single diner to dine alone, as mobile devices now allow them to access their friends when dining, and have replaced the book as their preferred 'dining companion'. A more positive perspective on dining alone is offered by Turkle (2011), who suggests that it can be a very basic spiritual practice, that enables you experience moments of solitude, to refresh and restore yourself. In the future, dining alone, whether in a restaurant or at home, may be an optional activity, as real-time, full-size interactive holographic images of your family and friends may be projected onto a screen that forms part of your dining table, so you never have to dine alone?

Changing dining trends

Over the last decade, there have been major structural changes in the way individuals in the West interact socially with others. There is much less formality and fewer hierarchical structures at work and home; partnership is emerging as the management model of the future. The Twitter generation has rewritten the rules of social engagement, where 'Hi' is an acceptable introduction to strangers, abbreviations are widely acceptable, informality is the norm when talking to professionals and dressing down is expected. This growth in informality is also affecting the way we consume food, but this trend is not new; for example, the growth of frozen TV meals since the 1950s and the widespread use of microwaves in the 1970s have restructured the way we eat at home. Supermarkets are also changing the way we access food, with, for example, prepared meals for one and individual breakfast snacks. We are also developing into a population which increasingly snacks and grazes and eats at non-conventional times (Future Foundation, 2011). Another indication of this growth in informality and changes to the way we eat is that business travellers (who tend eat on their own) submitted more expenses forms in 2012 from fast food restaurants than all other types of restaurants (Lindeman, 2013). There are also signs that single-person households are adopting different and flexible living and dining arrangements. Single-person flats are now being designed with a range of facilities beyond the usual gym and garden, to include more shared social space, such as a party room, library and even a large communal kitchen, in which the residents meet and dine together every few weeks (Fardknappen, 2013).

So how can tourism and food providers respond to such trends: by embracing the trend rather than rejecting a market segment. Just as cinemas responded to DVDs/home entertainment by improving and upgrading the quality of the cinema experience, and shops have recognised that online shopping offers convenience by improving the quality of the technical knowledge of their staff about the products they sell, so restaurants will have to change to satisfy the needs of the single diner. In the future, we will increasingly see restaurants offering all day menus, with the menu not tied to a particular time, as this better suits the single diner lifestyle. This raises an interesting research question as to why eating some types of meals alone in public places is more acceptable than other meals. For example, the business person eating breakfast alone in an airport hotel, the office worker eating lunch alone in a fast food restaurant or a retired person enjoying an afternoon snack in a coffee shop by themselves are all acceptable, but the single diner enjoying an evening meal in a local suburban restaurant is viewed with suspicion.

Ten Future Options for Managing the Single Diner

It is rare for new tourism products to suddenly appear without them developing somewhere in the world before their popularity spreads. Therefore, the following suggested 10 future dining options for the single diner, ranked by their likely degree of occurrence, have been driven partly by the expansion of products already established in some parts of the world (particularly in the US and the Far East), but have also been shaped by the societal trends previously discussed.

(1) *The bar/lunch counter*: Common in US restaurants, where the single diner is invited to sit at the bar, but the full dinner menu is provided. This design offers individuals the opportunity to socialise or not with their dining neighbours. The social aspect of dining with others is replaced by the presence of the server and chefs who directly face and interact with the diner, and offer entertainment and small talk, as well as food. This has not really developed in Europe as a dining concept (due to the limited bar space in many restaurants), but in Japanese-style restaurants this is usually the only option, and this layout may gain in popularity in the future.

(2) *Exhibition kitchens*: Similar to the above, but where the activity of preparing meals acts as a displacement for conversion, and provides for the

single diner to engage in the dining experience, without the need to speak to strangers.

(3) *The communal table/table of new friends*: This is a special table in a restaurant where staff may invite single diners, groups and even couples to share their meals with complete strangers. This may work if the food is not ordered individually, but is offered as a fixed price buffet style meal, as this aids social interactions as diners make suggestions to other diners about the food.

(4) *Supper clubs*: There could be a reinvention of locally managed supper clubs, where on a regular basis single diners (both friends and tourists) have the opportunity to eat with others single diners at a selection of different restaurants.

(5) *Your own confirmed table*: If staying at a hotel for a number of days/or if you choose to eat regularly at the same local restaurant, it is sometimes possible to reserve the same table. The advantage of this arrangement is that the diner feels more comfortable (just like at home) by eating in the same place. A variation of this concept may be your own single personal named table in a restaurant.

(6) *Restaurants with private single-person dining booths*: This may be seen as a high-tech option, with the restaurant recognising that the single diner wants the dining experience to meet their specific needs. Where the provision of ipad docking stations, charging points, small TV screens, internet connections for meeting their Facebook and Twitter friends acts as a displacement activity from any discomfort caused by dining alone.

(7) *Mobile restaurants*: There has always been an assumption that the restaurants are fixed in time and space, but why? In the future, it should be possible for purpose-built restaurants to be mobile (restaurants on wheels!), that move as the source of the demand changes over the day/week/season. For example, in the city centre at lunchtime, but moving in the evening to locations where there is a high number of single-person households, or from cities in the winter to tourism destinations in the summer.

(8) *Single person restaurants*: Although rarely discussed as a feasible option, usually on grounds of cost, this concept may be feasible in the future at locations with a high number of single diners/tourists. This option may be particularly attractive for the 'gastrosexual' market, where the single diner may want enjoy the pleasure of eating as an activity, without the distraction of human company.

(9) *Regular restaurant, with a single-person take-away section*: Such places would have a separate entrance and space where singles would order and collect their meals from specially designed single-person menus, for dining at home.

(10) *Single sex restaurant/private membership clubs*: Developed from the concept of the US sorority/fraternity students' clubs, such clubs will

positively welcome the single diner who can choose to eat alone or in company with like-minded professionals. For the single diner such clubs provide both a lifestyle base and professional support function for their members.

Implications of Future Trends and Key Questions for Future Research

As the number of single-person households increases, because they tend to spend more of their disposable income on leisure activities (including dining out) than other forms of households, their importance as a market segment will grow. Their future impact will not only be felt in the dining-out market, but will also be reflected in the growing demand for single-person food offers from food stores. Although single persons may be less likely to go to out-of-town shopping centres for their weekly shopping, they will make more visits to local convenience shops. Therefore, we may expect to see in the future the continued development of local versions of national food chains close to single-person places of work and homes, which along with specialised local shops will provide premium food products, as single people may be willing to pay higher prices for both quality and convenience. As we move into a society where 365/24/7 service is not only demanded, but also expected, shops will never close so they can better cater for those on three-shift working patterns, or indeed no formal working patterns at all. In the future, the norm may be the 24-hour restaurant, which serves breakfast at midnight, dinner as the sun rises and lunch at the end of the 5.00 pm shift. A place where meals are no longer labelled as breakfast, etc., but where single diners select five/six small meals a day from a grazing menu?

As to any future role that the restaurant may play in social cohesion, perhaps restaurant managers already see this as their responsibility, although this may have something to do with the expectation of a larger tip! We have already seen a notable increase in the past few years in takeaway/to-go orders from single diners to eat alone at home, and in the future, this trend may result in more demand for quality meals from regular rather than fast food restaurants, for single diners to take home.

Just as in the past, we have seen a decline in manufacturing and an increase in service industries, but we still measure the success of the economy in terms of growth in manufacturing, so there is likely to be political pressure to support the family, at the expense of single-person households. However, in the future the single diner and tourist will no longer be quiet and passive. We have already seen the development of organisations such as the Single Tourist Action Centre (2013) whose aim is to end discrimination against single travelers, and for single women travellers there are social networking sites such as Invite for a Bite (2013) where they can meet and share meals. In the future, such political action groups will continue to grow and lobby for the rights of the single diner/tourist.

Future research and policy issues impacting the single diner and their eating trends include:

- Do they add to the quality of life by encouraging diversity in the provision of dining outlets?
- Do they assist in developing a multicultural society by supporting ethnic restaurants?
- Do they add to a location's social capital by harnessing their willingness to support a more vibrant local community?
- Do they encourage a more mixed development approach in the design of city centres?
- Do their dining styles at home vary when they are on holiday?
- Are there differences in dining companions/patterns when they dine at home, as opposed to dining out?
- What are the future different restaurant design options for the single diner?
- What are the emotional and psychological needs of the single diner when they eat alone in a restaurant?
- Are there differences in the dining patterns between those who choose to be single and those forced to be single?

Concluding Remarks: The Implications for the Future of Food Tourism

The implications for the future of food tourism are that the single diner is here to stay and they represent a future market segment that will demand that its needs be acknowledged. Positioning the individual single diner at the centre of the dining experience is the core attribute to developing this market segment, for dining alone means exactly what it says on the tin, providing a dining service that serves their needs, and not the restaurant's needs. Failure to respond to this market may result in further alienation of single people, and may even increase their isolation from mainstream society. However, it needs to be recognised that the single diner is a not a humongous entity, its sub-constituents are spread across and determined by factors such as age, income status, lifestyle choices (forced or elective choice to be single), gender, location (urban or rural), living costs and physical and emotional closeness to family, friends and work colleagues. Responding to the future single diner market will require a suit of different policy and management options, that not only recognise the size and diversity of the market, but also their different emotional and psychological needs and wants.

This chapter suggests that the single diner in the future will be much more demanding, and they will no longer accept poor quality or service. When dining alone at home or in a restaurant they will be expecting food that is geared towards their lifestyle choices, which combine quality, simplicity and portion size. We can also expect to see a growth in local quality food outlets as well as restaurants geared to the needs of the single diner. These places will be clustered around areas with a high number of single-person households, close to their workplaces and increasingly at tourism destinations popular with single tourists, and will be a mixture of both national chain restaurants and shops and local specialised restaurants and shops. There is also likely to be an increasing demand from single-person households and tourists for food bought from restaurants, so in the future we may expect to see the development of restaurants with no dining space, as they will only provide high-quality food to eat at home and in their holiday apartments. When single tourists dine out, we may expect them to demand either specialised single-person dining restaurants developed to meet their needs, or zones within more traditional restaurants, designed solely for their use.

The future growth in the number of single-person households will also influence both the design of cities and their own living spaces. Single people will accept small personal living spaces, in return for higher quality public spaces, where they can enjoy a better quality of life, and this includes both shared eating spaces built into their living spaces, as well as high-quality dining establishments. Therefore, it is likely that in the future the single diner will be a key driver in the development and shape of urban spaces. In terms of the type of food eaten in the future, the single diner will force a shift towards timeless and more frequent mini meals, where terms such a breakfast, lunch and dinner will be replaced on the 24/7 menu by meal number one, two, three, etc.

In the future, the single diner will be at the heart of food tourism, they will drive its development and product offers. They will not accept poor quality service or social rejection, and if existing restaurants do not offer products that suit their lifestyle, expect new single-person specialised restaurants to provide their meals. However, such a trend may have a detrimental long-term negative impact on the quality of all our lives, and the food tourism sector will have lost a developing and increasingly valuable income stream.

References

BBC (2013) Desk lunch: How can you make it a bit nicer? *BBC News Magazine,* 7 February.

Bennett, J. and Dixon, M. (2006) *Single Person Households and Social Policy: Looking Forwards.* York: Joseph Rowntree Foundation.

Communities and Local Government (2009) *Household Projections to 2031, England. Housing Statistical Release March 2009.* London: Communities and Local Government.

Department for Work and Pensions (DWP) (2005) *Households Below Average Income Series 1994–2004.* London: TSO.

Euromonitor International (2012) *Special Report: Rise in Single-Person Households Globally Impacts Consumer Spending Patterns.* See http://blog.euromonitor.com/2012/03/special-report-income-inequality-rising-across-the-globe.html (accessed 13 February 2013).

Fardknappen (2013) See www.fardknappen.se/fardknappen.se/ (accessed 14 February 2013).

Feldon, D. (2003) *Living Alone and Loving It: A Guide to Relishing the Solo Life.* New York: Fireside Publications.

Future Foundation (2008) *The Emergence of the Gastrosexual.* Report for PurAsia. See http://nvision.futurefoundation.net (accessed 15 February 2013).

Future Foundation (2011) *The Rise of the Singleton Supper.* Report for Mars Food. See http://nvision.futurefoundation.net (accessed 20 February 2013).

Galbraith, J.K. (1969) *The Affluent Society.* Norfolk: Lowe & Brydone.

Gillespie, J. (2012) Does Facebook make us lonely. *Sunday Times*, 5 May.

Hartman Group (2012) Clicks & cravings: The impact of social technology on food culture. See www.hartman-group.com/pdf/clicks-and-cravings-report-overview-and-order-form-2012.pdf (accessed 18 February 2012).

Horwitz, J. (2009) Eating at the edge. *Gastronomica: The Journal of Food and Culture* 9 (3), 42–47.

Invite for a Bite (2013) The safe, friendly place for women to meet and eat. See www.inviteforabite.com (accessed 11 February 2013).

Jones, A. (2011) We may have 750 friends online, but we're lonely. *The Times*, 3 December.

Klinenberg, E. (2013) *Going Solo: The Extraordinary Rise and Surprising Appeal of Living Alone.* London: Duckworth Overlook.

Lewis, M. (2010) Spending cuts in Cumbria. *BBC Cumbria*, 16 June.

Lindeman, T.F. (2013) Work zone: Travelers value ease. *Pittsburgh Post Gazette*, 13 February.

Lucchesi, E. (2011) Is communal dining becoming a thing of the past? *Tribune News Service*, 3 August.

Murdock, P.G. (1949) *Social Structure.* Oxford: Macmillan.

Office of National Statistics (ONS) (2011) *Social Trends* 41. Cardiff: ONS.

Poulter, S. (2003) How dinner for one is becoming our staple diet. *Daily Mail*, 8 April.

Putnam, R.D. (2000) *Bowling Alone: The Collapse and Revival of American Community.* New York: Simon & Schuster.

Red Tractor (2013) Research reveals that Britain is a nation of dinner table dodgers. Report for Red Tractor. See www.redtractor.org.uk/research-reveals-that-britain-is-a-nation-of-dinner-table-dodgers (accessed 16 February 2013).

Riesman, D. (1950) *The Lonely Crowd.* New Haven, CT: Yale University Press.

Ryan, T. and Xenos, S. (2011) Who uses Facebook? An investigation into the relationship between the Big Five, shyness, narcissism, loneliness, and Facebook usage. *Computers in Human Behavior* 27 (5), 1658–1664.

Single Tourist Action Centre (2013) Ending discrimination. See www.singletourist.org.uk (accessed 11 February 2013).

Skidelsky, W. (2005) Food. *New Statesman* 18 (841), 56.

Summerfield, C. and Babb, P. (eds) (2004) Households & families. *Social Trends* 34, 25–36.

Turkle, S. (2011) Party of 4G? *The Washington Post*, 2 November.

VisitBritain (2010) Overseas visitors to Britain: Understanding trends, attitudes and characteristics. See www.visitbritain.org/Images/Overseas%20Visitors%20to%20Britain_tcm139-196119.pdf (accessed 17 February 2013).

VisitEngland (2012) *The GB Day Visitor: Statistics 2011*. Edinburgh: TNS.
VisitWales (2012) *Autumn in Wales. Have a Seat Survey.* Personal Communication from VisitWales.
Vittachi, N. (2002) Travellers' tales. *Far Eastern Review* 16 (5), 61–62.
Woolf, M. (2013) Dining rooms may be taxed? *Sunday Times*, 10 March.

15 Dimensions of the Food Tourism Experience: Building Future Scenarios

Gianna Moscardo, Christina Minihan and Joseph O'Leary

Highlights

- This chapter presents a conceptual model of food tourism experiences.
- This model provides a food tourism classification system and maps out supply chain issues.
- The model also suggests future directions for different aspects of food tourism.
- The chapter concludes with possible future food tourism scenarios.

Introduction

Food tourism, also known as culinary and gastronomic tourism, refers to travel activities that are motivated by, and focused on, food production and consumption (Ignatov & Smith, 2006) It results from the confluence of three forces demand from tourists for food-related experiences, preparedness on the part of food producers to offer food, and the organisation of supply by tourism and hospitality businesses. Together these forces create a wide variety of opportunities for food tourism experiences ranging from food and wine tasting, food-themed tours of regions, cooking classes, themed restaurants, food festivals and haute cuisine dining. Food tourism is seen as both meeting market demands for more specialised and experiential forms of tourism (Kim *et al.*, 2010), and offering a way for regions to use tourism to support local industries and develop competitive advantage (du Rand & Heath, 2006). Many destinations see food tourism as a way to generate more sustainable tourism benefits for local producers and businesses (Green &

Dougherty, 2008). But the rapid development of food tourism has meant that a confusing array of tourist opportunities have emerged with limited research evidence to guide practice or predict future developments.

The challenge for tourism researchers is to better understand this tourism phenomenon and provide robust classification systems that will allow for the development of explanatory models to guide improvements to practice and predict future directions. This chapter aims to address this challenge by reviewing the available evidence on food tourism and conducting research into tourists' perspectives on food experiences. It particularly focuses on identifying key food tourism experience dimensions and examines the implications of these for current and future demand. Using Bergman et al.'s (2010) typology of futures studies, this chapter seeks to make predictions about food tourism based on both claims about the nature of food tourism and providing explanatory mechanisms to support these claims.

Food Tourism Analysis and Discussion to Date

The academic literature on food tourism is developing rapidly, although it incorporates a wide range of different phenomena and provides only limited evidence from tourist perspectives. It can be organised around four main themes – the role of food tourism in regional development, the potential of food tourism in developing destination images, issues for food tourism supply chains and aspects of tourist motivations, expectations and behaviours. In the first theme are papers that describe the ways in which food tourism can be used to support local heritage and culture (e.g. Everett & Aitchison, 2008), as a regional development tool (Montanari & Staniscia, 2009) and case studies of different food tourism developments (Harrington & Ottenbacher, 2010). The second theme is about the role of food in the development of tourism and destination image. In this theme papers discuss food tourism marketing practices (Boyn et al., 2003), guidelines for using food in destination marketing (Hashimoto & Telfer, 2006), and analyses of food tourism developments (Tikkanen, 2007). The third theme reflects an emerging interest in supply chains and the issues faced by those who produce and present food tourism (Deale et al., 2008; Smith & Xiao, 2008).

Finally, there is a small but increasing number of studies of food tourists, their profiles, expectations and evaluations. These papers explore tourist perspectives on food as a part of their travel and demand for specific food tourism opportunities. Rising interest in the different types of food tourism have been linked to the broader rise of experience as a driving force in tourist behaviour (Povey, 2011; Quadri-Felitti & Fiore, 2012). Thus food tourism is seen as offering education, authenticity, engagement and entertainment.

It has also been suggested that tourists can be distinguished by the extent to which they are seeking specialist food experiences (Sanchez-Canizares &

Lopez-Guzman, 2012), with several studies outlining five tourist types defined by their orientation towards food and travel:

(1) Recreational tourists who are conservative in their approach to food, mostly seeking familiar food;
(2) Diversionary tourists who are described as seeking escape from every-day obligations and so focused on dining convenience and ease;
(3) Experiential tourists who are interested in food as a way to access and understand local cultures;
(4) Experimental tourists who want to try new and different cuisines and follow food fashions; and
(5) Existential tourists who adopt specific eating habits and cuisines consis-tent with their own identity and wider lifestyle such as organic or veg-etarian options (Cohen & Avieli, 2004; Kivela & Crotts, 2009).

Beyond this broad segmentation there have been some studies of tourist characteristics and evaluations at specific food-themed attractions (e.g. Smith & Costello, 2009) or in specific destinations (e.g. Ruzic & Medica, 2009).

A Preliminary Framework for Organising the Food Tourism Experience

Two key experience dimensions were identified, based on a review of the relevant literature, and were used to develop a concept map for food tourism (Figure 15.1). The first dimension was the level of visitor engagement required, ranging from low engagement on the left, as typified by selecting local dishes from a menu, to high engagement on the right, such as taking cooking classes. The second dimension distinguishes between experiences focused on the destination place and experiences focused on the interests of the individual tourist. At the place end of this dimension are food-themed regional tours, while at the personal end of the dimension there are two options – seeking healthy, safe, or organic food and seeking fine dining or fashionable cuisines. Local food markets sit at the centre of the model at the intersection between local culture and personal interests, offering varied levels of tourist interac-tion. This framework provides a way to conceptualise the domain of food tourism experiences that incorporates both form and type characteristics (Uriely et al., 2002) and provides direction for further research.

Food tourism can be seen as an 'umbrella concept', which is an idea at the beginning of its research development lifecycle (Hirsch & Levin, 1999). Hirsch and Levin (1999) refer to the first stage in this cycle as 'emerging enthusiasm' with rapidly growing interest in the concept after its initial introduction. In this stage the concept is applied to a wide range of situations

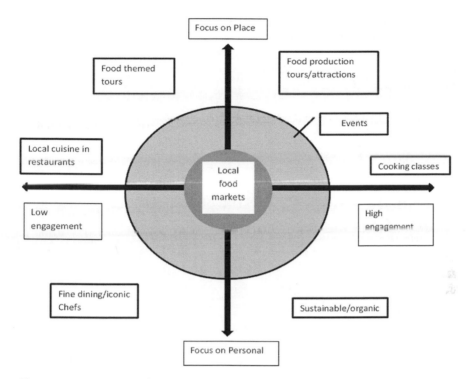

Figure 15.1 Preliminary food tourism experience framework

and linked to numerous other concepts. The literature review conducted for this chapter indicates that this is clearly the case for food tourism. This is then followed by a 'validity crisis' in which there is a critical response to the concept, with questions raised about the extent of its applicability and its value beyond existing theories (Hirsch & Levin, 1999). Responses to these challenges fall into third phase of 'tidying up typologies' where researchers begin to identify and classify which aspects of the phenomena under study are applicable to which parts of the concept of interest. According to Hirsch and Levin (1999) successful resolution of this stage is needed for conceptual coherence, otherwise there will be ongoing controversy and eventually the collapse of the concept.

The present analysis of food tourism experiences can be seen as an attempt to move beyond the stage of validity challenges by mapping out the key features of food tourism and suggesting some important typologies. The aim is to identify and use critical dimensions of food tourism experiences and to classify food tourism opportunities into coherent categories. This would then allow for an investigation of the supply side issues related to developing competitive and appropriate food tourism products, the identification of concepts and theories to explain tourist responses to different food tourism experiences, and an examination of potential future trends in the food tourism experiences. It is the latter objective that is of specific interest to this chapter and it requires an examination of tourist perspectives on food-related travel experiences.

Exploring Tourist Perspectives on Food Experiences

Method

In order to explore tourist perspectives the authors conducted a netnographic study (Kozinets, 2002) which gathered and content analysed 60 online tourist reviews of food tourism experience, 10 for each of the categories described in Figure 15.1. The sampling and analysis was conducted according to procedures described by Hsu *et al.* (2009). In the first stage of

Table 15.1 Summary of key experience themes for different types of food tourism experience

Themes	Cooking class	Product tours	Food tours	Food events	Sustain/ organic	Fine dining
Learning/knowledge 'learned the ins and outs of prosciutto' 'even more precious to learn the tradition behind this extraordinary product'	XXX	XXX	XX	X	X	X
Physical setting 'also get some photos of the buildings' 'the scenery [from the restaurant] is absolutely stunning'	XX	XX	X	XX	X	XX
Food quality 'after this you will never want to eat a Hershey bar again! – high quality chocolate' 'finest tasting [food] we've eaten'		XX	XXX	X	XX	XXX
Guide/teacher 'he provided a context to the naming of the wines' 'a great guide – very open'	XXX	XXX	X			

(Continued)

Table 15.1 *Continued*

Themes	Cooking class	Product tours	Food tours	Food events	Sustain/ organic	Fine dining
Service quality 'the staff is consistently helpful and friendly' 'service was very professional and friendly'					XX	XXX
Food variety 'three different dishes!' 'twenty different types'		XX	XX	XX		
Food quantity 'food portions were very generous' 'you will be stuffed'		X	XX	XX		X
Local culture 'excellent cultural experience – a lot of interesting local insight' 'it felt like a really authentic experience in a local home cooking with local grandmas and grandpas'	XX	X	XX	X		
Senses beyond taste 'a visual feast of colour and form…wonderful aromas to fill the air' 'the scent of garlic was wafting through the air'		XXX	XX	X		XX
Backstage access 'did you ever wish you knew someone from the city you are visiting so that you could experience a part of the city that the tourists don't see? Well now you do!'	XX	X	XX			
Fun/entertainment 'it was so much fun' 'very entertaining'		XX	X	XXX		

the sampling, targeted Google searches were used to identify a set of examples of food tourism experiences in each category from a range of different destinations. A random selection of five specific examples was then made from each category and in the second stage another internet search identified tourist reviews of these specific food tourism experiences. Two reviews were then chosen for each example using a systematic selection process to yield 60 reviews in total. The 60 examples came from a range of countries and included different cuisines, cultures and themes. These reviews were subjected to qualitative coding to identify key themes used to describe experiences and justify experience evaluations, both positive and negative.

Results

The thematic content analysis yielded 10 main themes and these are listed in Table 15.1 and described using quotes from the tourist reviews. The analysis focused on two questions – what were the main themes associated with all food tourism experiences and what themes or combination of themes could be used to distinguish between the different categories of food tourism experience? The marks in Table 15.1 are indicators of the extent of the use of the theme and the level of detail given to the links made between the theme and the experience with XXX meaning extensive and detailed links and X referring to some links but with little detail. Only two themes, a focus on learning and knowledge and recognition of the centrality of the physical setting, were consistently linked to all six categories. In the latter case this was mostly a concern with enjoying food experiences in a pleasant and/or interesting physical location. The learning and knowledge theme was, however, often mentioned in detail and/or several times across all the reviews indicating that food tourism is embedded in learning and self-development.

The analysis suggested a different cluster of themes was associated with each of the food tourism categories, confirming the usefulness of the initial framework. Thus cooking classes were described as providing backstage access to local culture and were influenced by the skills of the guide/teacher. The guide also played an important role in visits to places of food production with these experiences also characterised as multi-sensory and entertaining, with an emphasis on food quality and variety and, to a lesser degree, food quantity. Food-themed tours of destinations, both independent and guided, were focused simultaneously on both the food and local culture. For most tourists in this category food was a way to access and understand the place. Food events were primarily described in terms of fun and entertainment, with enthusiasm for food quantity and variety. By way of contrast, the last two groups strongly emphasised food quality and service staff with the main difference between them being the focus on food quantity and senses beyond taste for tourists reviewing their fine-dining experiences.

The Food Tourism Experience Framework

This exploratory study provided guidance for the further development of a food tourism experience framework and this is presented in Figure 15.2.

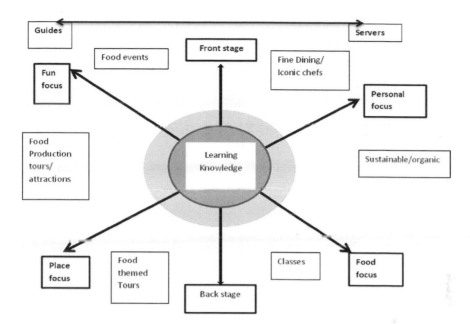

Figure 15.2 A conceptual framework for food tourism experiences

This framework is based on four experiential dimensions with learning and knowledge as a core element for all food tourism experiences. The figure retains the place versus personal dimension from the preliminary model but adds the dimensions of fun versus food focus and back stage versus front stage. Using these three dimensions it is possible to place the six main categories or types of food tourism experience around the model. Thus cooking classes are focused on food and access to the local culture beyond typical tourism spaces and opportunities, while food events tend to be staged and more about fun and entertainment. Regional food theme tours are an alternative way to access the back stage areas of a destination but with food being used as a means to interpret the place. The pursuit of famous chefs and fashionable or fine dining opportunities are, in turn, carefully staged and have a strong focus on self-image and self-development. Finally, food production attractions, such as distilleries and farms, are usually about a place and provide entertainment, with the pursuit of sustainable/organic food defined by a personal focus on the food itself. The model also includes a consideration of the role of staff in the food tourism experience, who were often described as critical to the tourist experience. On the left hand side of the model the staff are more likely to be seen as guides while on the right they are typically described as servers.

This conceptual framework can be used to map out and consider supply needs for each of the six types of food tourism experience. For example, the importance of learning and knowledge suggests that food tourism suppliers and presenters need to carefully consider the content and presentation of information about the food and its production. Combining this central element and the critical role of staff suggests resources should be invested in staff training that enhances their knowledge of the food being served and how to most effectively engage tourists in learning about it. The framework can also suggest relevant theories that could be applied to explain and guide practice in the different sectors. For example, the sector between front stage and personal focus, which includes an interest in fashionable cuisines, fine-dining and iconic chefs, might be best understood using ideas from the wider literature on connoisseurship (e.g. Brown, 2012; Manzo, 2010) or fashions in consumption (e.g. Moretti, 2011; Rafferty, 2011).

Food Tourism Futures

The framework can also be used to critically reflect on future directions and scenarios for food tourism using two approaches to understanding the pressures on the food tourism experience framework – general competitive pressures on products and services, and more specific predicted trends. Two related models are particularly appropriate for the discussion of general competitive pressures – the product lifecycle (PLC) and Porter's five competitive pressures (Porter, 2008). The basic PLC model suggests that products go through a similar set of stages including:

- an introductory stage when the first products are taken up by early adopters;
- a take-off stage where product information is disseminated and there is rapid growth;
- a slower growth stage with an increasing number of products being offered and substantial competitive pressure;
- movement into maturity with unsuccessful businesses leaving; and
- a final stage of product decline if alternatives or substitutes are developed (Golder & Tellis, 2010).

It might be argued that food tourism is in the early growth or take-off stage of the product lifecycle with rapid growth in both consumer interest and the number of destinations developing and promoting food tourism options. For both existing food tourism businesses and destinations seeking to develop tourism, this means that there is considerable and rapidly increasing competitive pressure. According to Porter (2008), options for responding to this pressure include increasing the value of the experience for consumers and finding ways to differentiate the product from others in the marketplace. Differentiation often involves the development of related products and new sub-categories of products (Calantone *et al.*, 2010). Tourism destinations, however, tend to engage in serial reproduction of experiences rather than differentiation or innovation (Richards, 2011). This presents a significant challenge for destinations using food in tourism development and marketing. Without product differentiation and attention to increasing consumer value it may be that many food tourism initiatives will fail. This does not mean that all food tourism experiences will decline, but rather that there will be consolidation with some destinations remaining strongly associated with food tourism experiences, while others may move to alternative tourism strategies. It is likely that over time successful food tourism experiences will become more differentiated and thus shift away from the centre of the framework and towards the outer rim of the framework, focusing on more specialised experiences.

The second way to examine food tourism futures uses the specific trends that might be connected to the dimensions in the food tourism framework. Table 15.2 provides a summary of four major current trends that have been reported as likely to influence consumer and business futures. The first and most dominant of these major trends is the continued pressure on businesses and individuals to adopt more sustainable actions (Bonini & Oppenheim, 2008; Esty & Winston, 2009). Widespread public discussion and media coverage of sustainability issues increases pressure on all businesses to address those issues in their products and services. In addition to this general move towards sustainability, there is a focus on the development of corporate social responsibility programmes to complement and balance pro-environmental activities (Eweje, 2011). Three predictions for food tourism futures can be developed from this trend. First, for those food tourism operations that get supplies from elsewhere, there will be increasing consumer, government and competitive pressure to consider the sustainability of the production of those supplies with greater use of sustainability labelling and accreditation. Second, this sustainability pressure will move beyond supplies to consider the actions of the food tourism business itself. In the shorter term there will be a market for sustainability-themed restaurants such as Billy Kwong's in Sydney (Kwong, 2013). In the medium term the adoption of sustainability programmes will become a widespread expectation of all food tourism businesses (Potts Dawson, 2011). The third prediction is the blending of food tourism and social enterprise with tourists likely to seek and support restaurants such as Jamie Oliver's Fifteen (Fifteen, 2013) and an expansion of other types of food experiences linked to social enterprises (Thompson, 2012).

The second major trend, related to sustainability, is the rise of concerns about health and well-being with continued growth in demand for organic, safe and healthy food options (Falguera *et al.*, 2012). One of the challenges will be meeting this demand worldwide with many consumers in developed and urban areas unlikely to be able to access organic food regularly and easily (Kearney, 2010). In this scenario, having easy access to locally produced, safe and/or organic food could become a major competitive advantage for some destinations. A second implication of this trend is that increasingly tourists will expect all food providers to offer organic, healthy and specific dietary options on their menus and to make this information easily available (Poulston & Yiu, 2011). Finally, it can also be suggested that demand for holiday cooking classes might emerge for programmes that are less about regional cuisines and more about healthy food options.

The third major trend reported in Table 15.2 is the rise of the middle class and consumers from what have been called the BRIC (Brazil, Russia, India and China) countries (Court & Narasimhan, 2010). This trend has several implications for food tourism futures. At the simplest level, increasing affluence in these countries generates increasing numbers of international travellers (Euromonitor, 2011; UNWTO, 2012), which in turn heightens demand for the provision of cuisines from these countries in the restaurants of popular destinations. These new international consumers have also been linked to high demand for luxury goods and services (Hennigs *et al.*, 2012; Yeoman & McMahon-Beattie, 2006). This interest in luxury goods reflects a desire to appear more sophisticated and Western/European in order to improve social status (Zhan & He, 2012). The implications for food tourism futures include greater demand from these markets for fine-dining, fashionable foods and opportunities to develop connoisseurship.

The fourth trend to be considered is the changing pattern of generational cohorts in tourist markets. Generational cohorts are groups of people born within a certain time period that share common life experiences and values

Table 15.2 Major future trends

Major trend	Predicted associated changes
Continued pressure for adoption of sustainability programmes	Sustainability becomes an expected operating standard for most businesses Shift to balance environmental sustainability with corporate social responsibility
Continued rise of concerns about health and well-being	Rapid growth in demand for organic/healthy food
Emerging markets and growing middle classes in Brazil, Russia, India and China	New groups of consumers eager to pursue luxury products and services Demand for a wider range of cuisines
Changing generational cohorts	As Generation Y matures it dominates consumer markets seeking experience, fun and entertainment Ageing Baby Boomers increasingly seek health and nostalgia

Sources: Global Trends (2013); Trendwatching (2013); Trends Research (2013).

that influence their behaviours (Noble & Schewe, 2003). In the last 30 years the two main cohorts of tourists have been Baby Boomers (born between 1940s and early 1960s) and Generation X (born in the early 1960s to the early 1980s). As Baby Boomers age the mix of generations in consumer markets is changing, with Generation Y (born between the early 1980s and early 2000s) becoming a dominant force (Moscardo & Benckendorff, 2010). Each of these groups has a different set of characteristics that influences their patterns of consumption. Generation Y have been consistently described as seeking experiences rather than products – especially those that offer entertainment, theming and diversity – as having a strong family and social orientation and as wanting meaningful travel (Moscardo et al., 2011). As they age and begin to travel as parents with children, it is likely that they will seek food tourism experiences that are themed, focused on fun, and that allow them to have quality social interactions with families and friends. Although Baby Boomers may become less dominant in the overall mix of tourists, they will still be an important market segment reflecting an ongoing interest in travel during retirement (Worsley et al., 2011). But as they age it has been suggested that they will be interested in both healthy food (Worsley et al., 2011) and nostalgia, seeking dishes popular in their childhood and youth (Parsons & Cappellini, 2011).

Concluding Remarks: The Implications for the Future of Food Tourism

The analysis of current food tourism products and services identified five key food tourism experience characteristics or dimensions which were used to create the food tourism experience framework. This framework can be used to describe the current situation and can assist in predictions about future food tourism directions. The exploration of future trends and competitive pressures within this food tourism experience framework identified three major themes that have implications for food tourism futures:

* The central importance of learning to food tourism experiences. In order to thrive into the future all food tourism experiences will have to recognise and address the importance of learning about the food that is being presented. More structured educational components will be developed and staff, including service staff, will be expected to be guides to the food experience with a detailed knowledge of the origin, production, varieties and social and cultural meanings associated with different foods.
* The move to sustainability in food tourism experiences, in all its aspects and dimensions. At first, growing concerns about environmental problems and social justice issues will create an interest in food tourism experiences built around sustainability and social responsibility. But these

will quickly become an expected element of all food tourism experiences. Future food tourism experiences will have to implement, promote and explain a variety of sustainability programmes and initiatives to meet demands from stakeholders.

- The need to adapt to rapidly increasing competitive pressures. As food tourism moves through the product lifecycle and increasing numbers of destinations adopt food experiences as a tourism development and marketing strategy there will be considerable competitive pressure on all food tourism businesses. For existing food tourism operations this means a need to add value to the experiences offered and for both existing and new entrants in food tourism this means a need to specialise and differentiate offerings. Future food tourism suppliers will have to critically examine existing tourism opportunities, the nature of supply in their destination and changing and new market demands in order to find niches and gaps that can be exploited. Some opportunities that can be identified include: the development of cooking classes based on health foods and diets, food tourism experiences promoting local and organic food, nostalgia-themed food tourism options, more food-themed events and attractions for Generation Y travellers and their families, growth in restaurants offering cuisines from the countries of new travel segments such as Russia and South America, and growth in food tourism experiences that offer tourists the chance to develop as food and beverage connoisseurs.

References

Bergman, A., Karlsson, J.C. and Axelsson, J. (2010) Truth claims and explanatory claims an ontological typology of futures studies. *Futures* 42 (8), 857–865.

Bonini, S. and Oppenheim, J. (2008) Cultivating the green consumer. *Stanford Innovation Review* 6 (4), 56–61.

Boyne, S., Hall, D. and Williams, F. (2003) Policy, support and promotion for food-based tourism initiatives. *Journal of Travel & Tourism Marketing* 14 (3–4), 131–154.

Brown, J.C. (2012) Entering the era of convenience sushi: Changes in the cultural meaning of a connoisseur cuisine. *Intersect: Stanford Journal of Science, Technology and Society* 5, 1–13. See http://ojs.stanford.edu.elibrary.jcu.edu.au/ojs/index.php/intersect/article/view/327

Calantone, R.J., Yeniyurt, S., Townsend, J.D. and Schmidt, J.B. (2010) The effects of competition in short product life-cycle markets: The case of motion pictures. *Journal of Product Innovation Management* 27 (3), 349–361.

Cohen, E. and Avieli, R. (2004) Food in tourism: Attraction and impediment. *Annals of Tourism Research* 31 (4), 755–778.

Court, D. and Narasimhan, L. (2010) Capturing the world's emerging middle class. See www.mckinseyquarterly.com/Capturing_the_worlds_emerging_middle_class_2639 (accessed 25 August 2012).

Deale, C., Norman, W.C. and Jodice, L.W. (2008) Marketing locally harvested shrimp to South Carolina coastal visitors: The development of a culinary tourism supply chain. *Journal of Culinary Science & Technology* 6 (1), 5–23.

Du Rand, G.E. and Heath, E. (2006) Towards a framework for food tourism as an element of destination marketing. *Current Issues in Tourism* 9 (3), 206–234.

Esty, D.C. and Winston, A.S. (2009) *Green to Gold*. Hoboken: John Wiley & Sons.

Euromonitor (2011) Emerging outbound markets. See www.euromonitor.com/emerging-outbound-markets-looking-ahead-in-uncertain-times/report (accessed 25 August 2012).

Everett, S. and Aitchison, C. (2008) The role of food tourism in sustaining regional identity: A case study of Cornwall, South West England. *Journal of Sustainable Tourism* 16 (2), 150–167.

Eweje, G. (2011) A shift in corporate practice: Facilitating sustainability strategy in companies. *Corporate Social Responsibility & Environmental Management* 18 (3), 125–136.

Falguera, V., Aliguer, N. and Falguera, M. (2012) An integrated approach to current trends in food consumption: Moving toward functional and organic products? *Food Control* 26 (2), 274–281.

Fifteen (2013) About Fifteen. See www.jamieoliver.com/the-fifteen-apprentice-programme/about/story (accessed 16 April 2013).

Global Trends (2013) GT briefing January 2013. See www.globaltrends.com/monthly-briefings/178-gt-briefing-january-2013-looking-ahead-the-best-of-2013-trends (accessed 6 April 2013).

Golder, P.N. and Tellis, G.J. (2010) Product life cycle. *Wiley International Encyclopedia of Marketing*. See http://onlinelibrary.wiley.com/doi/10.1002/9781444316568.wiem05005/pdf (accessed 22 April 2013).

Green, G.P. and Dougherty, M.L. (2008) Localizing linkages for food and tourism: Culinary tourism as a community development strategy. *Community Development* 39 (3), 148–158.

Harrington, R.J. and Ottenbacher, M.C. (2010) Culinary tourism – A case study of the gastronomic capital. *Journal of Culinary Science & Technology* 8 (1), 14–32.

Hashimoto, A. and Telfer, D.J. (2006) Selling Canadian culinary tourism: Branding the global and the regional product. *Tourism Geographies* 8 (1), 31–55.

Hennigs, N., Wiedmann, K.P., Klarmann, C., Strehlau, S., Godey, B., Pederzoli, D. and Oh, H. (2012) What is the value of luxury? A cross-cultural consumer perspective. *Psychology & Marketing* 29 (12), 1018–1034.

Hirsch, P.M. and Levin, D.Z. (1999) Umbrella advocates versus validity police: A lifecycle model. *Organization Science* 10 (2), 199–212.

Hsu, S., Dehuang, N. and Woodside, A.G. (2009) Storytelling research of consumer's self-reports of urban tourism experiences in China. *Journal of Business Research* 62 (12), 1223–1254.

Ignatov, E. and Smith, S. (2006) Segmenting Canadian culinary tourists. *Current Issues in Tourism* 9 (3), 235–255.

Kearney, J. (2010) Food consumption trends and drivers. *Philosophical Transactions of the Royal Society B: Biological Sciences* 365 (1554), 2793–2807.

Kim, Y.H., Goh, B.K. and Yuan, J. (2010) Development of multi-dimensional scale for measuring food tourist motivations. *Journal of Quality Assurance in Hospitality & Tourism* 11 (1), 56–71.

Kivela, J. and Crotts, J.C. (2006) Tourism and gastronomy: Gastronomy's influence on how tourists experience a destination. *Journal of Hospitality & Tourism Research* 30 (3), 354–377.

Kozinets, R.V. (2002) The field behind the screen: Using netnography for marketing research in online communities. *Journal of Marketing Research* 39 (1), 61–71.

Kwong, K. (2013) Our guiding philosophy. See www.kyliekwong.org/BillyKwongs.aspx (accessed 15 April 2013).

Manzo, J. (2010) Coffee, connoisseurship, and an ethnomethodologically-informed sociology of taste. *Human Studies* 33 (2–3), 141–155.

Montanari, A. and Staniscia, B. (2009) Culinary tourism as a tool for regional re-equilibrium. *European Planning Studies* 17 (10), 1463–1483.

Moretti, E. (2011) Social learning and peer effects in consumption: Evidence from movie sales. *Review of Economic Studies* 78 (1), 356–393.

Moscardo, G. and Benckendorff, P. (2010) Mythbusting: Generation Y and travel. In P. Benckendorff, G. Moscardo and D. Pendergast (eds) *Generation Y and Travel* (pp. 16–22). Wallingford: CABI.

Moscardo, G., Murphy, L. and Benckendorff, P. (2011) Generation Y and travel futures. In I. Yeoman, C. Hsu, K. Smith and S. Watson (eds) *Tourism and Demography* (pp. 87–100). Woodeaton: Goodfellow.

Noble, S.M. and Schewe, C.D. (2003) Cohort segmentation: An exploration of its validity. *Journal of Business Research* 56 (12), 979–987.

Parsons, E. and Cappellini, B. (2011) 'Land of history and romance': Consuming nostalgia through the British Italian cookbook. *Advances in Consumer Research* 39 (1), 392–397.

Porter, M.E. (2008) The five competitive forces that shape strategy. *Harvard Business Review* January, 86–104.

Potts Dawson, A. (2011) Accidental expert: Experiments in sustainable restaurants and food retailing. *Journal of Urban Regeneration and Renewal* 4 (4), 388–395.

Poulston, J. and Yiu, A.Y.K. (2011) Profit or principles: Why do restaurants serve organic food? *International Journal of Hospitality Management* 30 (1), 184–191.

Povey, G. (2011) Gastronomy and tourism. In P. Robinson, S. Heitmann and P. Dieke (eds) *Research Themes for Tourism* (pp. 233–248). Oxfordshire: CABI.

Quadri-Felitti, D. and Fiore, A. (2012) Experience economy constructs as a framework for understanding wine tourism. *Journal of Vacation Marketing* 18 (1), 3–15.

Rafferty, K. (2011) Class-based emotions and the allure of fashion consumption. *Journal of Consumer Culture* 11 (2), 239–260.

Richards, G. (2011) Creativity and tourism: The state of the art. *Annals of Tourism Research* 38 (4), 1225–1253.

Ruzic, P. and Medica, I. (2009) Assumptions for including organic food in the gastronomic offering of Istrian agritourism. *Turizam* 13 (1), 45–51.

Sanchez-Canizares, S.M. and Lopez-Guzman, T. (2012) Gastronomy as a tourism resource: Profile of the culinary tourist. *Current Issues in Tourism* 15 (3), 229–245.

Smith, S. and Costello, C. (2009) Segmenting visitors to a culinary event: Motivations, travel behavior, and expenditures. *Journal of Hospitality Marketing and Management* 18 (1), 44–67.

Smith, S.L.J. and Xiao, H. (2008) Culinary tourism supply chains: A preliminary examination. *Journal of Travel Research* 46 (3), 289–299.

Thompson, J. (2012) Incredible edible–social and environmental entrepreneurship in the era of the 'Big Society'. *Social Enterprise Journal* 8 (3), 237–250.

Tikkanen, I. (2007) Maslow's hierarchy and food tourism in Finland: Five cases. *British Food Journal* 109 (9), 721–734.

Trends Research (2013) Top 10 trends 2013. See www.trendsresearch.com/reports/Winter13TrendsJournalPreview.pdf (accessed 6 April 2013).

Trendwatching (2013) 10 crucial consumer trends for 2013. See www.trendwatching.com/trends/10trends2013/ (accessed 6 April 2013).

UNWTO (2012) UNWTO tourism highlights. See http://mkt.unwto.org/en/publication/unwto-tourism-highlights-2012-edition (accessed 25 August 2012).

Uriely, N., Yonay, Y. and Simchai, D. (2002) Backpacking experiences: A type and form analysis. *Annals of Tourism Research* 29 (2), 520–538.

Worsley, T., Wang, W. and Hunter, W. (2011) Baby boomers' desires for future health and food services. *Nutrition & Food Science* 41 (5), 359–367.

Yeoman, I. and McMahon-Beattie, U. (2006) Luxury markets and premium pricing. *Journal of Revenue and Pricing Management* 4 (4), 319–328.

Zhan, L. and He, Y. (2012) Understanding luxury consumption in China: Consumer perceptions of best-known brands. *Journal of Business Research* 65, 1452–1460.

Part 4

Research Directions

16 Food in Scholarship: Thoughts on Trajectories for Future Research

Eunice Eunjung Yoo

Highlights

- This chapter presents insights into the contemporary stage of scholarship on food and directs the future of the field by providing trajectories for future research.
- There has been limited academic attention on food in tourism scholarship in that existing studies mostly focus on managerial and marketing perspectives.
- Tourism scholars need to pay more attention to the ways in which food plays a significant role in tourism as an essential cultural constituent both for the tourist and the host by acknowledging the interrelationship between food, culture and tourism.
- This interdisciplinary approach to studies on food in tourism scholarship will be beneficial for a better understanding of the intricate meaning of food in tourism and the relationship between food and tourism.

Introduction

As one of the single most significant trademarks of a culture, food has a symbiotic relationship with tourism. Historically, travelling for food is what humankind originally did to survive. Nowadays, people often travel for food as well, yet it has taken an entirely distinctive meaning that is different from what it used to be in ancient times. As the first way of entering into contact with different cultures, food plays a major role in the way tourists experience a destination. In many cases, tasting the food from other cultures is an easier way of experiencing cultures than learning and interpreting their language. In this respect, food can be an easier mediating tool in the experience of a place (Montanari, 2006).

Given the symbiotic relationship between food and tourism, and the importance of food as a form of cultural identity, food is becoming increasingly significant in tourism as an essential significant component of tourism consumption as well as production (Long, 2004). For tourists, food consumption is a necessary element of their experience of a destination because they need to experience not only the landscapes, but also the taste of a destination (Hjalager & Richards, 2002b). In this respect, food has come to be recognised as an essential element of the local culture of a destination consumed by tourists (Hall *et al.*, 2003). In the process of tasting local food, sharing it with local people, and understanding different eating manners from her or his own, the tourist becomes not just a passive visitor to the place, but an active participant in the particular culture and community (Long, 2004). Nowadays, a platform and circumstance have been laid for food, culture and tourism to feature and interact together. Tourists' culinary experiences convey unique adventure and enjoyment to tourists, influencing tourists' attitudes, behaviours and decisions (Hjalager & Corigliano, 2000) as well as determining perceptions of and satisfaction with their overall experience (Quan & Wang, 2004).

In response to the increasing tourists' demand on food, it is not surprising that food becomes an important place marker in tourism promotion given the strong relationship between food and culture from the tourism marketer's perspective (Hjalager & Richards, 2002a). Food is seen as an important source of marketable images and experiences for the tourist (Boyne & Hall, 2004) in that local food is an important attraction for a particular destination that influences the overall tourist experience (Henderson, 2004). Given the growing competition between tourism destinations, diverse cultural aspects of a destination are becoming more important in attracting tourists. Moreover, food images are used to depict tourists' overall cultural experience at destinations (Frochot, 2003). For both tourists and tourism marketers, therefore, food remains an essential part of tourism, and thus cannot be ignored. Acknowledging this symbiotic relationship between food and tourism, this chapter aims to present insights into the contemporary stage of tourism scholarship on food and direct the future of the field by providing trajectories for future research. Hence, this chapter reviews the existing academic research on food in tourism scholarship as well as in other social scientific disciplines, namely anthropology, sociology and cultural studies.

Food as a Topic of Scholarly Research

Food has permeated almost every scholarly field and has become a widely accepted research topic by embracing an interdisciplinary approach through multilayered investigations into the ways that food functions in the life complex (Hauck-Lawson, 1998). A series of reviews of relevant studies reveals that food as a topic for scholarly discussion appears in a variety of academic disciplinary fields, including anthropology, geography, philosophy, sociology, psychology, cultural studies and women's studies. All in all, scholars within the boundary of the social sciences have found that food plays a significant role as an insightful tool for understanding various aspects of a society (Counihan & Van Esterik, 2008). Most of all, however, social scientific research on food has predominantly based its roots within three major disciplines: anthropology, sociology and cultural studies.

Food as a subject of serious inquiry has engaged anthropology from its very beginnings (Mintz & Du Bois, 2002). In essence, anthropologists consider food as a culture that represents sophisticated symbolic systems of a particular society, and try to explain and interpret these discursive meanings (Anderson, 2005; Lévi-Strauss, 1966/1997). Early anthropologists recognised the central role of food in different cultures. Anthropologists primarily view eating behaviours and food preferences as indications of culture, as a significant marker that helps groups distinguish themselves from one another, and a means for transmitting cultural norms. In essence, seminal anthropological works on food help us understand how food is culturally constructed (Lévi-Strauss, 1966/1997). Most of the studies consider the expression of race, class, nation and personhood through food production and consumption. Several studies deal with the construction of national identity through the contested transformation of food (Appadurai, 1988; Counihan, 1999; Heldke, 2001).

From a sociological perspective, scholars investigate the social patterns of food consumption through societal structure. They look at how food consumption shapes those societal organisations and the actions of diverse members or agents of the society (McIntosh, 1996). In particular, scholars in the sociology of food emphasise the interrelationship between food and culture by looking at determining aspects that influence the relationship (Goody, 1982; Mennell, 1996). Hence, they acknowledge that food habits are greatly influenced by economic, ecological and social circumstances (Mennell, 1996). In this respect, sociological food scholars mostly examine food consumption, focusing on its role as a means of social differentiation (Warde, 1997) as well as the ways that globalisation and modernisation contribute to food consumption (Ritzer, 2001).

Cultural studies on food generally re-examine the interdisciplinary history of food studies, from the anthropology of Lévi-Strauss (1966/1997) to Bourdieu's (1984) work on the relationship between food, consumption and cultural identity. Works on food consumption in sociology, anthropology and cultural geography share with cultural studies an interest in the way food consumption involves the production of meanings and identities. Through cultural studies, a range of representations of food consumption applies a variety of socio-cultural aspects and informs our everyday practices. In this respect, cultural studies has been concerned with the manner in which food is represented (Ashley *et al.*, 2004).

All in all, studies on food from a variety of disciplines have utilised food as a critical lens of analysis. Despite the different perspectives, these academics have contributed to broadening the concept of food as a topic for academic discussion and have agreed that food as a focal point has the potential to yield information about meanings and roles in people's lives (Hauck-Lawson, 1998). They argue that food contains various aspects of a particular society's cultural traditions and conveys that society's collective cultural identity. In this respect, food plays an essential role in articulating cultural exchanges and self-represen-tation as a means of establishing identity (Warde & Martens, 2000).

In essence, the reviews of extant studies of food written by leading food studies scholars indicate that these studies commonly discuss food as an important medium that tells various stories as a means of communication. Given the multi-sensorial properties of taste, smell, sight, sound and touch, food has the ability to communicate in a variety of cultural and social con-texts (Counihan & Van Esterik, 2008). A number of scholars have articulated that food symbolises personal and group identity, and constructs founda-tional elements both for individuals as well as for ethnic groups or other societal communities at large. In this respect, food has a strong communica-tive power in conveying diverse messages in every society (Anderson, 2005), and as a dominant means of identity discourse, including symbolic, and sig-nifying a wide range of meanings of the economic, social, religious, ethnic and aesthetic aspects of a culture (Holden, 2008).

Food in Tourism Scholarship

Although food as a topic of scholarly inquiry remains relatively under-researched, there is evidence of growing awareness and interest in researching food in tourism. Given the increasing number of food tourists whose primary motivation for travelling to a destination is to experience food, culinary cul-ture, and/or food related activities and events, such as food festivals, scholarly attention to food tourism as a form of cultural tourism has been escalating throughout the years. A systematic and thematic approach has been adopted for the scholarly literature review for this chapter, reviewing more than 110 academic publications, including peer-reviewed journal articles, books and book chapters in the public domain from the 1980s to the 2010s. The schol-arly attention placed on food and tourism can be ascribed to the position food takes as the primary or supporting reason tourists travel to a particular desti-nation, hence tourist experiences are partly or largely motivated by their desire to experience different culinary particularities and traditions of destina-tions (Boniface, 2003; Hall & Mitchell, 2000; Henderson, 2009; Long, 2004). The currently emerging body of literature on the relationship between food and tourism can be divided into four spheres: food as a significant element of tourist experiences, food as a tourism product, attraction and marketing tool, food as a tool for regional development, and food as a sign of culture and cultural heritage.

Food as a significant element of tourist experiences

Placing food in tourist experiences, the first research domain investigates tourists' food consumption behaviour, including their food experiences, perceptions, preferences, motivations, characteristics, values, satisfaction and behavioural intentions. Scholars have examined a variety of elements related to tourists' food consumption behaviour: the role of food in tourism experiences (Cohen & Avieli, 2004; de la Barre & Brouder, 2013; Kivela & Crotts, 2006); tourists' food consumption, preferences and motivational factors (Chang et al., 2010; Torres, 2002); factors influencing tourists' food consumption and experiences (Chang et al., 2011; Mak et al., 2012); food tourists' perceived value, satisfaction, and behavioural intention (Kim et al., 2011). Particularly, this type of consumer behavioural research on food and tourism applied distinctive concepts, such as personality (Kim et al., 2010) and emotion (Mason & Paggiaro, 2012) in examining their relationship with tourist food consumption and experiences.

There are additional aspects of tourists' food consumption and its position in tourist experiences. Scholars have developed a conceptual model through incorporating tourists' food consumption patterns and their experiences, building a model of tourists' local food consumption (Kim et al., 2009; Quan & Wang, 2004). In a similar vein, scholars aimed to develop a scale and measure tourists' motivation to consume local foods (Kim & Eves, 2012). Moreover, others have examined the relationship between the role of food service on tourists' perceptions and their satisfaction (Nield et al., 2000) and classification of tourism dining (Au & Law, 2002). All in all, these studies have emphasised the potential of local food in enhancing the sustainable tourism experience (Sims, 2009)

Food as a tourism product, attraction and marketing tool

Considering food as a tourism product and attraction, a number of scholars have examined the role of food as an important tool for marketing and promotion of a tourism destination. In fact, this is the most prevalent topic in food tourism studies. From supply stakeholders' points of view, the second category of tourism research on food focuses on the role of food in marketing, branding and promotion of tourism destinations. The role of food in tourism marketing and promotion has been greatly recognised by tourism scholars (Du Rand et al., 2003). Several researchers have indicated that tourists' experiences with local food itself or food-related attractions or products, such as religious food (Son & Xu, 2013), food hawkers (Henderson, 2000; Henderson *et al.*, 2012), food festivals (Henderson, 2004), and historic restaurants (Josiam *et al.*, 2004), are considered to be tourism attractions, and these studies have recognised food's positive associations with general tourism destination management as well as tourists' overall experiences. These benefits and impacts of local food and the role of food as a tourism product and attraction have also been acknowledged as a driving force for enhancing destination competitiveness (Du Rand & Heath, 2006; Presenza & Del Chiappa, 2013).

This recognition leads the notion that the role of food in eminent tourism attractions and products contributes to destination promotion and marketing. Tourism scholars have identified how destination marketing organisations (DMOs) utilise food-related content in their marketing practices, including both print and e-marketing materials (Horng & Tsai, 2010; Okumus *et al.*, 2007). In a similar vein, studies have identified the role of food and food-related events as image-makers and/or image-enhancers for tourism destinations and have emphasised the opportunities for food as an important part of the branding of many destinations (Brouder & de la Barre, 2013; Hashimoto & Telfer, 2006; Lee & Arcodia, 2011; Lin *et al.*, 2011). These scholars have identified that traditional foods can affect the tourist experience positively and thus help to create a destination brand. Others have also examined the impact of food brand equity and the role of destination familiarity in travel intentions, in the context of food tourism (Horng *et al.*, 2012).

Food as a tool for regional development

Acknowledging the importance of food for development of a region, and understanding the economic power of food and tourism as a vehicle for regional development and regeneration, tourism academics have examined the successful key elements of strategic development. The earlier studies investigating the relationship between tourism and local food production highlighted the role of food tourism as an incentive for increased local food production (Belisle, 1983; Telfer & Wall, 1996). In a similar vein, tourism scholars are recognising the role of food in tourism as a vehicle of the experience economy for rural development strategies (Sidali *et al.*, 2013). Several scholars also investigated the success factors for the strategic development of food tourism (Horng & Tsai, 2012). In a similar fashion, Boyne *et al.* (2003) have investigated the development context for food-related tourism initiatives.

Another concern for tourism scholars regarding food in tourism is the perspectives of entrepreneurs, including their attitudes, perceptions and expectations of food in tourism (Alonso & Liu, 2012; Presenza & Del Chiappa, 2013), acknowledging the significant role of entrepreneurs and entrepreneurial networks in the process of food tourism (Mykletun & Gyimóthy, 2010). The relevant discussion goes on to investigate the significance of economic relationships and local partnerships between food production and tourism for positive regional development (Ohe & Kurihara, 2013). Similarly, Everett and Slocum (2013) have also highlighted the importance of effective and collaborative partnerships in food and tourism, focusing on the role of food tourism in delivering sustainability agendas. Recently, more scholars are incorporating particular considerations of sustainability in their research on regional development through food and tourism. Scholars have investigated how local food can contribute towards sustainable development, focusing on economic aspects of food in tourism and rural development. Scholars have particularly looked into the important synergistic relationships between food production and consumption in tourism that are of critical relevance to sustainability (Everett & Aitchison, 2008; Gössling et al., 2011; Hjalager & Johansen, 2013).

Food as a sign of culture and cultural heritage

The fourth sphere of food in tourism scholarship encompasses studies based on the notion of food as a sign of culture and cultural heritage by recognising the socio-cultural significance of food and its role in sustaining regional identity and cultural expression (Hegarty & O'Mahony, 2001). The concept of 'heritagisation', the use of food in the process of heritage construction (Bessière, 2013), is a recent, growing area of research interest for tourism scholars. Based on the notion of heritage as a social construction, the studies emphasise the role of food and food heritage in the construction of social identities. The scholars under this category acknowledge that food is not only a basic need for tourists, but also a cultural element that can positively represent a destination (Jones & Jenkins, 2002; Reynolds, 1993). Moreover, it is noted that the presentation of food heritage is not merely a staged and superficial phenomenon designed for tourists, but actually a self-generating multidirectional process that influences and alters the local foodscape (Avieli, 2013).

The most commonly discussed aspect of food as cultural heritage is the notion of identity, as food heritages help to establish and reinforce regional or national identity (Bessière, 1998, 2013; Timothy & Ron, 2013). It is through the inter-relationships between food, place and identity that food tourism's social and cultural impact can truly be explored, acknowledging that 'gastronomy has become a significant source of identity formation in post-modern societies' (Richards, 2002: 3). Taking a sociological perspective and identifying a social demand for food and tourism, scholars have investigated culinary heritage as a source of local initiatives and a factor in local distinctiveness and territorial identity construction (Bessière, 1998; Everett & Aitchison, 2008; Fox, 2007; Presenza & Del Chiappa, 2013; Staiff & Bushell, 2013). Focusing on the role of food as a sign of culture, these studies have investigated the ways in which food and culinary aspects contribute to national identity, and underlined the ways in which food and culinary culture reveal a rich host of cultural and historical information about destinations (Metro-Roland, 2013). These scholars, collectively, understand food as an important element of cultural heritage, a powerful marker of places, and its contributions to national identity.

Trajectories for Future Research

Close scrutiny of existing academic research on food in tourism and other social scientific disciplines reveals that food research embraces an interdisciplinary approach through multilayered investigations into the ways that food functions in the life complex. A wide range of research on food in non-tourism disciplines provides valuable insights into the future trajectories of food tourism scholarship. The review of food in tourism scholarship indicates that the recognition of the relationship between food and tourism has been increasing over the years. However, there has been uneven academic attention placed on food in tourism scholarship. The majority of the current research domains have been concentrated on commercial and managerial perspectives of food in tourism. What is needed within the literature of this burgeoning area of research is to engage more socio-cultural perspectives. In spite of the significant socio-cultural role played by food in tourism, it has not been widely discussed yet within tourism scholarship. The main focus of the current studies has been located in the role of food as a managerial tool without further discussion on the meaning of it.

Given the importance of food in understanding cultures and its symbiotic relationship with tourism, it is advisable for tourism scholars to pay more attention to the ways in which food plays a significant role in tourism as an essential constituent both for the tourist and the host by acknowledging the interrelationship between food, culture and tourism. Tourism scholars need to deconstruct the broader societal and cultural issues in greater depth and to expand knowledge about the relationships between food and tourism. These connections are manifold and complex. In this respect, it is important to shift from a managerial orientation to a more socio-cultural orientation. It is time to examine food tourism through a 'cultural lens' (Boniface, 2003; Everett & Aitchison, 2008) by acknowledging the critical and innovative future trajectories it offers to food and tourism studies, whilst presenting a new approach to achieving sustainable tourism development. All in all, scholars need to note the larger cultural context of a destination in which a substantial part of its intangible heritage is connected to food.

In essence, scholars should recognise the integral and integrated role of food in culture. They should consider food as a symbol of cultural identity, and the preparation and consumption of food as a culture in and of itself in that food permeates our lives and assigns meaning to our culture (MacClancy,

1993), and it plays a critical role in our societies and presents intricate cultural and societal symbols. In this respect, researching a particular food and culinary culture uncovers a variety of cultural and societal characteristics, including basic values and beliefs. More specifically, such characteristics include a wide range of society's economic, ethnic, religious and other socially constructed values. Given the interdisciplinary nature of food in scholarships, there is a need for a multidisciplinary approach in studying food and tourism. Therefore, tourism scholars should reflect on food in their research as a cultural means of communication and interpretation in that food becomes a meaningful text that can be analysed and interpreted (Anderson, 2005).

References

Alonso, A.D. and Liu, Y. (2012) Old wine region, new concept and sustainable development: Winery entrepreneurs' perceived benefits from wine tourism on Spain's Canary Islands. *Journal of Sustainable Tourism* 20 (7), 991–1009.

Anderson, E.N. (2005) *Everyone Eats: Understanding Food and Culture.* New York: NYU Press.

Appadurai, A. (1988) How to make a national cuisine: Cookbooks in contemporary India. *Comparative Studies in Society and History* 30 (1), 3–24.

Ashley, B., Hollows, J., Jones, S. and Taylor, B. (2004) *Food and Cultural Studies (Studies in Consumption and Markets).* London: Routledge.

Au, N. and Law, R. (2002) Categorical classification of tourism dining. *Annals of Tourism Research* 29 (3), 819–833.

Avieli, N. (2013) What is 'local food?' Dynamic culinary heritage in the World Heritage Site of Hoi An, Vietnam. *Journal of Heritage Tourism* 8 (2–3), 120–132.

Belisle, F.J. (1983) Tourism and food production in the Caribbean. *Annals of Tourism Research* 10 (4), 497–513.

Bessière, J. (1998) Local development and heritage: Traditional food and cuisine as tourist attractions in rural areas. *Sociologia Ruralis* 38 (1), 21–34.

Bessière, J. (2013) 'Heritagisation', a challenge for tourism promotion and regional development: An example of food heritage. *Journal of Heritage Tourism* 8 (4), 275–291.

Boniface, P. (2003) *Tasting Tourism: Travelling for Food and Drink.* Aldershot: Ashgate Publishing, VT.

Bourdieu, P. (1984) *Distinction: A Social Critique of the Judgement of Taste.* London: Routledge.

Boyne, S. and Hall, D. (2004) Place promotion through food and tourism: Rural branding and the role of websites. *Place Branding* 1 (1), 80–92.

Boyne, S., Hall, D. and Williams, F. (2003) Policy, support and promotion for food-related tourism initiatives: A marketing approach to regional development. *Journal of Travel & Tourism Marketing* 14 (3–4), 131–154.

Chang, R.C.Y., Kivela, J. and Mak, A.H.N. (2010) Food preferences of Chinese tourists. *Annals of Tourism Research* 37 (4), 989–1011.

Chang, R.C.Y., Kivela, J. and Mak, A.H.N. (2011) Attributes that influence the evaluation of travel dining experience: When east meets west. *Tourism Management* 32 (2), 307–316.

Cohen, E. and Avieli, N. (2004) Food in tourism: Attraction and impediment. *Annals of Tourism Research* 31 (4), 755–778.

Counihan, C. (1999) *The Anthropology of Food and Body: Gender, Meaning, and Power.* New York: Routledge.

Counihan, C. and Van Esterik, P. (2008) *Food and Culture: A Reader.* London: Routledge.

de la Barre, S. and Brouder, P. (2013) Consuming stories: Placing food in the Arctic tourism experience. *Journal of Heritage Tourism* 8 (2–3), 213–223.

Du Rand, G.E. and Heath, E. (2006) Towards a framework for food tourism as an element of destination marketing. *Current Issues in Tourism* 9 (3), 206–234.

Du Rand, G.E.D., Heath, E. and Alberts, N. (2003) The role of local and regional food in destination marketing: A South African situation analysis. *Journal of Travel & Tourism Marketing* 14 (3–4), 97–112.

Everett, S. and Aitchison, C. (2008) The role of food tourism in sustaining regional identity: A case study of Cornwall, South West England. *Journal of Sustainable Tourism* 16 (2), 150–167.

Everett, S. and Slocum, S.L. (2013) Food and tourism: An effective partnership? A UK-based review. *Journal of Sustainable Tourism* 21 (6), 789–809.

Fox, R. (2007) Reinventing the gastronomic identity of Croatian tourist destinations. *International Journal of Hospitality Management* 26 (3), 546–559.

Frochot, I. (2003) An analysis of regional positioning and its associated food images in French tourism regional brochures. *Journal of Travel & Tourism Marketing* 14 (3–4), 77–96.

Goody, J. (1982) *Cooking, Cuisine, and Class: A Study in Comparative Sociology.* Cambridge: Cambridge University Press.

Gössling, S., Garrod, B., Aall, C., Hille, J. and Peeters, P. (2011) Food management in tourism: Reducing tourism's carbon 'foodprint'. *Tourism Management* 32 (3), 534–543.

Hall, C.M. and Mitchell, R. (2000) We are what we eat: Food, tourism and globalization. *Tourism, Culture and Communication* 2 (1), 29–37.

Hall, C.M., Sharples, L., Mitchell, R., Macionis, N. and Cambourne, B. (2003) *Food Tourism Around the World: Development, Management and Markets.* Oxford: Butterworth-Heinemann.

Hashimoto, A. and Telfer, D.J. (2006) Selling Canadian culinary tourism: Branding the global and the regional product. *Tourism Geographies* 8 (1), 31–55.

Hauck-Lawson, A.S. (1998) When food is the voice: A case study of a Polish-American woman. *Journal for the Study of Food and Society* 2 (1), 21–28.

Hegarty, J.A. and O'Mahony G.B. (2001) Gastronomy: A phenomenon of cultural expressionism and an aesthetic for living. *International Journal of Hospitality Management* 20 (1), 3–13.

Heldke, L. (2001) *Let's Cook Thai. Pilaf, Pozole, and Pad Thai: American Women and Ethnic Food.* Amherst: University of Massachusetts Press.

Henderson, J. (2000) Food hawkers and tourism in Singapore. *Hospitality Management* 19 (2), 109–117.

Henderson, J. (2004) Food as a tourism resource: A view from Singapore. *Tourism Recreation Research* 29 (3), 69–74.

Henderson, J.C. (2009) Food tourism reviewed. *British Food Journal* 111 (4), 317–326.

Henderson, J.C., Yun, O.S., Poon, P. and Biwei, X. (2012) Hawker centres as tourist attractions: The case of Singapore. *International Journal of Hospitality Management* 31 (3), 849–855.

Hjalager, A.M. and Corigliano, M.A. (2000) Food for tourists – Determinants of an image. *International Journal of Tourism Research* 2 (4), 281–293.

Hjalager, A.M. and Johansen, P.H. (2013) Food tourism in protected areas – Sustainability for producers, the environment and tourism? *Journal of Sustainable Tourism* 21 (3), 417–433.

Hjalager, A.M. and Richards, G. (2002a) Still undigested: Research issues in tourism and gastronomy. *Tourism and Gastronomy*, 224–241.

Hjalager, A.M. and Richards, G. (2002b) *Tourism and Gastronomy.* London: Routledge.

Holden, T. (2008) Masculinities in Japanese food programming. In C. Counihan and P. Van Esterik (eds) *Food and Culture: A Reader* (2nd edn) (pp. 202–220). New York: Routledge.

Horng, J.S., Liu, C.H., Chou, H.Y. and Tsai, C.Y. (2012) Understanding the impact of culinary brand equity and destination familiarity on travel intentions. *Tourism Management* 33 (4), 815–824.

Horng, J.S. and Tsai, C.T. (2010) Government websites for promoting east Asian culinary tourism: A cross-national analysis. *Tourism Management* 31 (1), 74–85.

Horng, J.S. and Tsai, C.T.S. (2012) Culinary tourism strategic development: An Asia Pacific perspective. *International Journal of Tourism Research* 14 (1), 40–55.

Jones, A. and Jenkins, I. (2002) A taste of Wales–Blas Ar Gymru: Institutional malaise in promoting Welsh food tourism products. In A.M. Hjalager and G. Richards (eds) *Tourism and Gastronomy* (pp. 115–132). London: Routledge.

Josiam, B.M., Mattson, M. and Sullivan, P. (2004) The *historaunt*: Heritage tourism at Mickey's dining car. *Tourism Management* 25 (4), 453–461.

Kim, Y.G. and Eves, A. (2012) Construction and validation of a scale to measure tourist motivation to consume local food. *Tourism Management* 33 (6), 1458–1467.

Kim, Y.G., Eves, A. and Scarles, C. (2009) Building a model of local food consumption on trips and holidays: A grounded theory approach. *International Journal of Hospitality Management* 28 (3), 423–431.

Kim, Y.G., Suh, B.W. and Eves, A. (2010) The relationships between food-related personality traits, satisfaction, and loyalty among visitors attending food events and festivals. *International Journal of Hospitality Management* 29 (2), 216–226.

Kim, Y.H., Kim, M. and Goh, B.K. (2011) An examination of food tourist's behavior: Using the modified theory of reasoned action. *Tourism Management* 32 (5), 1159–1165.

Kivela, J. and Crotts, J.C. (2006) Tourism and gastronomy: Gastronomy's influence on how tourists experience a destination. *Journal of Hospitality & Tourism Research* 30 (3), 354–377.

Lee, I. and Arcodia, C. (2011) The role of regional food festivals for destination branding. *International Journal of Tourism Research* 13 (4), 355–367.

Lévi-Strauss, C. (1966/1997) The culinary triangle. In C. Counihan and P. Van Esterik (eds) *Food and Culture: A Reader* (pp. 28–35). New York: Routledge.

Lin, Y.C., Pearson, T.E. and Cai, L.A. (2011) Food as a form of destination identity: A tourism destination brand perspective. *Tourism and Hospitality Research* 11 (1), 30–48.

Long, L.M. (2004) *Culinary Tourism*. Kentucky: University Press of Kentucky.

MacClancy, J. (1993) *Consuming Culture: Why You Eat What You Eat*. New York: Henry Holt & Company.

Mak, A.H., Lumbers, M., Eves, A. and Chang, R.C. (2012) Factors influencing tourist food consumption. *International Journal of Hospitality Management* 31 (3), 928–936.

Mason, M.C. and Paggiaro, A. (2012) Investigating the role of festivalscape in culinary tourism: The case of food and wine events. *Tourism Management* 33 (6), 1329–1336.

McIntosh, W.A. (1996) *Sociologies of Food and Nutrition*. New York: Springer.

Mennell, S. (1996) *All Manners of Food: Eating and Taste in England and France from the Middle Ages to the Present*. Illinois: University of Illinois Press.

Metro-Roland, M.M. (2013) Goulash nationalism: The culinary identity of a nation. *Journal of Heritage Tourism* 8 (2–3), 172–181.

Mintz, S.W. and Du Bois, C.M. (2002) The anthropology of food and eating. *Annual Review of Anthropology* 31, 99–119.

Montanari, M. (2006) *Food is Culture*. New York: Columbia University Press.

Mykletun, R.J. and Gyimóthy, S. (2010) Beyond the renaissance of the traditional Voss sheep's-head meal: Tradition, culinary art, scariness and entrepreneurship. *Tourism Management* 31 (3), 434–446.

Nield, K., Kozak, M. and LeGrys, G. (2000) The role of food service in tourist satisfaction. *International Journal of Hospitality Management* 19 (4) 375–384.

Ohe, Y. and Kurihara, S. (2013) Evaluating the complementary relationship between local brand farm products and rural tourism: Evidence from Japan. *Tourism Management 35*, 278–283.

Okumus, B., Okumus, F. and McKercher, B. (2007) Incorporating local and international cuisines in the marketing of tourism destinations: The cases of Hong Kong and Turkey. *Tourism Management* 28 (1), 253–261.

Presenza, A. and Del Chiappa, G. (2013) Entrepreneurial strategies in leveraging food as a tourist resource: A cross-regional analysis in Italy. *Journal of Heritage Tourism* 8 (2–3), 182–192.

Quan, S. and Wang, N. (2004) Towards a structural model of the tourist experience: An illustration from food experiences in tourism. *Tourism Management* 25 (3), 297–305.

Reynolds, P.C. (1993) Food and tourism: Towards an understanding of sustainable culture. *Journal of Sustainable Tourism* 1 (1), 48–54.

Richards, G. (2002) Gastronomy: An essential ingredient in tourism production and consumption. In A.M. Hjalager and G. Richards (eds) *Tourism and Gastronomy* (pp. 2–20). London: Routledge.

Ritzer, G. (2001) *Explorations in the Sociology of Consumption: Fast Food, Credit Cards and Casinos.* London: Sage.

Sidali, K.L., Kastenholz, E. and Bianchi, R. (2013) Food tourism, niche markets and products in rural tourism: Combining the intimacy model and the experience economy as a rural development strategy. *Journal of Sustainable Tourism*, 1–19.

Sims, R. (2009) Food, place and authenticity: Local food and the sustainable tourism experience. *Journal of Sustainable Tourism* 17 (3), 321–336.

Son, A. and Xu, H. (2013) Religious food as a tourism attraction: The roles of Buddhist temple food in Western tourist experience. *Journal of Heritage Tourism* 8 (2–3), 248–258.

Staiff, R. and Bushell, R. (2013) The rhetoric of Lao/French fusion: Beyond the representation of the Western tourist experience of cuisine in the world heritage city of Luang Prabang, Laos. *Journal of Heritage Tourism* 8 (2–3), 133–144.

Telfer, D.J. and Wall, G. (1996) Linkages between tourism and food production. *Annals of Tourism Research* 23 (3), 635–653.

Timothy, D.J. and Ron, A.S. (2013) Understanding heritage cuisines and tourism: Identity, image, authenticity, and change. *Journal of Heritage Tourism* 8 (2–3), 99–104.

Torres, R. (2002) Toward a better understanding of tourism and agriculture linkages in the Yucatan: Tourist food consumption and preferences. *Tourism Geographies* 4 (3), 282–306.

Warde, A. (1997) *Consumption, Food and Taste: Culinary Antinomies and Commodity Culture.* London: Sage.

Warde, A. and Martens, L. (1998) A sociological approach to food choice. In A. Murcott (ed.) *The Nation's Diet: The Social Science of Food Choice* (pp. 129–146). Harlow: Longmans.

Warde, A. and Martens, L. (2000) *Eating Out: Social Differentiation, Consumption and Pleasure. Cambridge*: Cambridge University Press.

17 The Future of Food Tourism: A Cognitive Map(s) Perspective

Ian Yeoman, Una McMahon-Beattie and Carol Wheatley

Highlights

- A series of illustrative cognitive maps capturing the core concepts from preceding chapters' authors' thoughts about the future of food tourism.
- An aggregate cognitive map that represents the collective thoughts of leading academics and researchers about the future.
- The five core drivers of change that will shape the future of food tourism are identified as *food tourism as political capital; food tourism as a visionary state; what it means to be a foodie; the drive for affluence and exclusivity;* and *fluid experiences in a post-modernist world.*

Introduction

No one knows the exact future of food tourism but unravelling and making sense of the inevitable uncertainty through explanation is a purposeful way to understand the future. In the future studies literature (Yeoman, 2012; Bergman *et al.*, 2010) there has been a movement towards explanation through discussion of the layers, links and spaces that are the construction of the future. In order to do this in relation to food tourism a cognitive mapping approach has been adopted by the authors. Indeed, this approach been applied previously in tourism research (Yeoman *et al.*, 2006; Yeoman & Watson, 2011; Yeoman *et al.*, 2014). Each chapter of this publication has been interpreted through a cognitive map from which an aggregate map has been produced.

This aggregate map represents the contribution of this book to the future of food tourism clustered around five views and portrayed as *drivers of change* that will represent future discourses, actions and behaviours: namely, *food tourism as political capital; food tourism as a visionary state; what it means to be a foodie; the drive for affluence and exclusivity; fluid experiences in a post-modernist world.*

Conceptual Frameworks: A Cognitive Mapping Approach

Pearce (2012) has highlighted that conceptual frameworks can be used in a variety of ways and in different forms but are, nonetheless, purposeful in addressing emerging, fragmented or broad themes. They identify and bind knowledge and form a context to help researchers understand a particular phenomenon and thus make explanatory claims (Bergman *et al.*, 2010). Essentially, conceptual frameworks are concepts explained in diagrammatical form with relationships demonstrated through connections. Conceptual frameworks are not intended to be theories (Pearce, 2012: 13). As Brotherton (2008: 78) notes:

> Essentially, the conceptual framework is a structure that seeks to identify and present in a logical structure format, the key factors relating to the phenomena under investigation. Depending on the nature and purpose(s) of the research project, the conceptual framework maybe a correlational or causal in form.

Cognitive maps, as conceptual frameworks, are mental representations of an individual's understanding of a series of psychological transformations. Applied as a research methodology, cognitive maps are used to represent the cognition of researched thoughts utilising a series of links in the form of a map or picture. Jones (1993: 11) states that a cognitive map:

> ...is a collection of ideas (concepts) and relationships in the form of a map. Ideas are expressed by short phrases which encapsulate a single notion and, where appropriate, an opposite notion. The relationships between ideas are described by linking them together in either a causal or connotative manner.

The method used by the authors is based on the work of Eden and Ackermann (1998) whose approach to cognitive mapping is focused on the idea of concepts. Concepts are short phrases or words which represent a verb and ideas are linked as cause/effect, or means/end or how/why. As such a cognitive map is a representation of a respondent's perceptions about a situation. It relies on bipolar constructs, where the terms are seen as a contrast with each other. For example, 'foodie' may lead to 'seeking authenticity. . .exclusivity'. The result is not unlike an influence diagram or causal loop diagram, but different in that it is explicitly subjective and uses constructs rather than variables (Mingers, 2003). However, the literature on the application of cognitive mapping is often compromised as researchers adapt the theory based upon their own skills and research philosophies (Yeoman, 2004).

Decision Explorer

Computer assisted qualitative data analysis (CAQDAS) can help the researcher to capture and process concepts and data (Barry, 1998) thus helping a modeller to see the relationships, order and complexity of that data. In addition, a CAQDAS approach allows the modeller to track changes and make notes, which embodies the principles of grounded theory (Strauss & Corbin, 1994). DECISION EXPLORER (DE) (Jenkins, 1998) is a CAQDAS tool in the form of cognitive mapping developed by the team at Strathclyde University (Eden & Ackermann, 1998). DE allows a modeller to search for 'multiple viewpoints', 'the holding of concepts', 'tracing of concepts' and 'causal relationship management'. It allows the modeller to come to conclusions, connect thoughts and construct a purposeful interpretation of the phenomena (Levi-Strauss, 1966; Weick, 1979). What is critical to the success of DE is the ability to categorise concepts, values and emergent themes (Eden & Ackermann, 1998) thus allowing the modeller to elicit data and code concepts. This approach to modelling in tourism research is well documented by Yeoman *et al.* (2014), Yeoman and Schänzel (2012), Yeoman and Watson (2011) and Yeoman *et al.* (2006).

The Contribution of Each Chapter

In this section, we identify the contribution each chapter makes in the form of a cognitive map, underlying key concepts and summative meaning.

Chapter 2: The 'Past' and 'Present' of Food Tourism

From Figure 17.1, the key concepts are balanced between 'the past of food tourism' and 'the present of food tourism', emphasising the concepts of 'experience economy', 'emergence of food tourism within tourism academe', 'sub-types', 'marketing' and 'sustainability'. Thus Boyd (Chapter 2) sets out to position the future of food tourism against a narrative of evolution, development and specialisation of this field of tourism academe. His argument is that current trends have evolved from its infancy of research within rural tourism and the importance of the local in terms of production, consumption and experience. He notes that as the field has matured there is an absence of work that redefines established definitions and types;

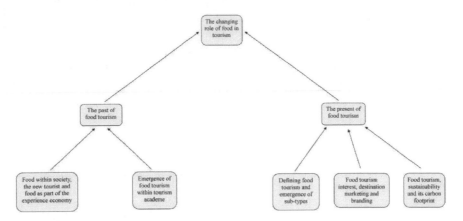

Figure 17.1 The past and present of food tourism

hopefully that redefining will not gain much traction in the future. Figure 17.1 portrays Boyd's thoughts that the 'local' must take prominence in the product offered, how it is marketed and the region branded, the experience that tourists seek, and that with the local placed front and centre economic development strategies should be able to ensure sustainability as well as have a response towards combating negative claims of creating large carbon footprints. Another development in the future of food tourism, he argues, will be the emergence of key destinations that are exclusively known for food, appealing to the serious food tourists over the casual and serendipitous food tourists. The future of food events, festivals and trails will play an increasing role in both production and consumption. In conclusion, in the future as tourists become more climate-aware and recognise the importance of food miles, authenticity should win out over contrived experiences around food in destinations.

Chapter 3: The Future of Food Tourism: The Star Trek Replicator and Exclusivity

Yeoman and McMahon-Beattie portray the future through two scenarios. The first one, *Wellington Food Festival: The Star Trek Replicator*, represents on one level the food tourist's desire for innovation and novelty. On another level, it portrays how science could change the food production process from a traditional land-based system to a laboratory-based one. The second scenario, *Exclusivity: The Future of Authentic Dining*, represents a number of drivers of change in society, particularly food scarcity. As a consequence real food becomes an exclusive experience for rich tourists, with the ultimate food experience focusing on authentic and rare foods from the past. The key concepts identified in Figure 17.2 are 'Star Trek Replicator', 'exclusivity',

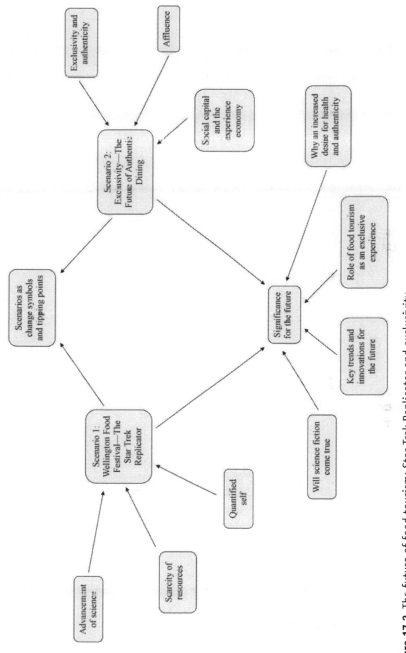

Figure 17.2 The future of food tourism: Star Trek Replicator and exclusivity

'significance', 'will science fiction come true', 'key trends and innovations for the future', and 'role of food tourism as an exclusive experience'. As food tourism has become the symbol of the experience economy, the social aspect of food (and wine) has come to the forefront. Many destinations are targeting high-yielding tourists using food as a symbol of authenticity and an important aspect of their offer is the opportunity to learn the craft of cooking. At the same time, the forecasts for food production and the growth in the world's population will create stress resulting in new forms of food and tastes. In addition, food tourism is an important form of entrepreneurship and innovation given the presence of small to medium enterprises and low barriers to entry and as such this will inject vibrancy and appeal into food tourism products and experiences. The activities of seriously wealthy and often very famous people will directly affect the shape of markets. The mega-rich often own or influence very potent cultural objects and favour certain social causes. In this way they drive both expectation and behaviour on the part of the more ordinary citizen. Their direct impact on the market for luxury and style (what it is and where it is to be found) is and will be immense. Their wealth and their tastes are a glorious incentivisation of food tourism markets and products. Another interesting observation made by Yeoman and McMahon-Beattie is that consumers are trying to extend their healthy years and reduce the chronic illness years. This means from a food tourism perspective that key issues are health and authenticity. Lastly, the authors highlight that innovations such as vertical farming and sea harvesting have brought about new forms of food. Overall they argue that the prospects for food tourism are bright, although at times scary.

Chapter 4: The Future Fault Lines of Food

The major argument portrayed in Figure 17.3 is that the interface between human beings and food occurs along scientific lines that can be partly, but imperfectly, scientific. The cognitive map highlights Hansen's arguments of 'flavour complexity', 'industrial agricultural method', 'food production system becoming bland' and 'uniformity of flavour'. The interface occurs on two fronts. The first is the interface between human survival adaptations and flavour perception. At this intersection we can study the human palate and its ability to discern 'flavour' as a conscious construct of perception, though in fact flavour is a combination of both taste and odour with the entire perception of the palate being actually a construct of not only these but also sensations in the tissues of the mouth, throat and nasal cavity. In this sense, the pleasure associated with certain flavours or gastronomical experiences (and in general the ability of human flavour detectors to discern thousands of different nuances of flavour, including distaste for certain bitter flavours that may be associated with poisons) confers a survival advantage on the individual organism. The second front is simply a statistical one

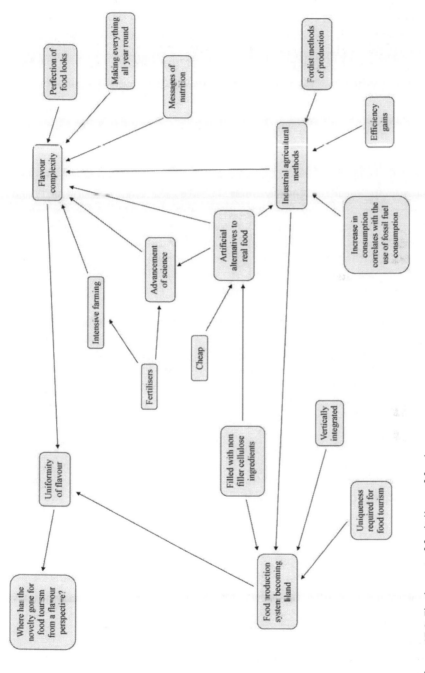

Figure 17.3 The impact of fault lines of food

related to the increasing use of genetic monocultures and uniformity in industrial-scale agriculture. Sensations constructed as 'flavour' are based in the sensing of soluble substances in food, and its subtle play and stimulation of those senses. On the other hand, Hansen argues, agriculture based in uniformity of soil, fertiliser, genetic strains and methodology is likely to produce food products with greater uniformity of soluble substances within the food product. Taken together, these two trends allow a prediction of increased demand in the food tourism sector for tourists seeking flavour novelty.

Chapter 5: The Impact of Future Food Supply on Food and Drink Tourism

Ells highlights the increasingly large number of considerations that need to be made when reflecting on the sustainability of current food tourism products and services. He also notes how issues of food security and related supply chains will influence the future shape of a global food tourism market. From Figure 17.4, we can observe a number of central concepts including, 'food choices', 'authenticity', 'ongoing food choice', 'activism' and 'value'. Ells argues that food tourism involves an increasing number of food policy networks and actors within government, supply chains and consumer-centred groups. As food, land and water supplies become more unstable (and potentially more expensive) it will be the food supply chain that ultimately shapes emerging food tourism formats. The future food tourist will need to more fully appreciate the underlying dynamics of the food supply chain and will be able to potentially engage with it in a wider variety of ways. These future activities will need to be more explicitly represented in revised conceptual frameworks of food tourism, particularly where culinary supply is concerned.

Chapter 6: Future Consumption: Gastronomy and Public Policy

Mulcahy argues that gastronomy has significance for all at some level, and it can transform a state, with each citizen and organisation doing their part, so that, collectively, the nation benefits. Figure 17.5 is focused on this argument through the concept 'gastronomy will be leveraged by governments' and then connected to a series of supporting arguments: 'level of engagement with food and tourism', 'experience economy', 'identity', 'stakeholders' and 'pursuit of exotic experiences in authenticity'. This national activism will not be found in elitist or high-profile restaurants, but in the authentic gastronomy of domestic and workplace kitchens, grown by, purchased from, prepared, and eaten by residents, supported and promoted by both a proactive business community and an engaged public service. This intuitively reflects history, geography, culture, landscape and all the other components that uniquely make a nation what it is, thereby providing compelling reasons to visit.

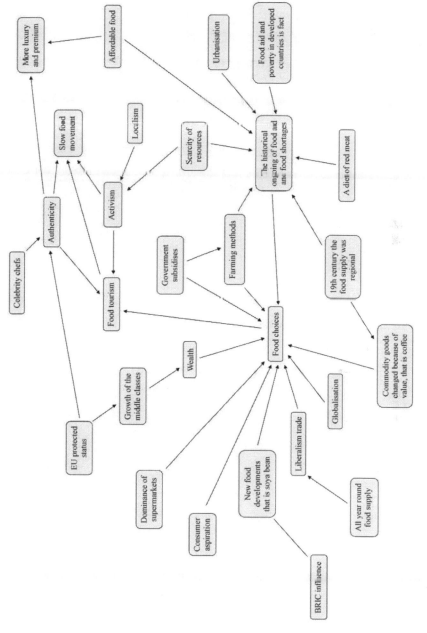

Figure 17.4 The impact of future food supply

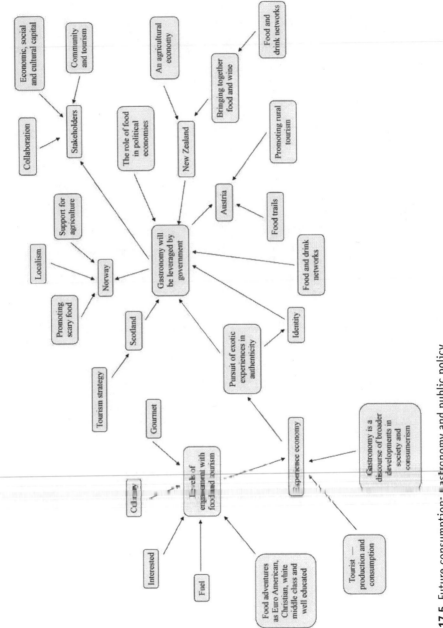

Figure 17.5 Future consumption: gastronomy and public policy

Given the state of many economies, Mulcahy argues that, especially in the developed world, resources are at a premium – both human and financial. The state will not be able to fund tourism as it has, unless it can be shown to be a net contributor to finances. In that event, gastronomic tourism is well placed to garner public policy support (strictly on the basis of a significant return on investment). Even then, high levels of collaboration between government, business and civil society will be required.

A gastronomy-driven economy is realistic, viable and sustainable, as gastronomy offers a scalable, cost-effective means of local and regional development, with the potential to strengthen identity, enhance appreciation of the environment, and encourage the regeneration of local heritage and the local economy. Such a commerce-focused business case gets the attention of policymakers and enterprises unaware of the centrality of gastronomy to economic strategy and indigenous profitable enterprises, and creates the necessary awareness and buy-in for success at national and local levels.

Chapter 7: Architecture and Future Food and Wine Experiences

Danielmeier and Albrecht highlight, through Figure 17.6, that due to changing wealth distribution, education, individualism, and marketing scepticism, in combination with the increasing importance of experience economies and growing expectations, the hospitality industry is about to change how and by what means it represents itself. Thus the roles of place and the narration of place will increase in importance as they are used in conveying uniqueness and points of difference. The concepts that are central to this interpretation are 'performative visitor experiences' and 'space'. It is argued that experiences and place performances will increasingly take precedence over the mere consumption of wine or food products. Focusing on the wine industry in particular, the authors thus examine how architecture enables the enactment and narration of company values by individual businesses. In doing so, they explore the role of actors, design and performativity; it is found that due to increasing expectations of consumers, personalised sensory and bodily place experiences will be offered in the future. These will cater for interactive enactments of place, people and produce. Architecture as place-making activity, it is argued, will increasingly be used to fulfil consumer desires, although this may occur entirely independently from localised wine and food production.

Chapter 8: Envisioning AgriTourism 2115: Organic Food, Convivial Meals, Hands in the Soil and No Flying Cars

Hurley envisions the future of food tourism through agritourism as an ecologically sound and socially just industry. As a vision, or preferred future,

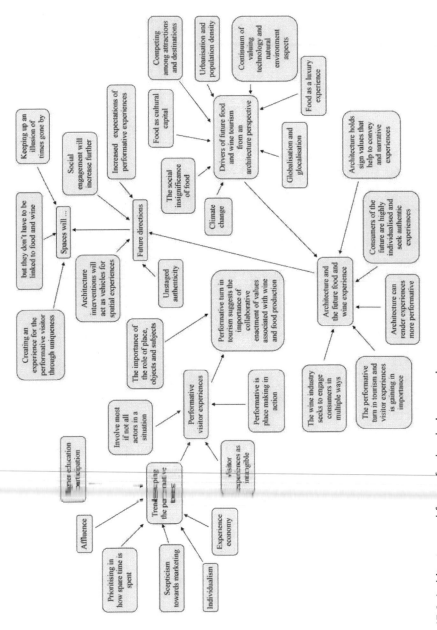

Figure 17.6 Architecture and future food and wine experiences

the chapter dares to be more than a projection or educated guess of future scenarios – it is a hope-filled desire for a future tourism based on travellers who have respect and compassion for their hosts as well as for the land and animals that provide the food and drink that they enjoy. These points are noted as concepts in Figure 17.7 as 'story based future', 'visioning future', 'community' and 'importance of consciousness'. Visioning is a scholarly approach that celebrates the best of humanity instead of the more conventional problematising of societal issues or offering a cautionary tale. However, Hurley does include a critical analysis of some of agritourism's present-day problems. But, inspired by Hopeful Tourism theory (Pritchard et al., 2011) these are presented with the hopeful assumption that a transformation has taken place and the suffering has ceased. Building on the work of many food and tourism activists, scholars and farmers this contribution offers a vision of a future of food tourism that is part of healthy, just and localised economies. It sees the future made up of many diverse futures including vibrant and sustainable rural communities and successful agritourism operations.

Chapter 9: Making the Difference: The Experience Economy and the Future of Regional Food Tourism

Meethan argues that future tourism developments need to be expressed in the context of globalisation, thus shaping national and regional identity. Central to this concept is how experiences are formed. In particular a focus on consumption as an active process that involves both producers and consumers creating experiences holds promise for future lines of research that focus on the micro and macro processes involved. The ambiguity and contradiction of authenticity has caused homogenisation and the eradication of difference in some sectors and sub-sectors, while at the same time, counter – globalisation encourages a celebration of the regional and the local. A drive towards localism is seen through individual experience. Foodstuffs and cuisines then assume a greater cultural significance as both a marker of identity as much as a distinct product for growing, niched, tourist markets. It is noted that small-scale development in turn relies on a number of institutional and regulatory frameworks that can assist the development of regionally-based foodstuffs. The use of policies which encourage the development of small to medium-sized enterprises through clustering is a crucial factor; they not only stimulate development but also help add value and can create the conditions in which a culinary experience economy can emerge. Thus tourism needs to seek tourism developments and experiences that are experiential, thus driving up demand for localised produce. These arguments are observed through a series of concepts in Figure 17.8 as 'regional identity', 'food and an association with place', 'experience economy', 'individualism' and 'homogenisation effect as a result of McDonald's'.

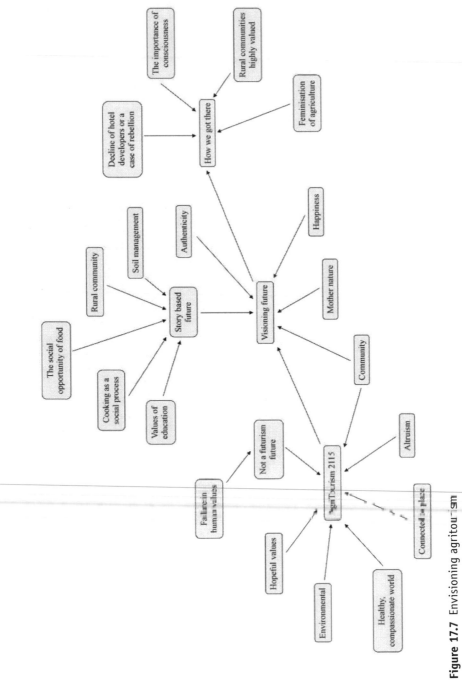

Figure 17.7 Envisioning agritourism

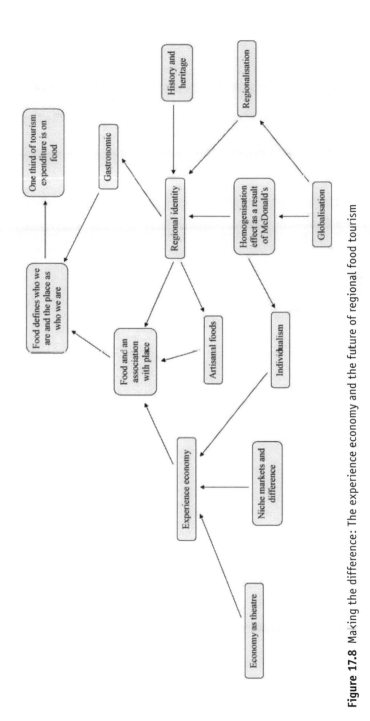

Figure 17.8 Making the difference: The experience economy and the future of regional food tourism

Chapter 10: Food and Intellectual Property Rights

Figure 17.9 highlights a number of concepts including 'geography', 'developed word thinking', 'who owns the intellectual property of chefs' recipes', 'protecting food issues', 'statutory monopolies', 'destination image' and 'legislation'. Fields sets out to indicate how intellectual property rights (IPR) will shape food tourism in the future. Rather than use IPR to strongly promote a destination or region connected to specific food and drink (the cost of application then policing of the system would be substantial), it is far better as a tool for protection of history, culture, tradition, society, etc., then using those for the promotion of tourism. The reason he provides for taking this stance is that eventually the effect of IPR will be diluted over time as more and more food and drink become protected. Currently, it is news when a product achieves IPR status, but for how long will it continue? If a tourism destination is too closely allied with an IPR-protected food or drink product, what happens if global warming prevents the production of those food and drink items in the locality at some point in the future?

Chapter 11: Back to the Future: The Affective Power of Food in Reconstructing a Tourist Imaginary

The significance of Scott and Duncan's contribution revolves around how we see food as a significant motivation to travel and so the chapter focuses on future food experiences through the tourist imaginary. Thus, the authors suggest that food tourists make sense of the world around them as an inherently imaginative process. The chapter identifies a number of concepts shown in Figure 17.10 namely 'imaginary', 'tourist and food imaginary', 'west meets east', 'the future – reflexivity in action', 'gaze...reality', and 'imaginary is becoming virtually mobile as food as an experience to illustrate the future'. Scott and Duncan reflect on what might influence the future imagination of the individual rather than the future of the tourist. Thus they problematise the term 'food tourist' and the unproblematic notion of the 'gastronomic' individual as a cover-all for anyone with an interest in food. They argue that the performance of gastronomy is not available to all and, for their purposes, the 'food tourist' encompasses the reflective (reflexive), experiential, local and global nature of much food-related tourism. They explore the idea that to consume food-as-culture is pitted against the need to mitigate the risk of food to the 'body'. Consequently, Scott and Duncan's imaginings of future (touristic) food experiences comprise this friction between desire and risk. In conclusion, Scott and Duncan draw out a change in the demographic of those motivated by 'food', from an ageing Western tourist to a younger Eastern (Asian) tourist, as being of importance. This is discussed by considering their (future) shared and parallel imaginaries. They see the future as being

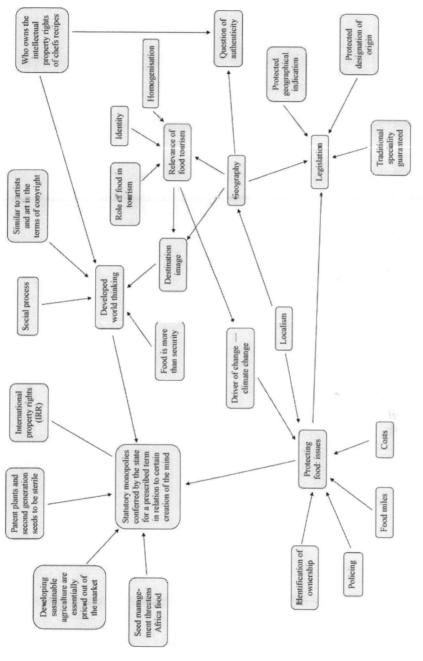

Figure 17.9 Intellectual property rights and food

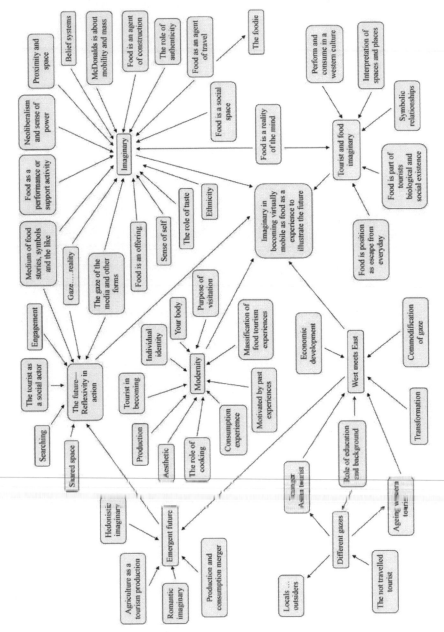

Figure 17.10 Back to the future

about an emergent, hopeful food tourist where there is a blurring of cultural boundaries – where the shared production and consumption of food, at multiple scales and spaces, results in food tourism as a truly cosmopolitan endeavour.

Chapter 12: The Changing Demographics of Male Foodies: Why Men Cook But Don't Wash Up!

Yeoman and McMahon-Beattie argue that men see cooking as a leisure activity whereas washing up is a chore, hence the central proposition of the chapter. Further, men are claiming a stake in the kitchen in a particular way These are young, upwardly mobile and unabashedly masculine men who love to cook and love to be seen to cook. This trend has been created by a wide range of forces from multiculturalism, travel and the single lifestyle and is one which will continue to grow in the future. The key concepts identified in Figure 17.11 include 'gastronomy is the new rock 'n' roll', 'men see cooking and food as a leisure activity not a chore', and 'The new foodies from a tourism perspective is about authenticity, place, foodies and craftsmanship.' From a food tourism perspective the authors highlight three dimensions. First, the consumer's desire for new, authentic food experiences is increasing. Authenticity is about food that is simple, rooted in the region, natural, ethical, beautiful and human. Second, the visibility of the male celebrity chef along with books, magazines and blogs about men cooking seem to indicate a growing enthusiasm for cooking. Finally, men are foodies in the sense that cultural capital defines identity and status; it becomes the critical currency of conversation, notably in phrases like, 'have you been to France and dined at the Hotel George V' or 'made authentic Thai Green Curry at the Elephant Cookery School in Krabi'? It is the knowledge and experiences of the food, hobbies and craft that help define who foodies are rather than their socio-economic grouping. Yeoman and McMahon-Beattie argue that consumers are moving from an era of industrial to cultural capitalism, where cultural production is increasingly becoming the dominant form of economic activity and securing access to the many cultural resources and experiences that nurture human psychological existence becomes an important aspect in shaping identity. The well-travelled *Man Foodie* can be viewed as a foodie and food tourist.

Chapter 13: The New Food Explorer: Beyond the Experience Economy

Laing and Frost highlight the emergence of the food explorer as a niche market, against the backdrop of trends in food tourism. Their contribution is based upon a number of key concepts identified in Figure 17.12, namely 'manifestations and trends', 'food explorer as a growing futures niche market', 'supporting experience . . . peak performance' and 'the food tourist is

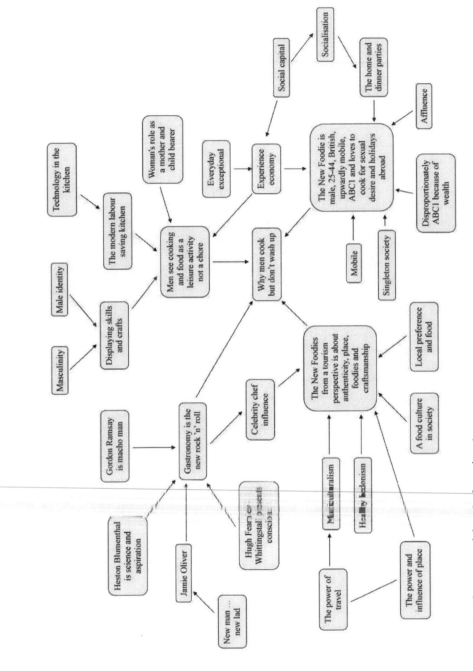

Figure 17.11 Why men cook but don't wash up!

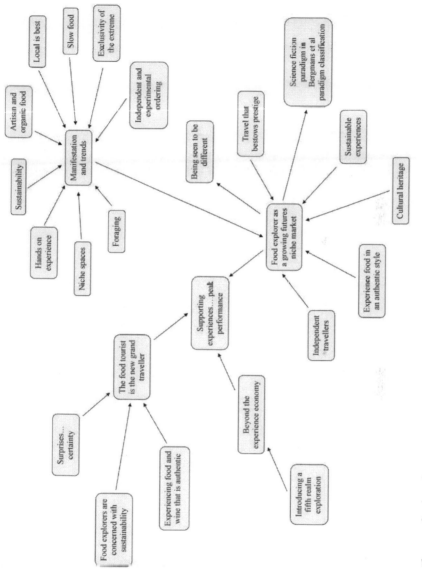

Figure 17.12 The new food explorer

the new grand traveller'. The chapter identifies nine trends: slow food, artisan or organic food and produce, a desire for hands-on experience, sustainability, niche spaces, the exclusivity of the extreme, a preference for independent or experimental ordering or tasting, the view that local is best, and a rise in an interest in foraging. Laing and Frost argue for a new dimension or realm of Pine and Gilmore's experience economy (2011), which covers exploration, given that the food explorer does not seek out scripted and staged experiences. Instead, they search for authenticity, sustainability and prestige or distinctiveness in their food tourism experiences.

Chapter 14: The Future of Dining Alone: 700 Friends and I Dine Alone!

The known long-term changes in the structure of the population, the changing construct of the meaning of 'family' and the expected growth and dominance of single-person households in the Western world, will all have a profound impact on the future evolution of the single diner states Hay. The key concepts identified in Figure 17.13 include 'the single diner', 'key trends' and 'future options'. Hay argues the traditional dining model of three square meals/day at set times was driven by the regularity needs of the industrial society. In the future, this will change, as both work and lifestyle patterns continue to adapt to the demands of the 365/24/7 society. One consequence of which will be the development of 24-hour local restaurants, with the type of meals not determined by time, but by the needs of the largest market segment, the single diner. As a result of these changing work and lifestyles choices, restaurants will develop different dining options for the single diner (smaller and more frequent meal choices), different eating layouts (special spaces for the single diner) and changes in attitudes (welcoming the single diner as a new source of income). These changes will be necessary to better meet the needs of the much more politically powerful, single-person households.

The continuing development of new communications technology and the adoption of increasingly informal communications structures will result in a meshing and merger of functional and leisure activities, and in the future dining alone will become part of a multifunctional leisure activity. Dining alone will no longer be associated with the lonely nor seen as an unacceptable social activity, but as a positive lifestyle choice. In the future, the new companion of the single diner will not be the traditional book or even their twitter friends, but through the projection of full-size holographic images, the single diner will have the option of sharing their meal experiences in real time with their friends and family.

The future of food tourism, Hay argues, is dependent on the acceptance, and meeting the social needs, of the single diner, and failure to meet these needs may have a detrimental impact on the quality of all our lives.

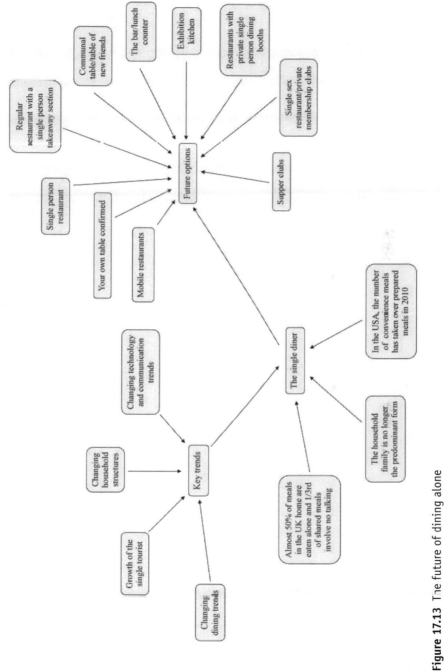

Figure 17.13 The future of dining alone

Chapter 15: Dimensions of the Food Tourism Experience: Building Future Scenarios

Moscardo and colleagues take the perspective that food tourism is an umbrella concept that can include many different things. These concepts include 'framework for organising food tourism experiences', 'conceptual framework', 'importance of learning', 'sustainability', 'consolidation of experience' and 'serial reproduction...differentiation' as seen in Figure 17.14.

Moscardo *et al.* use both existing food tourism research and a study of tourist reviews to develop a conceptual model of the food tourism organised around key consumption experience dimensions. The four key dimensions identified include: the central role of learning about food for all types of food tourism experience; focus on the destination place versus a focus on personal issues and development; fun rather than food; and back stage versus front stage.

These dimensions have then been used to suggest a preliminary food tourism classification system which includes six main categories of food tourism experience: food events, fine-dining, sustainable/organic food, food classes, food-themed destination tours, and food production tours/attractions. Each of these categories of food tourism is associated with different experiences features, different tourist activities and motivations and different supply chain issues. This model and the classification system can be used to develop more robust and specific explanatory models that can assist both the practice of food tourism provision and also be used to generate food tourism future scenarios. The theoretical development for the category of fine-dining, for example, could be informed by the wider literature on connoisseurship. In the case of the category of sustainable/organic food a consideration of food tourism futures suggests that in the short term this is likely to be a growth area within food tourism, but that in the medium term it will become less attractive to consumers who will increasingly expect all their food tourism experiences to consider issues around sustainability and organic food production. One option that could be considered within this food tourism category is a move to social enterprises and an expansion of the corporate social responsibility aspects of food production. These two examples, the authors argue, demonstrate the value of the model for better understanding current food tourism experiences in order to better predict possible food tourism futures.

Chapter 16: Food in Scholarship: Thoughts on Trajectories for Future Research

Yoo's chapter contributes to food tourism scholarship through its adoption of an interdisciplinary lens that links tourism and food studies, and present insights into the contemporary stage of tourism scholarship on food

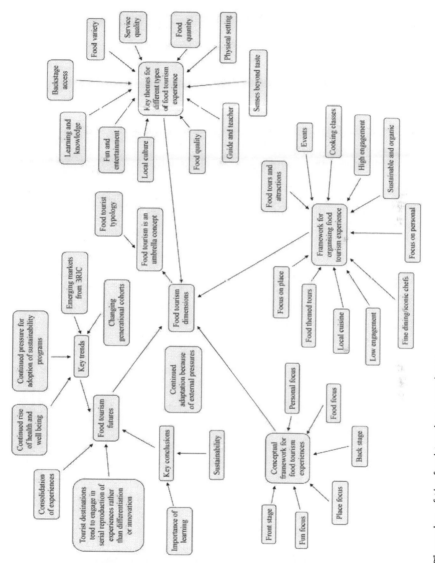

Figure 17.14 Dimension of the food tourism experience

and directs the future of the field by providing trajectories for future research. By reviewing the existing academic research on food in tourism scholarship as well as in other social scientific disciplines, such as anthropology, sociology and cultural studies, this chapter provides research areas for scholars to explore. Given the importance of food in understanding cultures and its symbiotic relationship with tourism, Yoo indicates that tourism scholars need to pay more attention to the ways in which food plays a significant role in tourism as an essential constituent both for the tourist and the host by acknowledging the interrelationship between food and culture and tourism. This interdisciplinary approach to studies on food in tourism scholarship will be beneficial for a better understanding of the intricate meaning of food in tourism and the relationship between food and tourism. All of the above are summarised in Figure 17.15 as 'food as cultural heritage', 'food in scholarship', 'food as tourism attractions and marketing tool' and 'tourist food consumption behaviour and dining experience'.

Developing an Aggregate Map of the Future of Food Tourism

The purpose of this section is to demonstrate how a construction of the aggregate cognitive map took shape; it combines the individual cognitive maps constructed in the previous section. Because of the complexity and subjectivity of the construction, the section is only an illustration of the process in order to guide readers' understanding of how the process happened. The merger of the individual cognitive maps into an aggregation is a process in which the researcher immerses him or herself into the maps and searches for concept connections, driven by semantic similarity. These allow the drawing out of key concepts from each individual map and the remapping of the concepts using DE. Once this was complete and, after several iterations, an aggregate cognitive map was formed (see Figure 17.16).

As this aggregate map is complex, and given there are a great number of connections, DE has a number of features which allow the breaking up of the aggregate map into viewpoints. From this the researcher can build, explore and reflect on these maps as component parts of the total aggregate map. The 'central' command looks at specified band levels which are connected to the concepts. This allows the researcher to view the importance of the length of linkage between concepts. Each concept is weighted according to how many concepts are traversed in each band level. Fundamentally, the central command shows how many concepts are dependent upon one concept. Image 17.1 demonstrates this view.

The 'domain' (Image 17.2) command performs a hierarchical domain analysis which lists each concept in descending order of the linked density around that concept. Those concepts with the higher link density are listed

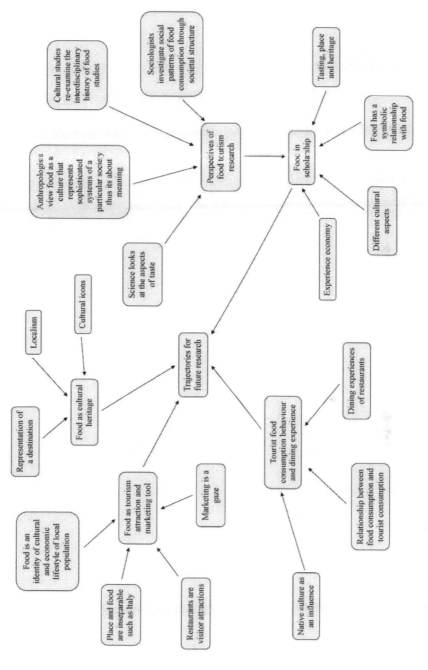

Figure 17.15 Food in scholarship

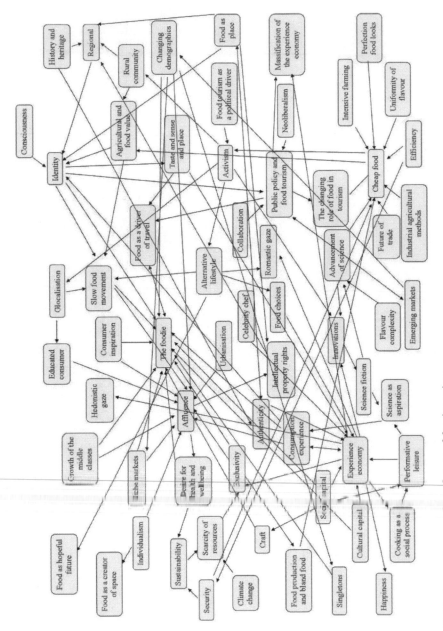

Figure 17.16 Aggregate map of the future of food tourism

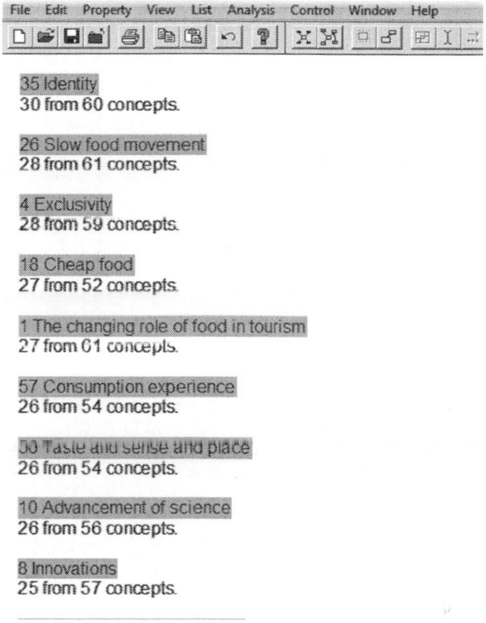

Image 17.1 Central analysis

first. The importance of the 'domain' command highlights the importance of the closeness of the local links between concepts. The researcher used both the 'central' and 'domain' commands as a means to identify the most important concepts in order to explore and construct maps. Further, both the 'central' and 'domain' commands identify a number of concepts to map and the modeller makes a judgement to construct and explore these concepts while holding them as a central view.

Image 17.3 shows a DE screen of the construction of a viewpoint drawing out the concepts 'cheap food', 'experience economy' and 'the foodie', etc. By using the command 'show unseen links', the modeller is able to find the connection between the concepts and thus start to build and feel a cognitive map. From here the researcher can start to build a map, explore links and reflect upon them.

Viewpoint 1: Food tourism as political capital

Why should the public sector be involved in food tourism? As the experience economy has evolved, political power and political discourse have moved from manufacture to experiences, especially in the advanced economies of the world. Thus tourism now has a political discourse of identity, consciousness and national heritage through food tourism. In addition, this political discourse is a representation of the land, tastes and cultural aspects of a place.

File Edit Property View List Analysis Control Wir

Al concepts in descending order of value

19 links around
2 Experience economy

18 links around
61 The foodie

14 links around
6 Affluence

11 links around
18 Cheap food

9 links around
35 Identity

8 links around
31 Public policy and food tourism

6 links around
23 Activisim
26 Slow food movement

5 links around
4 Exclusivity
10 Advancement of science
25 Alternative life style
48 Regional
50 Food as place
57 Consumption experience
63 Changing demographics

Image 17.2 Domain analysis

Food tourism is a process in which political discourses are easily forged between consumer and supply. It is a means of collaboration by which communities can find a common bond. From a political perspective, food tourism has political power as the creative class evolves (Florida, 2014) in many countries, especially in emerging nations. Figure 17.17 is a portrait of food tourism as economic, social and cultural capital, which means political leaders see food tourism as political capital from a public policy perspective.

Viewpoint 2: Food tourism as the visionary state

The present food production system is focused on producing cheap food for the masses, shaped by the concepts (in Figure 17.18) 'intensive farming', 'efficiency' and 'perfection'. Tourism is an escape from reality and it allows tourists to be transformed into a temporal liminal state; food plays a part in

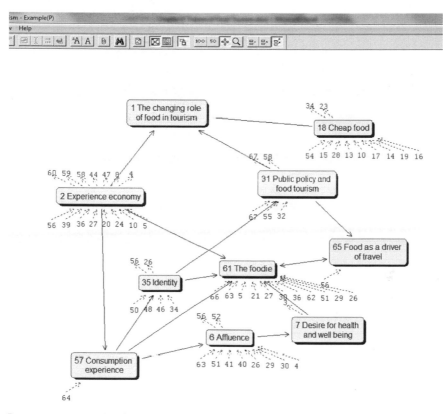

Image 17.3 Example of cognitive map construction

this temporal state. On the one hand, tourists seek an alternative and a visionary world of perfection, with food tourism representing a back-to-basics philosophy of localism and authenticity. The tourist acts out a Bohemianism alternative, even though it is temporal. Food tourism is a visionary futures world where perfection is portrayed as guilt free and sustainable. Here food tourism is a portrayal of everything that society is not; it is essentially about everything tourists are escaping from.

Viewpoint 3: What it means to be a foodie

As the experience economy matures, the foodie emerges as a tourist who has a passion for food and this engenders social and cultural capital (Grenfell, 2012). Social capital is derived from being part of the network of foodies and cultural capital develops due to the associated expertise, exclusivity and knowledge. Today, and in the future, being a foodie is a way of life brought about by changing demographics and the desire to do something as 'I am single'. This foodie is mainly from an urban centre and is someone who sees

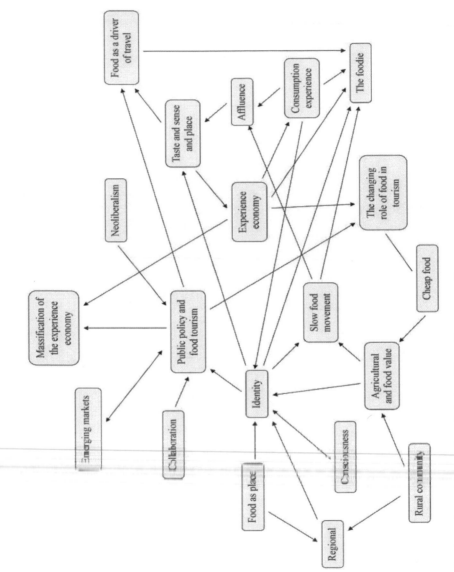

Figure 17.17 Food tourism as political capital: A public policy perspective

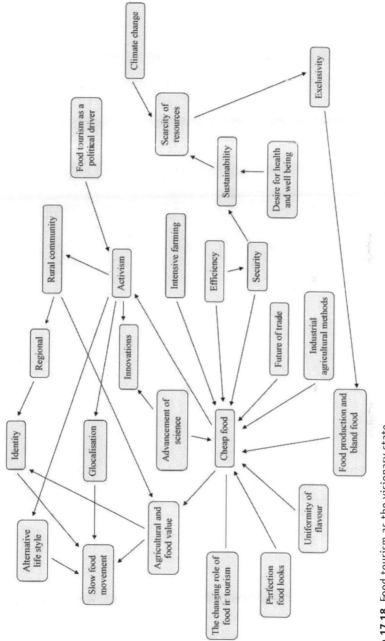

Figure 17.18 Food tourism as the visionary state

food as an ancient craft to be learned and practiced. There are links to Bohemianism-shaped identity and the slow food movement. Basically, a foodie is a professional amateur or connoisseur whose main reason for travel is food (see Figure 17.19).

Viewpoint 4: The drive for affluence and exclusivity

The political drive to increase the economic value of tourism shapes the future of food tourism. In the future, food becomes more expensive for a number of reasons including food inflation, urbanisation, changing diets and population growth. As food becomes a source of social capital, it will also become a more exclusive experience as luxury providers look for ways to distinguish their products. Additionally, as world tourism is forecasted to grow through demand from the emerging middle classes of Asia, providers will look to offer exclusive products and experiences in order to attract these affluent consumers. As we can see from Figure 17.20, the cognitive map is centred on the following concepts, 'exclusivity', 'affluence' and the 'desire for health'. Thus exclusivity will be founded based on the relationship between 'the foodie' and 'the desire for health' which is supported by a second loop in Figure 17.20 which identifies 'scarcity of resources' and 'sustainability' as driving forces.

Viewpoint 5: Fluid experiences in a post-modernist world

The connections and flows in Figure 17.21 highlight the central focus of food tourism as an experience but, at the same time, the contradictory concepts of 'hedonistic gaze' and 'authenticity' portray the fluidity of food tourism. Food and food tourism are a point of differentiation: they are a luxury to some and a hobby to others. But what combines both hedonism and authenticity is the experience. In a post-modernist world shaped by affluence consumers live longer, travel more frequently and celebrate more often. At the core of a fluid identity is the notion of sampling and novelty: simply put, consumers want to try new things. Fluid identity is about the concept of self, where self cannot be defined by boundaries. The consumer's desire for new experiences results in both authenticity and hedonism being complimentary concepts.

Concluding Thoughts: Explaining and Conceptualising the *Drivers of Change*

Figure 17.22 represents the drivers of change that will shape the future discourses, actions and behaviours around food tourism.

As society has advanced, the consumption of both food and tourism has changed. In 1950, 25 million tourists took an international holiday, today

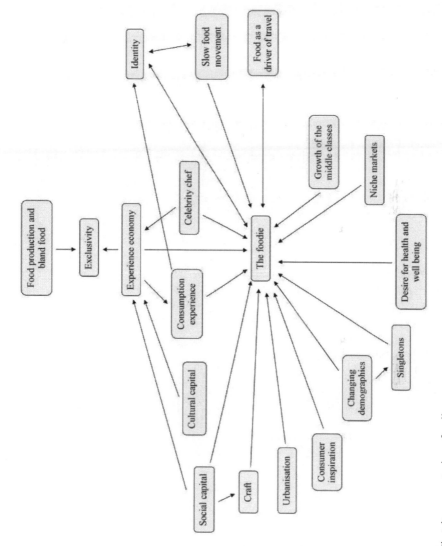

Figure 17.19 What it means to be a foodie

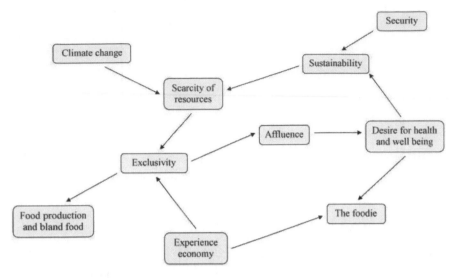

Figure 17.20 The drive for affluence and exclusivity

that number is over 1 billion and Yeoman (2012) optimistically forecasts that this is set to rise to 4.2 billion by 2050. Food tourism without doubt is a major component of the tourist's itinerary and a focus of destination strategies. Food is symbolic of a country, a passion of tourists and something that binds communities, tourists and businesses together. Indeed, food and holidays are the top two topics that consumers talk about (Yeoman, 2012).

Food tourism as political capital

Food is one of the key elements of a nation's culture and identity, along with its history, symbols, myths and discourses (Smith, 1995). In line with this there is a connection between food and capital. Capital can be the economic, social, cultural and political (Bourdieu, 1984; Bennister & Worthy, 2012; Dubois, 211; Grenfell, 2012) and it can be objectified or embodied. Boyd argues in Chapter 2 that food and tourism have a strong historical connection which binds them together as a political force. Additionally, food and agriculture have been traditionally strong economic sectors with associated public policies and strategies. These now often encompass food tourism and, as such, it drives political capital. Food and tourism are outputs, symbols and rituals of the food production system and, often, they cannot be separated. For example, a farmers' market is both a food tourism experience and farm retail outlet. In Chapter 3, Yeoman and McMahon-Beattie argue that the political capital of food tourism is captured in destination strategies as destinations chase high-yielding tourists to bring wealth and economic prosperity. Politically, food tourism generates employment and economic activity. The

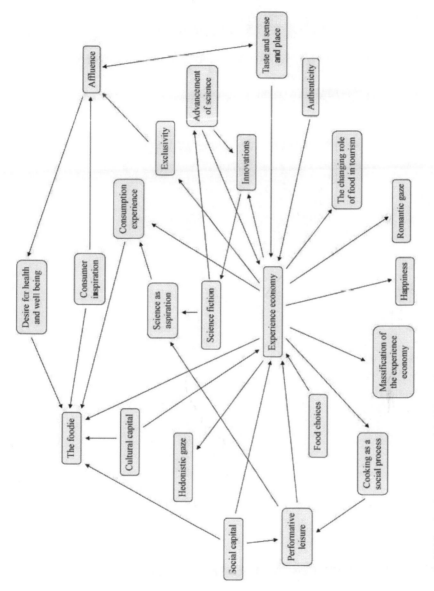

Figure 17.21 Fluid identity in a post-modernist world

Figure 17.22 Drivers of change

demonstration of political involvement in food tourism is identified in Chapter 6, as Mulcahy argues that gastronomy is leveraged by governments for political and economic reasons. Supporting Smith's (1995) gastronomic theory of nations from a political capital perspective is the link between 'authenticity' and a destination or country's history, place and culture. Here, authenticity is nationalism as food tourism is a symbol of ritual and identity. This form of protecting identity is drawn out by Meethan in Chapter 9 as food is a form of national and regional identity in an increasingly globalised world. Hence, political leaders should champion and protect local foods and cultures.

Food tourism as a visionary state

Closely linked to the driving force of food tourism as political capital is that of food tourism as a visionary state. Visions and political utopias are closely associated (Shklar, 1965). Ideologies are political utopias, paradises and perfect worlds in which those ideologies are presented as visions (Bergman *et al.*, 2010). Utopian entities are often portrayed in tourism as romantised images of destinations where tourists desire to be (Yeoman *et al.*, 2014). As food tourism has political capital it is portrayed as a vision through the use of words such as 'authenticity' and 'activism' in relation to how food tourism can react to the problems of humankind and climate change. In Chapter 2, Boyd portrays a visionary gaze of food tourism as 'local', 'regionality branded', 'authentic' and the 'focus of economic development strategies' in which tourists are 'climate aware' and want a 'sustainable' experience. Yeoman and McMahon-Beattie (Chapter 3) envision how science, through innovation, can provide a plentiful food supply. In Chapter 4, Hansen is critical of the present food supply poducers' homogeneous food that is bland and tasteless and advocates a vision of sustainability and an alternative lifestyle. Ells (Chapter 5) highlights issues in the food chain supply regarding security and globalisation and advocates a solution based upon the concepts of 'authenticity', 'activism' and the 'slow food movement'. In Chapter 6, Mulcahy has a vision of the future in which food tourism offers a 'scalable cost-effective means of local and regional development, with the potential to strengthen identity, enhance appreciation of the environment and encourage the regeneration of local hertiage and the local economy'. Hurley, in Chapter 8, sees the future of tourism through agritourism as an ecologically sound and socially just industry. Meethan (Chapter 9) envisions a future in which producers and consumers create experiences which are characterised by a drive towards localism. Within his vision, food and cuisines assume greater cultural significance, create market identity and grow niche tourist markets. Scott and Duncan (Chapter 11) explore the imaginings of future (touristic) food experiences which comprise the friction between desire and risk and Yoo (Chapter 16) agrues for a strong relationship between food and local culture as a vision for the future. Hence, drawing on the past, the editors of this book advocate a utopian vision of nostaligia where localism and authenticity provide a basis for the escapist nature of food tourism. Food tourism is therefore a 'gaze' for both producers and tourists to imagine a future in which stakeholders, communities and political groups can bond through a common language.

What it means to be a foodie

Food tourism and foodies are well documented in the literature (Henderson, 2009; Yeoman, 2008, 2012; Getz et al., 2014). A picture has developed of a future consumer that is better educated, wealthy, has travelled more extensively, lives longer and is concerned about their health and wellbeing. Foodies are those tourists who are passionate about food and where food is the main reason for travel. Food to the foodie is the source of all moods and all sensations (Yeoman, 2012) and is the signifier of culture and symbolic order. To the foodie, food is a focus for socialising and a means for simultaneous enriching experiences, expressing personal identities and adding to quality of life. In this book, the foodie and food tourist are a central construction of the future. In Chapter 12, Yeoman and McMahon-Beattie note that consumers are moving from an era of industrial to cultural capitalism where cultural production is increasingly becoming the dominant form of economic activity. Securing access to the many cultural resources and experiences, such as food and food tourism, becomes an important aspect in shaping identity. From a masculine perspective, Yeoman and McMahon-Beattie identify how young, upwardly mobile men see cooking as a leisure activity but washing up as a chore. *The Man Foodie* is unabashedly masculine, loves to cook and be seen to cook – all in the cause of trying to impress a potential partner. In Chapter 13, Laing and Frost examine the emergence of the food explorer based upon a number of driving forces in society, including the desire for hands-on experiences and the rise in the interest in foraging, thus authenticity, sustainability and prestige are important for the future of food tourism and foodies.

The drive for affluence and exclusivity

The importance of affluence and exclusivity is shaped by the proposition that rising income (and the wealth improvement connected with it) has been the driving agent of modern society. It is a key indicator of societal success and responsible for the empowerment of consumers in relation to tourism. Increased personal prosperity creates an emboldened consumer-citizen, a more demanding, sophisticated and informed actor with intensified expectations of, for instance, quality innovation and premium choices in every market. It seems every destination for political and economic reasons is chasing high-value tourists in order to increase revenues. Yeoman (2012) points out that with the arrival of mass tourism for the middle classes the definition of luxury within tourism becomes diluted thus luxury providers need to redefine luxury as exclusivity. Yeoman recognises a future society where food is scarce and consumers' access to and ingestion of food will reshape identity and cultural class. Showing culinary prowess will bring recognition and honour. Food could become a luxury, with expensive, rare and exotic foods marketed for their authenticity, local nature and cultural identity. In Chapter 2, Boyd highlights that affluence is resulting in destinations shaping their food tourism propositions for the serious, high-spending, food tourist. Yeoman and McMahon-Beattie (Chapter 3) draw attention to the fact that the activities of the seriously wealthy and celebrities can shape markets and consumer trends. Laing and Frost (Chapter 13) draw attention to the food explorer who is shaped by increased wealth and prosperity and seeks exclusiveness and prestige through social and cultural capital. In Chapter 7, Danielmeier and Albrecht highlight that increased wealth is making the place experience, through architectural design, more of a talking point.

Fluid experiences in a post-modernist world

Rising incomes and wealth accumulation distributed in new ways alter the consumer balance of power as new forms of connections and associations allow a liberated pursuit of personal identity which is fluid and less restricted by background or geography. Tomorrow's tourist wants dynamic escapist experiences but at the same time social responsibility and authenticity. This is about diversity of experiences through sampling a wide range of novel and familiar experiences (Yeoman, 2008). Fluid food tourism experiences means undertaking an authentic Turkish cooking class but at the same learning to cook with liquid nitrogen. Food tourists of the future will have so much choice: consumer volatility will increase and a high entropy society will exist. Food tourists are and will be excellent at using social network tools to search for better deals, become communities, be informed and influence. This is a tourist that wants to experience food in several ways, reflecting increasing aspirations and higher-order expectations. The changing meaning of luxury raises the importance of cultural and social capital, and this will be reflected in how tourists talk about destinations and experiences. The importance of cultural capital defines identity and status and it becomes the critical currency of conversation, e.g. 'have you been to Heston Blumenthal's Fat Duck Restaurant or the Blue Oyster in Los Angeles?' From a food tourism perspective, Yeoman and McMahon-Beattie's scenarios in Chapter 3 are a typical demonstration of fluid identity in action. The scenario *Wellington Food Festival: The Star Trek Replicator* represents the food tourist's desire for novelty and adventure whereas the second scenario, *Exclusivity: The Future of Authentic Dining,* is shaped by the concepts of 'social capital' and 'authenticity'. Scott and Duncan in Chapter 11 emphasise the importance of hedonistic imaginary and explore how the food tourist balances indulgent behaviour and risk. The search for new forms of experience is the central proposition of Yeoman and McMahon-Beattie (Chapter 12) where masculine identity is constructed through men who love to cook and love to be seen to cook.

Therefore…

In conclusion, these five drivers of change are at the centre of discourses about the future of food tourism. The drivers overlap, influence and integrate with each other. Food tourism as a collective discourse binds farmer, producer, distributor, retailer and consumer together thus providing stakeholders and communities with a utopian vision of the future. Through the creation of visions, political capital is created as political leaders see the opportunity to create dialogue through common purpose, i.e. the land, food and the tourist. These are the elements of policy and strategy which focus on the high-value tourist, characterised by affluence and exclusivity. To the food tourist, food is their identity. This identity is fluid and is shaped by authenticity and hedonistic experiences.

References

Barry, C.A. (1998) Choosing qualitative data analysis software: Atlas/ti and nudist compared. *Sociological Research Online* 3 (3), http://socresonline.org.uk/3/4/4.html (accessed 10 September 2012).

Bergman, A., Karlsson, J. and Axelsson, J. (2010) Truth claims and explanatory claims – An ontological typology of future studies. *Futures* 42 (8), 857–865.

Bennister, M. and Worthy, B. (2012) Getting it, spending it, losing it: Exploring political capital. Presentation at the Political Studies Association, London. See www.ucl.ac.uk/constitution-unit/research/foi/political-capital.pdf (accessed 12 September 2014).

Bourdieu, P. (1984) *Distinction: A Social Critique of the Judgement of Taste*. Cambridge, MA: Harvard University Press.

Brotherton, B. (2008) *Researching Hospitality and Tourism: A Student Guide*. London: Sage.

Dubois, V. (2011) Cultural capital theory vs cultural policy beliefs: How Pierre Bourdieu could have become a cultural policy advisor and why he did not. *Poetics* 29, 491–506.

Eden, C. and Ackermann, F. (1998) *Journey Making*. London: Sage.

Florida, R. (2014) *The Rise of the Creative Class – Revisited*. New York: Basic Books.

Getz, D., Andersson, R., Robinson, R. and Vujicic, S. (2014) *Foodies and Food Tourism*. Oxford: Goodfellows Publishing.

Grenfell, M. (2012) *Pierre Bourdieu: Key Concepts*. London: Routledge.

Henderson, J. (2009) Food tourism reviewed. *British Food Journal* 111 (4), 317–326.

Jenkins, M. (1998) The theory and practice of comparing casual maps. In C. Eden and J.C. Spender (eds) *Managerial and Organizational Cognition* (pp. 196–219). London: Sage.

Jones, M. (1993) *Decision Explorer: Reference Manual Version 3.1*. Glasgow: Banxia Software Limited.

Levi-Strauss, C. (1966) *The Savage Mind*. Chicago: University of Chicago Press.

Mingers, J. (2003) A classification of the philosophical assumptions of management science. *Journal of the Operational Research Society* 54 (6), 559–570.

Pearce, D. (2012) *Frameworks for Tourism Research*. Wallingford: CABI.

Pine, J.B. II and Gilmore, J.H. (2011) *The Experience Economy*. Boston, MA: Harvard Business School Press.

Pritchard, A., Morgan, N. and Ateljevic, I. (2011) Hopeful tourism: A new transformative perspective. *Annals of Tourism Research* 38 (3), 941–963.

Shklar, J. (1965) The political theory of utopia: From melancholy to nostalgia. *Daedalus* 94 (2), 367–381.

Smith, A.D. (1995) Gastronomy or geology? The role of nationalism in the reconstruction of nations. *Nations and Nationalism* 1 (1), 3–23.

Strauss, A. and Corbin, J. (1994) Grounded methodology: An overview. In N. Denzin and Y. Lincoln (eds) *Handbook of Qualitative Research* (pp. 263–272). Sage: London.

Weick, K.E. (1979) *The Social Psychology of Organizing*. New York: Random House.

Yeoman, I. (2004) The development of a soft operations conceptual framework. PhD thesis, Edinburgh Napier University.

Yeoman, I. (2008) *Tomorrow's Tourist: Scenarios and Trends*. Oxford: Elsvevier.

Yeoman, I. (2012) *2050 – Tomorrow's Tourism*. Bristol: Channel View Publications.

Yeoman, I., Munro, C. and McMahon-Beattie, U. (2006) Tomorrow's world, consumer and tourist. *Journal of Vacation Marketing* 12 (2), 174–190.

Yeoman, I., Robertson, M., McMahon-Beattie, U. and Mysarurwa, N. (2014) Scenarios for the future of events and festivals: Mick Jagger at 107 and the Edinburgh Fringe. In I. Yeoman, M. Robertson, U. McMahon-Beattie, E. Backer and K. Smith (eds) *The Future of Events and Festivals* (pp. 36–51). Oxford: Routledge.

Yeoman, I. and Schänzel, H. (2012) The future of family tourism: A cognitive mapping approach. In H. Schänzel, I. Yeoman and E. Backer (eds) *Family Tourism: Multidisciplinary Perspectives* (pp. 171–193). Bristol: Channel View Publications.

Yeoman, I. and Watson, S. (2011) Cognitive maps of tourism and demography: Contributions, themes and further research. In I. Yeoman, C. Hsu, K. Smith and S. Watson (eds) *Tourism and Demography* (pp. 209–236). Oxford: Goodfellows.

Endnote: The Future of Food Tourism

New Zealand's reputation for world-class produce and culinary innovation continues to draw visitors, increasing gastronomic tourism both in and around the country.

However, what is the future given consumers' price sensitivity, desire for novel experiences, climate change, a growing world population, changing diets and higher expectations? Ian Yeoman and colleagues present an insightful road map about the future of food tourism through imaginative scenarios, identifying the key drivers of change and an analysis of the key issues and decisions.

Today, street and produce markets are favourites for visitors and locals alike, while national and regional food events encourage tourism through the celebration of local food and beverage industries.

Over the past five years, Visa Wellington On a Plate (VWOAP) has established a reputation as New Zealand's premier culinary event – showcasing the capital's flavour and finesse. The festival has quickly gained support from the Wellington regional food and beverage industry, suppliers and producers, who now rely on the annual celebration as a cornerstone to the marketing of their industry in both domestic and international markets. VWOAP is a representation of the changes that have occurred in society and the consumers' desire for experience and their interest in food.

VWOAP not only works as a dedicated food brand for Wellington but also provides economic benefit to the Wellington economy, attracting out-of-town visitors and providing a launch pad for both artisan and growing producers to share their passion with our hungry audience. Our goal is for VWOAP to become an event of world culinary standard, firmly etched on the bucket lists of global foodies.

Events such as VWOAP – or the Melbourne Food & Wine Festival, SF Chefs in San Francisco and Dine Out Vancouver – not only meet market demand, but also encourage a sense of community. Culinary festivals give participants the opportunity to work together, identify their strengths, and promote this through the menus and events presented to consumers. This attracts visitors and consequently expenditure and exposure for those participants and also other businesses throughout the region.

An additional benefit of the festival is VWOAP's contribution to the cultural experience of Wellington. VWOAP supports, strengthens and highlights a key component of the Wellington offering – the café and cuisine culture, making the city an attractive place to visit.

The festival may only take place for a fortnight each year, but it has provided the wider region with a platform on which a year-round proposition can be based – encouraging food tourism to the capital any time of the year.

Television has led to the rise of the celebrity chef, and as the popularity of food events and food as entertainment grow, there has been a shift in the way people view restaurants. Once a magnet for special occasions, eateries are now taking the place of our dining rooms. The way we enjoy food has also changed. Food is now just as much about the social experience as it is sustenance. Everyone can cook, be it simple or complex, but it is experiencing new tastes, flavours and textures that have visitors following their noses. Food is a contributing factor when deciding where to visit, with our stomachs acting as guides.

Sarah Meikle
Festival Co-Director, Visa Wellington On a Plate 2013

Index